Kurt Weill

Photograph of Kurt Weill at work by Lotte Jacobi, 1926.

Kurt Weill

AN ILLUSTRATED LIFE

Jürgen Schebera   Translated by Caroline Murphy

Yale University Press   New Haven and London

Published with the assistance of the Kurt Weill Foundation for Music.

This is an authorized translation and licensed revised and expanded edition of *Kurt Weill: Eine Biographie in Texten, Bildern und Dokumenten,* published in 1990 by Breitkopf & Härtel in Wiesbaden.

Printed in the United States of America.

Library of Congress Cataloging-in-Publication Data
Schebera, Jürgen, 1940– . [Kurt Weill, 1900–1950. English] Kurt Weill : an illustrated life / Jürgen Schebera ; translated by Caroline Murphy. p. cm.
"Published with the assistance of the Kurt Weill Foundation for Music." Includes discography (p.   ), bibliographical references (p.   ), and index.
ISBN 0-300-06055-6 (cloth), 0-300-07284-8 (pbk.)
1. Weill, Kurt, 1900–1950. 2. Composers—Biography. I. Title. ML410.W395S3513 1995
782.1′092—dc20 [B] 04-41444 CIP MN

A catalogue record of this book is available from the British Library.

The paper in this book meets the guidelines for permanence and durability of the Committee on Production Guidelines for Book Longevity of the Council on Library Resources.

2 4 6 8 10 9 7 5 3

The translator gratefully acknowledges Stephen Hinton's advice on various matters pertaining to this translation, as well as the assistance of the Kurt Weill Foundation and the Yale Music Library in locating English-language sources for a number of quotations.

Contents

v

Preface

After the composer Kurt Weill died on 3 April 1950 in New York's Flower Hospital, from complications of coronary disease, it seemed for more than two decades as if all that might survive of his music would be a few catchy tunes—from "Mack the Knife" to "September Song"—whistled on the streets of Europe and the United States. The dramatist Maxwell Anderson foresaw the problems of reception when he remarked at the memorial concert held on 10 July: "How great Kurt Weill was as a composer of music the world will slowly discover—for he was a much greater musician than anyone now imagines. It takes decades and scores of years and centuries to sift these things out, but it's done in time—and Kurt Weill will emerge as one of the very few who wrote great music."[1]

Since the late 1970s a remarkable Weill renaissance has taken place. New performances and recordings and a rapidly growing body of literature are finally opening up our perspectives on the extraordinarily multifaceted oeuvre

of this composer. "Classical" instrumental works, especially from the early compositional phase of this pupil of Busoni, are being rediscovered, along with important art
songs and choral compositions. But above all, it is Weill's works for the stage—both in
the musical theater of the Weimar Republic and in the very different world of Broadway—
that make him one of the great innovators and avant-gardists of the twentieth century.

While working on the Broadway opera *Street Scene* in 1946, Weill reflected: "Ever
since I made up my mind, at the age of nineteen, that my special field of activity would be
the theatre, I have tried continuously to solve, in my own way, the form-problems of the
musical theatre, and through the years I have approached these problems from all different angles."[2]

In his collaborations with leading dramatists of his day—from Georg Kaiser to Bertolt
Brecht, from Maxwell Anderson to Elmer Rice—Kurt Weill created works in Germany
and later in the United States which, for all their versatility, consistently express an
unmistakable stylistic principle which he formulated shortly before his death as follows:
"I have learned to make my music speak directly to the audience, to find the most
immediate, the most direct way to say what I want to say, and to say it as simply as
possible."[3]

Kurt Weill shared the fate of most progressive artists and thinkers in the Weimar
Republic. With the establishment of the Hitler dictatorship in 1933 he was banned from
his homeland, at the height of his creativity thus far. He was one of the very few German
émigrés to become fully assimilated into the world of American theater; indeed, he
became an American composer. Ever since, the musical world has thought in terms of
"two Weills" and has been busy weighing the European and American works against each
other—not a terribly productive pursuit. David Drew rightly points out that we can do
justice to the composer only if we "view his work as a whole, and not just in . . . parts."[4]
It is in this spirit that I offer this book.

Owing to the complicated situation regarding sources, the literature on Weill before
the 1970s is hardly worth mentioning. Not until 1975 did the London-based musicolo-
gist David Drew publish two volumes of writings by and about Weill, which provided a
preliminary selection of the scattered written material. In 1977 a book by Gottfried
Wagner appeared on the collaboration between Weill and Brecht; it was followed in 1979
by the penetrating analytical monograph *Kurt Weill in Europe*, by Kim H. Kowalke.
Three biographical works have appeared since then: one in the United States in 1980 (by
Ronald Sanders), one in the United Kingdom in 1982 (by Douglas Jarman), and one in
Japan in 1985 (by Tatsuji Iwabuchi and Erina Hayasaki).

The Deutscher Verlag für Musik published my biographical sketch of Weill in the
series *Für Sie porträtiert* (Portrayed for You) in 1980. This was followed in 1983 by a first
biography I wrote, *Kurt Weill: Leben und Werk* (The Life and Work of Kurt Weill), with
an appendix of material written by and about Weill.

A new phase of Weill research was ushered in by the death of Lotte Lenya in 1981, after
which the extensive papers of the composer and his wife were sorted, organized, and
archived for scholarly use. With the opening of the Weill–Lenya Archive at Yale Univer-

sity and the Weill–Lenya Research Center at the Kurt Weill Foundation for Music in New York in 1983, all these materials (manuscripts, correspondence, music, documents, photographs, programs, and so on) became available. The *Kurt Weill Newsletter*, which the Kurt Weill Foundation has published semiannually since 1983, disseminates information worldwide on new research, as well as on performances and new releases of printed music, recordings, and books.

A first international scholarly conference on Kurt Weill, in New Haven in November 1983, brought together musicologists from four continents. The expanded versions of the presentations published in *A New Orpheus: Essays on Kurt Weill* (1986) can be seen as the first fruits of this new research phase.

The publication of David Drew's *Kurt Weill: A Handbook* in 1987 is of fundamental significance. The result of decades of research, the *Handbook* offered the first comprehensive overview of Weill's compositions. A second international conference took place in Duisburg, Germany, in 1990; the results of this conference were published in *A Stranger Here Myself: Kurt Weill-Studien* (1993). Weill's collected writings were also published in 1990 under the title *Musik und Theater: Gesammelte Schriften*. And in 1991 the British writer Ronald Taylor presented a literary-historical biography of Kurt Weill, *Kurt Weill: Composer in a Divided World*. Further source publications are under way: the Weill–Lenya correspondence, a selection of Weill's correspondence with Universal Edition in Vienna, and—most important of all—a major edition of Weill's music, which is to be published starting in 1995 and is expected to comprise some forty volumes.

It seemed appropriate in light of the new state of research to take my 1983 book, which had rapidly gone out of print, and thoroughly revise and reconceptualize it. Thanks to numerous helpful critical comments after its publication, I was able to clarify or correct quite a few facts. I was also able to draw on new material; the availability of Weill's correspondence in particular has helped me to illuminate the contours of Weill's life and works. Thus the book now appears in a completely new form, with both the text and the illustrations considerably expanded. Following the principle of "work in progress," it marks my third approach to this subject. But it still adheres to the premises of its forerunners of 1980 ("This volume is intended to help convey a picture of the entire Kurt Weill") and 1983 ("The book is intended to foster an interest in delving more intensively into Weill's life and work as well as into his music").

Just as the first biography would not have been possible without the active participation and support of Lotte Lenya, this new book would not have been possible without the generous help and support of the Kurt Weill Foundation for Music in New York, especially of its president, Kim H. Kowalke, and of the director of the Weill–Lenya Research Center, David Farneth. My first thanks go to them. They have been both gracious and patient in answering my many questions, placing all the materials I requested at my disposal during my visits to New York. I am especially grateful for permission to reproduce passages from the correspondence, as well as many new photographs and documents.

Thanks are likewise due to the staff of the John Herrick Jackson Music Library at Yale University, who granted me access to the manuscripts and materials in the Weill Papers.

David Drew in London has encouraged and supported my work. Without his pioneering work over decades in editing and interpreting Weill's music, this book would not be imaginable. The following people have helped me further with material: Peter Frank of the Stanford University Library, Peter Knudson of the University of Southern California, and the libraries of the Academy of Motion Pictures and Arts in Beverly Hills and UCLA. James K. Lyon in La Jolla, California, and Mordecai Bauman in New York have also generously supported me.

Special thanks go to Günther Glaeser of the Bertolt-Brecht-Archiv at the Akademie der Künste der DDR in East Berlin, Jutta Theurich at the music division of the Deutsche Staatsbibliothek in East Berlin, and Ulla Jablonowski at the Stadtarchiv Dessau, who helped fill in a number of gaps in Weill's childhood and youth.

I am indebted to the staff of the Deutsche Bücherei in Leipzig, the Deutsche Staatsbibliothek in East Berlin, the Staatsbibliothek Preußischer Kulturbesitz in West Berlin, as well as the archives of the Akademie der Künste in West Berlin.

The dedicated record collectors Bernd Meyer-Rähnitz in Dresden and Klaus Hohn in Nuremberg have supplied me with valuable information and record documents, for which I am very grateful.

Finally, Irene Hempel and Thomas Frenzel of the Deutscher Verlag für Musik were open, receptive companions on this project. My concluding thanks go to them and to Stephen Hinton for his critical reading of the manuscript.

After the German edition of this book was printed, the Kurt Weill Foundation obtained a large sheaf of letters that Weill wrote in his youth to his brother Hans and the family. Selected passages from these letters, as well as some newly unearthed photographs and documents, have been included in the English-language edition. The bibliography and discography have also been updated.

I am grateful to Harry Haskell of Yale University Press for his commitment to seeing this edition into print and to the Kurt Weill Foundation for its financial support of the translation. May it now find its way to readers in the English-speaking world!

Photographic Acknowledgments

Weill–Lenya Research Center, Kurt Weill Foundation for Music, New York, for photos on pp. xii, 2, 8, 13, 14, 16, 24, 25, 60, 61, 63 (bottom), 64–66, 69, 73, 79, 104, 106, 110, 127, 147, 153, 163 (bottom), 170, 175 (top), 188, 197, 202, 217, 219, 223, 225–28, 233, 234, 236, 238, 245, 247–52, 254, 255–80, 282–94, 297–99, 301–06, 313, 314 (bottom), 317, 318, 320, 322–26, 328–30, 333, 335 (top), 336, 337.

Weill–Lenya Archive, Yale University, New Haven, for photos on pp. 48, 62, 103, 128 (right), 132, 166, 167, 243, 284, 298 (bottom), 315, 321, 327, 332, 334.

Collection of Dr. Jürgen Schebera, Berlin, for frontispiece and photos on pp. 5 (left), 18, 27–39, 42, 45, 50–57, 63 (top), 67, 68, 70–72, 74–78, 82–101, 105, 108, 111, 114–23 (left), 124–26, 128 (left), 129, 130, 131, 133–35, 137–46, 148, 154, 158 (bottom left and right), 160–63 (top), 164, 165, 169, 171–74, 175 (bottom), 176, 177, 179–86, 189, 193, 198, 201, 205–15, 232, 242, 246, 251, 253, 281, 296, 300, 308, 314 (top), 319, 335 (bottom).

Stadtarchiv Dessau, for photos on pp. 5 (right), 6, 7, 9, 11, 12, 23, 44, 59.

Stadtarchiv Lüdenscheid, for photo on p. 28.

Staatsbibliothek Preußischer Kulturbesitz, Musikabteilung, Berlin, for photos on pp. 41, 42, 46, 123 (right), 136, 159, 178, 200 (right).

Museum für Geschichte der Stadt Leipzig, for photos on pp. 83, 150, 151, 156, 157, 158 (top), 196, 200 (left).

Akademie der Künste Berlin-Brandenburg, Bertolt-Brecht-Archiv, Berlin, for photo on p. 109.

Akademie der Künste Berlin-Brandenburg, Nachlaß Ernst Busch, Berlin, for photo on p. 198.

Pascal Huynh, Paris, for photo on p. 220.

Berliner Ensemble, Archiv, Berlin, for photo on p. 113.

I

Early Years

Kurt Weill's parents, Albert Weill (1867–1955) and Emma Weill, née Ackermann (1872–1957), in 1897, the year of their marriage.

Facing page 1: Kurt Weill, aged one, with his mother, in 1901.

I

Childhood and Youth in Dessau

On 2 March 1900, in the town of Dessau, the third child of the Weill family was born. The entry in the town records states that the son was "given the name Curt Julian."[1] His brothers, Nathan and Hans Jakob, had been born in 1898 and 1899; he was followed by a sister, Ruth, in 1901.

The father of the family, Albert Weill, was a Jewish cantor and instructor of religion. Born in 1867 in Baden, in the south of Germany, at age thirty he had married Emma Ackermann, who came from a family of rabbis in Wiesloch.

(Her brother Aaron became a rabbi in Brandenburg in 1908.) In 1898 Albert Weill was offered the position of cantor by the Jewish community of Dessau. Accordingly, he moved to the north German region of Anhalt at the end of the year and took up his new duties at the beginning of 1899.

Curt Julian—from now on we shall call him Kurt, following the spelling he himself later used—spent his early childhood with his siblings in the house at Leipziger Straße 59 in Dessau. Although, as we can see from a surviving photograph of the house, the family did not live in great prosperity, the children grew up in a culturally rich atmosphere nourished by their father's love and knowledge of music and their mother's literary ambitions. Emma Weill had a particular fondness for nineteenth-century French literature; Kurt Weill's middle name, Julian, is drawn from the character Julien Sorel in Stendhal's *The Red and the Black*. Works of Goethe and Heine had their place in the family library, next to those of Herder and Moses Mendelssohn; among contemporary writers Rilke was the preferred poet. Albert Weill was not only a performing musician and a good pianist but also a composer. In 1893 a Frankfurt publisher brought out a collection of his hymns for the synagogue under the title *Kol Avraham: Synagogengesänge für Kantor and Männerchor* (The Voice of Abraham: Synagogue Songs for Cantor and Male Chorus).

The history of Dessau's Jewish community dates back to the year 1621, when the first three Jewish families were granted permission to settle in the town. Within a little more than a century, by around 1750, two hundred Jewish families were living in Dessau, making up 9 percent of the population. The community had had its own synagogue since 1687. In the eighteenth and nineteenth centuries the Jewish community in Dessau became one of the most enlightened in all of Germany. An organization of Jewish philanthropists committed to the ideals of Dessau's native son Moses Mendelssohn (born in Dessau in 1729) succeeded in founding both a Jewish Gymnasium and a Jewish Volksschule for poor children of both sexes. The reform of the Jewish liturgy began in Dessau: the first German-language sermon was preached in the Dessau synagogue on 22 October 1808, and, starting in 1810, marriage ceremonies and confirmations based on the Christian model were performed there. In addition, the first German-language Jewish newspaper, *Sulamith*, was published in Dessau.[2]

At the time of Kurt Weill's birth, Dessau counted about six hundred Jewish citizens among its 15,000 inhabitants. The synagogue formed the natural center of this community. When Julie, Baroness of Cohn-Oppenheim and daughter of the former court banker Moritz Cohn, died in Dessau in 1903, she left much of her extensive property to the Jewish community, with the stipulation that a new, more attractive synagogue be built on part of it. When the cornerstone for the new synagogue (designed by the Berlin architects Cremer and Wolfferstein) was laid in 1906, the ceremony also signaled an end to the rather cramped living situation of the Weill family, since the cantor was to live in an apartment on the ground floor of the parish house next door.

Construction was completed in less than two years: by Passover of 1907 the Weills were able to move from Leipziger Straße to the nearby corner of Steinstraße and Askanische Straße. The apartment of the "Cantor and Religious Instructor" Albert Weill

Entry in Dessau's records noting the birth of
Curt Julian Weill.

Kurt Weill's birthplace at Leipziger Straße 59 in Dessau's "Sand Suburb," as the Jewish quarter was called. This photograph was taken in 1947, long after the family had left. In the 1960s the house was torn down.

was on the ground floor of the parish house, next to the administrative rooms. The spacious rooms of the second floor were given over to the social life of the community, and the brothers of the Jewish Anhalt Lodge met in conference rooms on the third floor.

Adjoining the parish house was the imposing synagogue itself, built in the Romanesque-Byzantine style and decorated with traditional Jewish motifs. Its copper-clad dome, crowned with the Star of David, rose high above the surrounding "Sand Suburb." In keeping with its progressive goals, the community had a magnificent organ by the Dessau organ-builders Fleischer and Kindermann installed in the main room of the synagogue, where it provided the musical framework for the services. Next to the main room, between the synagogue and the parish house, there was a small room for weekday devotions.

On 18 February 1908, nine months after the parish house was completed, the synagogue was consecrated in a service attended by Duke Frederick II. This was one of the first high points in young Kurt's life: "Meanwhile the organ, at which the Court Organist Professor Richard Bartmuss sat for this occasion, began a softly played prelude, which led into the first choral selection. At the prayer-leader's stand appeared Cantor Weill, who led the first part of the service singing responsively with the chorus."[3]

It is clear that Kurt Weill received a strictly Jewish upbringing in the family of Cantor Albert Weill. His father was proud to be able to trace his German-Jewish family line back

Dessau's new synagogue with its parish house, Steinstraße 14.
The Weill family moved into the apartment on the ground floor
at Passover of 1907. The synagogue was dedicated on
18 February 1908.

to 1360 in southern Germany, and the children learned both to take pride in their Jewish ancestry and heritage and to practice their religion seriously. These are important roots of Weill's music; though they are expressed differently in different periods of his creative output, they are always there and are especially evident in some of his early work, as well as in several works composed after 1933 in France and the United States.

The boy's musical education came first from his father, who, quickly recognizing Kurt's musical gifts, taught him to play the piano and took him to the synagogue as often as he could. By the age of seven, Kurt was already able to play the piano competently, and at age twelve he began filling notebooks with compositional efforts.

In 1909 Kurt Weill entered the Herzogliche Friedrichs-Oberrealschule, which shared a building with the Herzogliches Friedrichs-Gymnasium. One of his fellow pupils, Willy Krüger, remembers Kurt as "a talented pupil. Never a teacher's pet, though—he was content for years to be fourth or fifth or sixth best in the class. While most of us went off to play ball after school, Kurt would practice the piano or the organ for three to four hours almost every afternoon."[4]

Two teachers in particular furthered Weill's musical education decisively: the music teacher August Theile, who was responsible for the chorus and school orchestra, and the German teacher Dr. Max Preitz. The latter was an enthusiastic bibliophile. Since Albert Weill also had quite a respectable library, Kurt's classmates often got him to distract the

The Weill siblings Ruth, Hans, Kurt, and Nathan in 1910.

Cantor Weill with his sons in 1909; *left to right:*
Kurt, Nathan, and Hans.

Program from a performance of the Dessauer Feldkorps, given in January 1915, with Kurt Weill, aged fifteen, accompanying on the piano. This was his first public performance.

teacher before difficult lessons. He usually succeeded. "Kurt would raise his hand and ask Dr. Preitz about some rare edition of the classics. The teacher was only too glad to get into that kind of discussion and would forget all about looking over our homework assignments."[5]

Next to the school stood another building that was to become a second home for the boy: the Herzogliches Hoftheater. Rebuilt after a fire in 1856 that destroyed the interior, the new theater—with its weighty Corinthian columns, modeled on the facade of Pozzi, extending out to the street, and particularly with its devotion to Wagner following the 1857 premiere of *Tannhäuser*—became a "north German Bayreuth" and one of the most important musical theaters in Germany.

The theater stood right across Kavalierstraße from the ducal palace, where Duke Frederick lived. Years later, in an interview in New York, Weill recalled that "every morning between 10 and 11 [the duke] drove out of the palace courtyard and across the square, to attend rehearsals of the local theatre which presented plays and operas under his patronage."[6] The musical son of the cantor caught the duke's attention, and in 1910 Weill started receiving free admission to theatrical performances and rehearsals. In 1916 he was also often called to the court to give piano lessons to the duke's two nephews and niece. From time to time he was asked to accompany singers at musical evenings in the palace. After the concert he would be given tea and pastries and would spend time with the ducal children. Weill always remembered "one conversation he had with the nephew of the duke, a child about his own age, who was very curious about the subjects being taught in the public schools. Weill recited the list of things his class was studying. At first the little aristocrat was swamped by it, but he quickly recovered with 'I have just learned to make the letter I.' "[7]

Weill's school friends from 1912 on were Martin Friesleben, son of an Evangelical elder, and the son of the physician Dr. Schmidt. Kurt often made music with them in the Weill apartment. Once the whole class was allowed to participate in Sukkoth (the Festival of Booths) in the synagogue.

The wave of nationalism that swept over Germany with the outbreak of World War I left its mark on Dessau's Oberrealschule. Military poems and national anthems dominated school instruction in both German and music. Kurt Weill participated actively in the fervor of the day. He joined a national boy scout organization which called itself the Dessauer Feldkorps (Dessau Military Corps). Under the direction of a teacher named Gerlach, this group practiced military scouting games and staged patriotic evenings. A program from one such evening in January 1915 has survived. It included recitations and singing in the Restaurant Zentrale; accompanying at the piano was the "scout" (one of the designations of rank within the "military corps") Kurt Weill. At this time he also composed a number of military choruses himself, which were rehearsed at school— among them "Ich weiß wofür." A lost one-act opera based on Theodor Körner's *Zriny* (1812), a play glorifying love of the fatherland, also dates from those early war years.

Pupils from the Oberrealschule were first conscripted into the Imperial Army in 1915–16. Soon thereafter the first announcements of casualties reached Kurt Weill, who was asked to represent his schoolmates in saying some words of remembrance. "He always found the right words," Willy Krüger remembers. Another former schoolmate recalls, "All of us, Kurt Weill included, were, in our political naiveté, caught up by the national spirit that prevailed in Germany at the time."[8]

Just two years later, in the wake of the defeat of the German Empire, tens of thousands of deaths, and the deprivation and hunger of 1918–19, Kurt Weill had changed his mind. Looking back in 1930, he reflected, "I . . . even wrote—amazingly enough, considering who I am today—war choruses."[9]

On 1 October 1913 Albert Bing, who had studied with Hans Pfitzner, was engaged as the Hoftheater's opera conductor. He had an important influence on the young Kurt Weill's further musical and general education, giving him his first systematic instruction

The music room in the ducal palace at Dessau. Here the young
Kurt Weill instructed the duke's two nephews and niece and
performed on the piano in 1916.

in composition. Now, in addition to playing the piano, Kurt could flesh out his first untutored compositional efforts on the basis of a solid theoretical education.

Many of these early compositions were long thought to be lost, but in 1983 a number of manuscripts from the family belongings of Kurt's sister, Ruth, were made public. In addition to compositions for religious occasions in the synagogue—such as "Gebet" (Prayer), an a cappella piece for mixed chorus on a text by Emanuel Geibel composed "for Ruth's confirmation," and "Mi Addir: Jüdischer Trauungsgesang" (Jewish Wedding Song)—Weill wrote a number of songs with piano accompaniment in these early years (on texts by Otto Julius Bierbaum, Joseph von Eichendorff, Richard Dehmel, Hermann Löns, Arno Holz, and others); there is also a "character piece for piano," entitled *Intermezzo*. The outstanding work is unquestionably *Ofrahs Lieder*, a cycle of five songs with piano accompaniment written in 1916 on Hebrew verses by Jehuda Halevi.

Kurt's class at the entrance to the salt mines of Leopoldshall,
during a trip to Straßfurt in 1915. Kurt is seated at the far right
of the front row.

About his instruction Weill wrote to his brother Hans: "I'm working away furiously with Bing—a couple of times a week. Alongside the usual technical and clef-reading exercises, we are now doing the following: We take an opera score and its piano reduction. First Bing plays from the reduction while I conduct from the score, and then we trade parts. So now he has given me the first scene from *Fidelio* as homework."[10]

Through Albert Bing, Weill's connections to the theater were also strengthened. From 1917 on he was a regular "adjunct" *répétiteur* there. As a pianist he had already taken part in an official palace concert in December 1915, playing Chopin and Liszt. At the same time he of course continued to attend the Oberrealschule. His music teacher there was very taken by his pupil's musical ambitions. Weill later reported: "The director . . . and the professor of the upper classes showed the greatest interest in music. At that time already they vigorously encouraged me."[11]

The intimacy of the relationship between the young Kurt Weill and the Bing couple is shown in a letter Kurt wrote to his brother Hans, in which he describes going to a performance of Verdi under Bing's direction and then continues: "The three of us then celebrated the occasion over tea and hot chocolate, and Bing told stories of *Rigoletto* performances with Caruso and Baklanow. You can imagine that the last thing I felt like doing this morning was going to school. But what could I do?"[12]

It was undoubtedly through Bing's recommendation that the young *répétiteur* and schoolboy met the Hoftheater's celebrated soprano Emilie Feuge in 1918. When she put together a pupils' concert on 6 February 1918 in Dessau, she handed over the piano accompaniment to Weill (the program included songs and arias by Bellini, Mozart, and Wagner) and also agreed to have two of her pupils sing duets by Weill: "Abendlied"

(Evening Song) and "Maikaterlied" (May Tomcat Song), on texts by O. J. Bierbaum. The next day, the press had this to say about Weill's performance:

> As an opening, Madam Feuge sang the Rose Friquet aria from Maillart's *Bell of the Hermit* and unleashed a veritable storm of excitement. What then followed was a true string of pearls—arias, songs, duets, and trios—with which her pupils gave proof of what they had learned in Madam Feuge's singing school. . . . Mister Kurt Weill, a pupil of the music director Mister Bing, rendered great service toward the success of the evening by providing piano accompaniment that was technically accomplished and sensitively attuned to the singers. Mister Weill was also represented by two duets of his own composition, which were well received.[13]

Apparently the young pianist was well received by the singer, too; in subsequent years she frequently asked him to accompany her daughter Elisabeth on song recitals.

The war left its mark on the Weill family as well as the larger community. Whereas a characteristic picture in 1914 was of the six Weills taking walks through Dessau, "the father always wearing a hat and conversing full of harmony and ease with his wife and four children,"[14] by 1916 the picture had changed. Nathan had been sent to the French front as a medical orderly, and Hans was conscripted at the end of 1917. Although Kurt reached draft age in April 1918, he never entered the army. A letter to Hans shows how relieved he was about this: "It's better to go hungry than to play soldier, don't you think?"[15]

Cantor Weill was not spared the economic hardships of the war. His earnings were drastically reduced, and hunger entered the house next to the synagogue. Although Kurt brought in a modest income with the piano lessons he gave, "the small, delicately constituted young musician fainted from hunger that year more than once and he greatly welcomed his opportunities to have dinner as well as music" when invited to wealthier households.[16]

In August 1917 he wrote longingly to his brother: "Oh, I would so like to have a nice little room somewhere in Berlin, Leipzig, or Munich, with shelves full of scores and books and piano reductions and manuscript paper, and I'd like to work like the blazes—for

Manuscript of the title page of one of Weill's earliest compositions, *Ofrahs Lieder*, written in Dessau in September 1916.

**Kurt, aged fifteen, seated at the piano in his parents'
apartment in Dessau.**

once without having to worry over and over again about household cares or school or the
draft, all of which sometimes makes my head almost burst open—but just to hear music
and be music!"[17]

It had long been clear that music was what Kurt would pursue in his higher education.
Shortly before he graduated from the Oberrealschule in March 1918, he gave an hour-
long lecture (it was customary at the time for pupils to give practice lectures) on Felix
Mendelssohn, at which he played the musical examples on the piano. Decades later, his
schoolmates still remembered the impressive clarity of his musical analysis. A nine-page
paper by the fifteen-year-old ("Richard Wagner's *Meistersinger von Nürnberg*, an address by Kurt Julian Weill") has survived and provides ample evidence of his abilities.

In April 1918 Kurt Weill traveled to Berlin for the admission test to the Staatliche
Hochschule für Musik. He passed the test and matriculated. His childhood and early
youth lay behind him; now, as a highly gifted young musician, he set out to learn the craft
of composition in the cultural center of Germany.

First Period of Study in Berlin

At the end of April 1918 Kurt Weill began his studies at the Hochschule für Musik in Berlin. His teachers were Friedrich E. Koch (counterpoint), Rudolf Krasselt (conducting), and Engelbert Humperdinck (composition). About the last of these he wrote to his brother, "I came to Humperdinck by pure coincidence. I had been confused with another student who had simply asked at one point if he could study with Humperdinck."[1]

The eighteen-year-old pursued his studies with great intensity; in addition,

Envelope of a letter from Kurt to his brother
Hans (which he always spelled "Hanns"),
written in Berlin on 30 August 1918.

Hans was a merchant's apprentice in Halberstadt—hence Kurt's playful use of the term
"conductor's apprentice" in the return address.

he took philosophy courses at the University of Berlin. On 9 May he was already writing with some pride, "You could admire me here as a stud. mus. (war mousse!) and a philosophy student. . . . I've already been to two wonderful lectures at the university. In Dessoir's 'Philosophy of Art' every word is a revelation to me, and I am also following Cassirer's discussion of Greek philosophy with much joy and interest."[2]

Very soon Weill formed an initial opinion of the Hochschule. After a month of study he wrote, "The instruction at the Hochschule is certainly not modern; the closest it comes is in Humperdinck's clever disregard for contrapuntal writing. Koch is a rigid contrapuntalist and as a composer a hypermodern much-ado-about-nothing writer."[3]

Nonetheless, he did not dismiss the technical progress his instruction brought him. At the beginning of the summer recess in July 1918 he wrote to his brother: "Looking back at the results of my first semester I believe . . . that I got some idea about what composing is, that I benefited a great deal from my instruction in score reading, organ and even piano playing. . . . What I otherwise learned about life is of inestimable worth: from how to cook gruel to how to deal with immodest female choristers."[4]

Weill returned home to Dessau for just two months, where he wrote at the beginning of August: "As easily as I was working in Berlin, it is now coming to me with great difficulty in this desolate place. So you can see how very dependent I still am on stimulation from teachers, fellow students, operas, and concerts. I wonder if I can ever create real art unless I shed that dependency. Well, we both know that I'm not going to turn into a second Beethoven or Schubert, and I believe the rest have mostly suffered from the same 'illness.'"[5]

Returning to Berlin at the end of August 1918, he lived through the last weeks of the German Empire. Germany had in fact already lost the war, though the armistice of November 1918 was still three months away. The revolutionary situation was heightened when the sailors' mutiny of 3 November in Kiel led into the upheaval of the November Revolution. In Berlin the general strike organized by the Spartacus Union forced the emperor to resign, and Germany became a republic. Everywhere soldiers' and workers' councils were being set up. Kurt Weill followed the events of those weeks and months with keen attention; they sharpened his political views, which had hardly had a chance to develop in Dessau.

On 12 November he reported to his brother:

The great revolution broke out with such elemental force and such fabulous speed on Saturday that it must be utterly incomprehensible to people out in the countryside. I was out the whole previous night and noticed then how carefully everything had been prepared. Of course at that point there were only precautionary rules against the revolution. On Saturday I spent the whole day at the Reichstag, saw the surprise attack on the barracks, the formation of the workers' and soldiers' councils, the parades, the speeches by Liebknecht, Hoffmann, Ledebour, etc., and finally in the evening the heavy fighting at the Marstall. And I witnessed the real battle at the Reichstag yesterday.[6]

And three days later he wrote, "The revolution has been steered into a calmer course even here, and a few outstanding, completely trustworthy men have taken over the reins. It would all be fine were it not for one fear: that in place of a dictatorship of the aristocracy we could get a dictatorship of the proletariat. Of course that is only the goal of the Spartacus Union." He continues: "Jews are being used by every party that feels oppressed as a means of deflection. Naturally, we can work against that. . . . But the kind of politics that those German citizens of Jewish faith are pursuing who want to observe everything without participating is impossible. . . . I wish you cordial *Maseltov* on the first sabbath of peace."[7]

Nor did the events of the day go unfelt at the Hochschule für Musik. In December 1918 a student council was formed in which Weill took an active role. His motivation is worth noting: "I have now been voted into the student council of the Hochschule. Have accepted only to fight against *risches* [Yiddish for anti-Semitism]."[8]

The first demand made by the student council was that the seventy-year-old conservative director of the Hochschule, Hermann Kretzschmar, be dismissed. This happened at the beginning of 1919, and it was more than a year, until spring of 1920, before a successor was found in Franz Schreker. By this time, however, Weill was no longer there to meet him.

In spite of all the unrest, Weill's studies continued. He benefited most from his conducting teacher, Rudolf Krasselt, then principal conductor of Berlin's Städtisches Opernhaus. "Krasselt makes increasing demands on the evolving *répétiteur*. He wants to arm me with what Bing simply let me learn in Dessau. He is also requiring me to take a further step in my piano technique, and I myself can see that I'll have to practice diligently over the summer to recover my technique."[9] Under the influence of Krasselt, as he acknowledged in the spring of 1919, he "almost came to the point of deciding to let go of this writing business"[10] and throw himself entirely into becoming a conductor.

Nonetheless he completed Humperdinck's course in composition and assisted him in orchestrating the opera *Gaudeamus: Szenen aus dem deutschen Studentenleben* (Gaudeamus: Scenes from German Student Life). He reported to his brother, "Yesterday

Engelbert Humperdinck and his dog on the porch of his Berlin
house in 1919. Humperdinck was Kurt's composition teacher at
the Hochschule für Musik in Berlin.

Humperdinck had me come to his apartment for my lesson; he had me stay for tea, and I learned some new things about him and his son. The young H. literally said to me, 'If I had your talent in composition, I would become solely a composer, whether my name was Weill or Humperdinck. Write an opera and you are a made man!' "[11] Under Humperdinck's tutelage he wrote further compositions of his own, including the String Quartet in B minor (1918) and an Orchestral Suite in E major (dedicated "to my father in grateful admiration").

The string quartet consists of four movements, marked moderato, in 6/8; allegro ma non troppo (im heimlich enzählenden Ton [in a secretly narrating tone]), in 2/4; langsam und innig [slow and intimate], in 3/3; and lustig und wild [jovial and wild], in 12/8. The third and fourth movements are played without a break. The opening theme of the first movement is reminiscent of Mozart; the second movement, by contrast, evokes Brahms. It also pays homage to Mahler's Sixth Symphony by incorporating the Alma theme. The finale of the quartet, in the form of a fugue, is indebted to many of Reger's chamber music works. The eighteen-year-old was naturally paying tribute to his immediate musical predecessors. But the new, chromatic harmony is equally pronounced; Weill's music clearly shows every sign of post-Wagnerianism. In this quartet a descending figure of related fourths and fifths—which David Drew has called a "Weillian Ur-Motif" and which recurs in later works, from the First Symphony through *Die Dreigroschenoper*— first appears as a melodic motif. Certain rhythmic figures—the beginnings of a toccata style that will be developed in many later works, through *Die Bürgschaft*—are also evident in the string quartet.

The orchestral suite consists of a total of seven movements and already shows an astonishing assuredness in the handling of individual groups of instruments. This composition was long thought to have disappeared but was rediscovered in 1983.

But Weill's most important work from these months in Berlin was a symphonic poem based on Rilke's *Weise von Liebe und Tod des Cornets Christoph Rilke* (Tale of the Love and Death of Cornet Christopher Rilke). Telling his brother Hans about his work on this, he wrote:

> I want to grow to the point—this would be possible only because of Schönberg— where I write only when I must, when it comes to me most honestly from the depth of my heart; otherwise it becomes rational music, and I hate that. . . . The *Weise* comes to me from my heart; I am really living in this music—but at the same time I am ashamed of it! I need verses to set my imagination in motion; and my imagination is not a bird, it is an airplane! . . . Now you must not think that I sit around all day feeling sorry for myself. No, the orchestration makes me very happy, even though all sorts of mistakes creep in, since I am foolish enough to do it all myself.[12]

Here a working principle appears that Kurt Weill adhered to all his life.

The symphonic poem was premiered in March 1919 by the Hochschule orchestra. As the work is now considered lost, let me quote an excerpt from Heinrich Strobel's essay on the young Weill, which appeared in 1927 in the journal *Melos:* "A symphonic poem on Rilke's *Weise von Liebe und Tod* seeks, in the style of Schönberg's *Pelleas und Melisande*, a stronger concentration of the expressively suspended melos in the superimposition of lines that are also carriers of tones. Here one first sees indications of development: a cautious turning away from the external pathos of late romantic epigones. It is characteristic enough that the brilliance of Straussian instrumentation does not overlay even these first works."[13]

Numerous reports in the surviving correspondence of that time show that Kurt Weill attended plays and concerts regularly during his years as a student at the Hochschule. He speaks enthusiastically of Else Lasker-Schüler's play *Die Wupper,* admires the comic Max Pallenberg, goes to the opera, and, again and again, attends performances of works by Beethoven. Emphatically he writes to his brother: "I would like to fall in love some time to the point of going mad so that I could forget everything else; I believe that would do me good. There is only one other thing that has the kind of effect on me that I imagine love would: Beethoven. I just heard the Kreutzer sonata again at the Hochschule. It could bring me to tears; it alone could make me well if I were ill."[14]

Weill financed his visits to Berlin's theaters and concerts and his purchases of books through his income as choir director at the Jewish synagogue in Berlin-Friedenau, a position he held from May 1918 through the spring of 1919. This brought him 250 marks a month, but it also meant that he had to put up with a lot. "On Sunday in rehearsal we got up to Rosh Hashanah, and this evening I hope to go into exile. The men (there are ten of them) are all *goyim* and hack through the text. But they don't want to rehearse more than twice a week. And so one has to sit here."[15] Sometimes it was even worse: "Yesterday evening, after two composition lessons, I had a choir rehearsal from 7:45 till 11:45 in which I had to simultaneously direct, sing tenor, play the organ, and yell at the women— so I'm fairly exhausted now. Nothing is working; the organ motor is defective and the cantor is singing in the movie house."[16]

But, as he admitted to his brother, all this had to be put up with, "since I am so down and out that without my Friedenau gig I wouldn't be able to pay for my trip home or my food."[17]

Although Weill received, thanks to Humperdinck, a stipend of 300 marks from the Felix Mendelssohn-Bartholdy Institute after the warm reception of his setting of the Rilke poem, it was already clear to him that he was ready to leave the Hochschule, since it had nothing else to offer him. But where to go? Weill sought advice from the leading representative of the musical avant-garde in Berlin, Hermann Scherchen. On 20 June 1919 he wrote to his brother:

> This morning I finally had an interview with Scherchen. He advised me to go to Vienna; he doesn't know Schreker well, though, and thinks that there is really only one person from whom someone who is gifted (he had glanced at my string quartet) could learn something and through whom I would really get an idea of where the young generation is in music and what it wants: Arnold Schönberg, the acknowledged apostle of a new music, who is accomplishing extraordinary things in a private composition school. . . . But this private study probably costs so much money that I can't even contemplate going there, at least not for now. In any case, I'm still going to write to Schönberg today.[18]

A week later he writes:

Why am I not as thick-headed as the rest, who consider it their greatest good fortune to spend five years and more at the Hochschule, who don't even think about there being music out there that they don't know and wouldn't understand? Thank providence that I'm not like that! Thank providence that I seek the new and understand the new. Strauss is faded. Imagine everything that is artificial, trivial, whitewashed, studied about Strauss being replaced by the height of modernity in the Mahler vein, by something drawn deeply from within a great personality: then you have Arnold Schönberg as I have now come to know him through his *Gurrelieder,* a grand work for soloists, chorus, and a huge orchestra based on absolutely heavenly poetry by J. P. Jacobsen. This work and Cassirer's lectures on Spinoza have given me peace in my inner struggles. Whatever happens now will be all right with me, but I must go to Vienna—sooner or later. This Schönberg has brought me something so new that I was left completely speechless.[19]

Schönberg replied quickly to his letter, as Weill reported to his brother on 14 July:

Have I written you yet that I had an extremely nice card from Schönberg from Vienna in which he declares his receptiveness in the most elegant manner. The phrasing of the card is so modern that we're all in raptures over it here. I will give you the exact wording in my next letter. Nonetheless, I can hardly expect to get to Vienna before next spring and have already written to this effect to Schönberg. . . . In any case the date is approaching when I must reach a decision without my knowing what to do. By the 26th I have to be officially withdrawn from the Hochschule. . . . So that leaves Dessau, but only if all else fails.[20]

The family's ailing financial situation ended up keeping Kurt Weill from becoming Arnold Schönberg's pupil in the fall of 1919. What would this have meant for his further development? But the answer to that question already leads us into the realm of speculation. The fact is that Weill had to earn some money and that he had already responded to various job openings (including a position as assistant conductor at the theaters of Cologne and Tilsit). But all this came to naught, and in the end he decided to accept a position as *répétiteur* in Dessau. What clinched this important decision—to take a paid musical position instead of continuing his studies somewhere—was above all the material situation of his family, which had worsened to the point where the support he could provide was urgently needed. The synagogue, experiencing tremendous financial difficulties, let his father go in the early summer of 1919; the family was allowed to stay on in the parish house until he found a new position (which he did in May 1920, as director of a Jewish orphanage in Leipzig).

There was no question for Kurt Weill—either now or in later years—but that he would fulfill his filial duty. A position as *répétiteur* was available to him at the Dessau theater (partly because of his earlier adjunct work there), and so he determined to break off his studies and return from Berlin to Dessau. At first he lived with his parents and his sister, Ruth. Both his brothers had left Dessau after being discharged from the Imperial Army; Nathan was studying medicine in Leipzig, and Hans was a merchant's apprentice in Halberstadt.

Theater Experience in Dessau and Lüdenscheid

At the beginning of the 1919–20 season Kurt Weill assumed his duties as *répétiteur* at Dessau's Friedrich-Theater, as the earlier Hoftheater was now called, following the demise of the German monarchy. It was his first job as a professional musician, and he was proud of the monthly salary he brought home. Hans Knappertsbusch, then already a well-known conductor, was the new musical director of the Friedrich-Theater. Weill's earlier teacher and friend Albert Bing was continuing as conductor.

Announcement of a recital by soprano
Elisabeth Feuge, accompanied by Kurt Weill, in
Dessau's *Anhalter Anzeiger*, 3 September 1919.
Two songs of Weill's were on the program.

Weill had an immediate, big success both as a pianist and as a composer. He prepared a concert of arias and songs with the young soprano Elisabeth Feuge, daughter of Emilie Feuge, who had been a successful chamber singer in Dessau for more than twenty years. A dress rehearsal on 3 September in the nearby town of Köthen was followed the next day by their premiere in Dessau. Along with arias by Meyerbeer and Rossini, as well as songs by Liszt, Wolf, Reger, Pfitzner, and others, two songs of Weill's were included in the program. The review made special mention of Weill's part in the evening: "At the piano Frl. Feuge had in Kurt Weill an accompanist who was outstanding in every respect, one who shone in his exemplary technical mastery and in his musical, poetical nuancing. Two songs composed by this promising young musician were also met with much interest. Avowedly expressionistic—especially the first—they betrayed a strong, independent talent. The audience, which filled the concert hall to capacity, practically showered the two performers with applause."[1]

Which two songs of Weill's were performed is not known; but he himself described the concert's reception quite differently: "The Hoftheater's hall was bursting at the seams with a top-drawer audience, including a lot of nobility, since the entire court appeared. Especially my songs she sang with spell-binding beauty, but their strict modernity was met with stupid misunderstanding from most of the audience. Elisabeth was with the prince afterward, and she and I were invited to visit the crown princess next week for more music-making. In Dessau that still means something, even after 9 November 1918! All the people from the theater came, too, so I have established myself splendidly in my new position."[2] His collaboration with Elisabeth Feuge continued, as a program from a concert of contemporary songs (by Schreker, Pfitzner, Schönberg, and Weill) on 22 June 1920 in Halberstadt testifies.

But for Weill, once the novelty of the eagerly awaited work had worn off, his responsibilities as *répétiteur* quickly became restricting. After a short time, tensions developed between Weill and Knappertsbusch. What had been standard practice under Bing— namely, that the young Kurt Weill was encouraged to participate in all musical discussions and to express his opinions freely—did not sit well with Knappertsbusch. The new

**Kurt Weill (*kneeling in the front row, left*) with his colleagues at
Lüdenscheid's Stadttheater in May 1920. He held the position of
conductor there for six months.**

director admonished his *répétiteur* to stay within the bounds of his prescribed duties. For
the young, multifaceted Weill, this meant being locked into the purely mechanical task of
preparing singers. One incident shows clearly what the atmosphere was like between
Weill and his boss. "During one evening's performance the diminutive *répétiteur,* just as
he was about to prompt the entrance of the tenor, fell through a trapdoor backstage and
was knocked unconscious. The tenor was late for his cue, and Knappertsbusch stormed
backstage at the end of the act, in search of his missing assistant. 'He was always so small,'
he shouted. 'Now he's disappeared completely!' "[3]

It is hardly surprising that Weill latched onto the first chance he could find to leave the
Friedrich-Theater. That opportunity arose in December 1919. In the small Westphalian
town of Lüdenscheid, a certain Arthur Kistenmacher had determined to found a town
theater; the position of conductor was among those that needed filling. On the recommendation of his former teacher Humperdinck, Weill applied for the post and was hired.
After only three months of working in Dessau, he resigned from the Friedrich-Theater
and at the end of November 1919 left his birthplace for good. Thereafter, he returned to
Dessau on only two occasions, for short visits in 1923 and 1928 when his works were
being performed there.

What Kurt Weill found in Lüdenscheid was a typical little third-rate theater. Plays,
operettas, and operas were performed in a hotel lounge. The orchestra was similarly
third-rate; and rehearsal time was much shorter than in Dessau, since there was a new
show nearly every week and, audience size being small, only a few performances of each
show. The repertoire ranged from Wagner to Kollo, with a predominance of operettas and
farces.

Weill was expected not only to conduct but also to rework the orchestral music as
necessary to accommodate Lüdenscheid's orchestra, to add or adjust parts, to work the

**Postcard from Kurt to his brother Hans, 5 March 1920. It reads:
"I wish the two months in this dump were already over."**

singers into the production, and to provide all sorts of musical assistance to his colleagues in the theater. An interview conducted in the United States in 1941 tells of his adventures beginning his job in Lüdenscheid as a completely inexperienced conductor:

> The greenhorn sped to his new job and was only mildly surprised, on his arrival in the late afternoon, at the instruction that he was to conduct the local company in a performance of *Martha* that same evening. His consternation grew a little when he was informed that no score of the opera was available; the publishers parsimoniously kept such scores in whirlwind circulation. But he was told not to worry; it would arrive in time for the performance.
>
> Waiting for the score, he painfully spent his time trying to remember what it was all about. Then his most nightmarish apprehensions became a reality. When the score did arrive, hardly a page of it was in its original state. Instead there was a maze of incomprehensible pencil markings, green denoting "Hamburg cuts," red "Dresden," blue "Munich" and so on. The concertmaster said that the local company used some of the cuts but not others; he wasn't clear on which.[4]

Yet Kurt Weill threw himself into his work there. To his sister, Ruth, he wrote: "You can imagine how much I have to do. Sunday afternoon *Fledermaus*, in the evening *Cavalleria Rusticana*, Monday afternoon *Zigeunerbaron*, in the evening the premiere of a new operetta. How I am to finish rehearsing is a mystery to me; no one here seems to have any idea what it means to perform *Cavalleria* with this orchestra and chorus."[5] How must he have felt at the conductor's podium during *The Flying Dutchman*? Having to work on pieces a level below operettas must have been especially depressing. "Tomorrow I have another premiere," he writes "a horribly foul sung burlesque called *Im 6. Himmel* (In Sixth Heaven)."[6]

Program from a March 1920 performance at the town theater in
Lüdenscheid. Kurt Weill is listed as musical director.

In spite of these working conditions and in spite of many low points, this was where Weill learned the craft of the theater and the orchestra. From now on, no one would be able to hoodwink him in this area. "I learned everything I know about the theater there," he later declared and said, in a similar vein, that it was during his half-year in Lüdenscheid that he realized that "my special field of activity would be the theater" and determined to make this the focus of his work.[7]

That the barely twenty-year-old Kurt Weill still found time alongside such exhausting theatrical work to compose speaks for his energy and iron determination. In Lüdenscheid he undertook his first real work on opera (other than the *Zriny* project begun in 1916), a one-act opera based on Ernst Hardt's play *Ninon von Lenclos*. He wrote to his sister, "In case my theater life leaves me a little time and energy for my own work again, I intend to finish setting the one-act play of Ernst Hardt's that I have started. If it works out, it could even lead the way toward a new, thoroughly lyrical direction in the production of musical drama. If I were now to create a piece of art in collaboration with a poet, I would have wholly new ideas for it. . . . But for now I can't even think about composition work; no one can imagine how that makes me suffer."[8] Whether Weill finished the one-act opera at that time is questionable, since we have no existing evidence of it. The situation is quite

The young Kurt Weill as a champion of contemporary music.
Program from a concert of the Jewish cultural association of the
town of Halberstadt, given on 22 June 1920.

different with another composition likewise begun in Lüdenscheid, the choral fantasy *Sulamith,* based on verses from the Song of Songs. Did Weill wish to withdraw from the extreme secularity of the theater world into the fold of his faith? Parts of the manuscript have survived, and Heinrich Strobel must have known the entire work when he wrote that Weill

> is plugging away through the most insignificant little ditties. He is comfortable with the hands-on work of theater. If one looks at any one of the composition drafts from this period, the musical sphere in which the twenty-year-old lives broadens. It extends to Debussy, to the early Schönberg. Impressionistic sound and expansive melody flow together in the choral fantasy *Sulamith*. Only in fleeting moments do clearer contours stand out from the dramatically rippling movement. Already significant is an angular voice-leading, which disrupts tonal boundaries, and also the effort to articulate clearly and distinctly the poetry sung by soprano and women's chorus."[9]

Letters show that as early as March 1920 he was already thinking seriously about his next step. Seek a new, better theater position? Go to Schönberg in Vienna after all? Or continue studying in Berlin? On 14 March he wrote, "By the winter I'll be turning my back on operetta for good. Maybe I can somehow realize my Vienna plan. In any case, I no longer have to starve for my art."[10] A month later, at the end of April, he wrote: "I am determined, should I not find a truly attractive position for the winter, to go to Berlin in the fall to prepare for my doctorate and, if I can, study with Schreker."[11]

After working there for six months, Weill left Lüdenscheid with the following assessment: "Looking back, I can see that I have learned a lot. I feel so secure now as a conductor that I am no longer fearful of anything."[12]

From Westphalia Weill went to Leipzig, where his parents had moved from Dessau. For one last time he now lived in his parents' home for a few months. He stepped in as substitute director of two Leipzig choruses so as to make his contribution to the still modest resources of his family. He had not yet made any decisions about his future. At the end of July 1920 he wrote to his brother, "I just spent a few days in Berlin. . . . I am eagerly seeking a dissertation topic, probably from the realm of symphonic music. It's not such an easy thing."[13]

During these months in Leipzig Kurt Weill finished a composition that he had begun during his time at the Hochschule in Berlin and then continued in Lüdenscheid: the Sonata for Violoncello and Piano, dedicated to Fritz Rupprecht, solo cellist at the Dessau theater, and Albert Bing.

The sonata consists of three movements, marked allegro ma non troppo in 4/4; andante espressivo in 7/8; and allegro assai, wild bewegt, grotesk vorzutragen [to be performed grotesquely, with wild movement], in 3/8. It demonstrates—even before he began to study with Busoni—Weill's remarkable control of diatonic harmonic material. At the same time, the characteristic elements of the String Quartet in B minor are retained. The thematic construction of this work could be called cyclical. "One of the most persistent characteristics of his harmony is what could be called 'semitonal instability,' whereby one chord or harmonic complex dissolves into the next through the chromatic shift of a semitone by one or more of its notes. The result is a continual hovering between major and minor keys."[14] This harmonic trait (the "chromatic shift of a semitone") being characteristic of many of Ferruccio Busoni's compositions, the sonata shows how much Weill had already absorbed of Busoni's style, and the degree to which he had already taken him as a model, even before he joined Busoni's master class.

So the normal life of a conductor could have begun for Kurt Weill, in the theater or the concert world, perhaps. But just to compose on the side, more or less as a break from his conducting work? This was not an option for the twenty-year-old Weill. He had long since laid aside the one-time thought of giving up his "scribbling." His father supported him in his decision to seek to perfect his compositional abilities with a real teacher. Franz Schreker, who in the meantime had become the new director of the Hochschule für Musik in Berlin, seemed to him to offer the best possibilities. So in the late summer of 1920 Kurt Weill decided to try his luck once more in the capital.

At the beginning of September he bade his parents farewell in Leipzig and moved to Berlin to start a new, important stage of his life. His *Wanderjahre* were over; now came the decisive phase in the forming of the composer.

Master Pupil with Busoni

Kurt Weill arrived in Berlin in September 1920 as one of a veritable throng of young intellectuals and artists who were drawn from all over Germany to the capital city, which was fast becoming the new intellectual and cultural center of the Weimar Republic. With the decree by the Prussian Landtag of 1 October 1920 uniting eight urban and fifty-nine rural districts into the new metropolis of Greater Berlin, a city of three and a half million emerged, second only to Los Angeles in population and area. In the years that followed, Berlin developed into an artistic mecca of European stature. Many obstacles of the Wilhelminian era gave way to a broad opening for the democratic exchange of ideas, and in this center of industrialization and urbanization numerous new institutions and opportunities for the production of art were created on a scale not previously known. The flourishing world of journalism, publishing, and theater offered many employment possibilities; in short, any young person who wanted to get somewhere in the early 1920s went to Berlin. Carl Zuckmayer reflected this feeling of a whole generation: "You could already sense something of that incomparable intensity, that stormy upsurge which within a few years made Berlin the most interesting and exciting city in Europe. . . . Berlin smacked of the future. For the sake of that you were willing to brave the cold, the filth, the ill-treatment."[1]

Alongside the opulence of the city's cultural life, a grave social and political polarization was taking place. Berlin at this time had the largest concentration of tenements in the world and—especially in the final years of the Weimar Republic—it became a battleground for embittered class warfare and clashes between progressive and reactionary forces.

In the twenties Berlin's musical life also attained world stature. The city offered musicians many teaching and working possibilities, as well as first-class performance opportunities for their own works. Kurt Weill would become well acquainted with both in the rich, fruitful decade to follow.

But his star had not yet risen. Equipped with a stipend of over fifty Reichsmarks a month from his uncle Leopold, who wanted to help support his nephew's studies in music, Weill rented a modest furnished room and set out to seek some first contacts. Berlin's musical world was just then celebrating the return of Ferruccio Busoni after a five-year sojourn in Zurich. We do not know if Weill attended either of the two triumphant piano recitals that Busoni gave in November 1920 at the Berlin Philharmonie and about which the Englishman Edward J. Dent (who in 1921 became the first president of the newly formed International Society for Contemporary Music) wrote, "The great hall was filled to overflowing, and he was greeted with such demonstrations of enthusiasm as that room had seldom seen. . . . These recitals left no doubt that Berlin welcomes him with open arms."[2] The press was already announcing in the summer of 1920 that Busoni would conduct a master class in composition at the Preußische Akademie der Künste.

It was Leo Kestenberg, himself a former pupil of Busoni's and since 1919 responsible for music within the Prussian Ministry of Culture, who had taken the initiative. In 1919 he had sent an offer to Busoni in Zurich that could hardly be refused: a class limited to six months a year and two days of instruction a week in his Berlin apartment. Busoni accepted the offer. He was to select his pupils by December 1920 and begin the master class in January 1921.

This news prompted Weill to set aside his original plan to return to the Hochschule and to apply for Busoni's master class instead. Under whose auspices this happened is impossible to reconstruct precisely; but a letter Weill wrote to his father in late November 1920 shows that the critic Oskar Bie played a part, and the very same month the young composer received an invitation to visit Busoni. He handed in a number of compositions to be looked over along with his application. "You can hardly believe how hard it is to get

**Ferruccio Busoni (1866–1924) in 1921, the year in which Kurt
Weill started studying with him.**

to Busoni; the doorman is instructed to send everyone away. Nonetheless, I spent an
extremely interesting afternoon with him. His talk is tremendously stimulating, and he
requires complete freedom and openness, even in a social setting, making it hard for
someone like me to know how to be with him. I've not yet accomplished anything
positive. He is astonished at my youth, has kept my compositions but does not want to
decide, since so many people have applied that there is hardly any room left for a young
whippersnapper such as me. Oh well."[3] Kurt Weill's joy must have been all the greater
when, a little later, in December 1920, news reached him that Busoni had accepted him
into his class.

Ferruccio Busoni, born in 1866 near Florence, was one of the decisive forces in the
musical development of the first decades of our century. He grew up as a child prodigy
and made his debut while still very young as a piano virtuoso and a composer. From 1888

on, he was increasingly involved in teaching piano at, among other places, the conservatories of Helsinki, Moscow, and Boston, where he also taught music theory. In 1894 he settled in Berlin, but each year he spent a few months away, giving master classes for pianists, in Vienna in 1907–08 and Basel in 1910, and in 1913–14 serving as director of the Liceo musicale in Bologna. In between times there were also extended concert tours. In the fall of 1915 Busoni moved to Zurich.

He had begun to compose as a seven-year-old, and his music showed the strong influence of the classical and romantic German musical tradition of the eighteenth and nineteenth centuries. In addition, he edited numerous works of Bach's, earning him an outstanding reputation as "Bach-Busoni." Even in his youthful works he had forged ahead into new harmonic realms; and his compositions from about 1909 on are characterized by radical bi-, poly-, and atonal extensions of harmony.

Busoni had formulated his aesthetic views in 1907 in his *Entwurf einer neuen Ästhetik der Tonkunst* (Sketch of a New Esthetic of Music), which was widely circulated among young musicians, especially in its second, expanded edition of 1916, where one could read: "The harmony of *to-day,* and not for long; for all signs presage a revolution, and a next step."[4] The thoughts in this book grew out of a fundamental misgiving over the dogmatization of traditional rules and its implication in the stagnation of musical progress—a misgiving that was shared by people working in all the arts at this time and which focused a great deal of energy around questions of artistic revolution and renewal. This explains the widespread appeal of Busoni's book, which became a programmatic document for an entire generation of young musicians. It discusses the most diverse problems of musical production and reproduction but does not offer finished solutions; rather, it seeks to provide critical stimulus—as does Busoni's concept of a "comprehensive, youthful classicism which incorporates all that is experimental from the beginning of the twentieth century."[5] In the last section of his *Entwurf* Busoni develops, in the place of the two modes of major and minor, 113 scales of seven tones within an octave; with a "kaleidoscopic blending and interchanging of twelve semitones."[6] He comes quite close to Schönberg in his atonal period.

The book's reception can be understood only in the context of the time. Busoni wrote in a letter to his wife, Gerda: "In a voice shaking with excitement, a young student spoke to me on the street, in order to tell me about the great impression my little book had made on him."[7] The *Entwurf* was a call to set out for new shores and reflected exactly what had been taking place in musical development since about 1910. Naturally it sparked great controversies. The conservatives, led by Hans Pfitzner, saw a "futuristic danger" entering German music; at least, so read the title of a polemic by Pfitzner written in reaction to the *Entwurf einer neuen Ästhetik der Tonkunst.*

Busoni had also made significant contributions to the development of musical theater by the time Weill met him. Although he wrote only four works for the stage in all, it was above all the two one-act operas *Turandot* and *Arlecchino* (both premiered in 1917), as well as *Doktor Faust* (first performed posthumously, but it was being composed in 1920–21 and Busoni had already presented parts of it), that put his thoughts about operatic theory into practice and had an extraordinarily strong influence on contemporary discussions. Busoni asserted that "opera as a musical composition always consisted in a series of short, concise pieces and that it will never be able to exist in any other form."[8]

Furthermore, Ferruccio Busoni was a famous personage, thanks to his aristocratic appearance and his contacts with many leading representatives of the intellectual life of his day; in short, by around 1920 he had become the musical and also the personal idol of an entire generation of young musicians in Germany and Europe. Though he was certainly not of Schönberg's lasting, school-building significance and though his works are now, unjustly, almost forgotten, Busoni lives on as the second great central figure of late bourgeois musical development in our century. A synthesis of him and Schönberg is hardly possible, since they represent opposed paths of musical development, but as David Drew has said of Weill and Schönberg, they are "linked by their irreconcilable differences no less than by their secret affinities."[9] Jutta Theurich adds, "If one wishes to assess both the mutual effect these two artists had on each other and their personalities, one cannot help but realize that in spite of the divergences, even oppositions, in the artistic solutions they proposed, these were only different answers to general problems of a particular historical phase. In this respect their outer and individual differences come to appear as an inner commonality manifesting itself in different ways."[10]

It was clearly a great honor for Kurt Weill to be accepted into Busoni's master class, which began in January and was officially inaugurated on 1 July 1921. It consisted in the end of only five pupils—all of them, in spite of the fears Weill expressed to his father, "young whippersnappers"! Along with Weill, three Swiss—Luc Balmer (born 1898), Robert Blum (born 1900), and Walther Geiser (born 1897)—were selected, as well as the native Muscovite Wladimir Vogel (born 1896). Here too Busoni's sense of being a world citizen was reflected.

The instruction took place in Busoni's elegant apartment on the Viktoria-Luise-Platz; a photograph shows the teacher, seated in a dignified pose, as *spiritus rector* amid the young men. He received his pupils twice a week: "The young men come on Mondays and Thursdays, but I can send them away after an hour or an hour and a half."[11] Busoni's teaching has been described by the composer Philipp Jarnach, who became a friend of his in 1914 and worked in the conservatory in Zurich from 1918 to the middle of 1921, as follows:

> Busoni was not a teacher in the narrow sense of the word. He lacked both any kind of educative impulse and, self-evidently, the passionate impartiality of a pedagogue. Although he himself had undergone complicated schooling in theory, he did not believe in instructional systems. As he saw it, only intellectual independence and insight could penetrate the practical to the point where art, rather than mere routine, might come into being. The sensibility of the individual was the sole force able to overcome the resistance of the material; and though he considered a flawless assimilation of empirical experience to be indispensable, he demanded that an artist never rely on what he had learned but instead draw from the idea itself the means with which to formulate it. This heroic view, which consciously ignored all the intermediate stages of ability and also shifted technical problems into the creative sphere, shows adequately

Ferruccio Busoni with the pupils in his master class in 1922; *left*
to right: **Kurt Weill, Walther Geiser, Luc Balmer, Wladimir Vogel.**

Busoni's impatience with all systematizing, with all rhetorical lack of expressive originality. Nonetheless, he did not tire of pointing toward the formal world of a Bach or a
Mozart, toward the infinite capacity of a supreme freedom of imagination to fill
seemingly narrow formulas with new life in the free play of the powers of melody. His
own example and this attitude were the great teaching the young artists received from
him.[12]

In 1925 Kurt Weill wrote about his experience of the classes: "At this stage there were
no longer any 'pupils.' He called us 'disciples'; he gave no lessons but let us breathe his
being, which, though manifesting itself in all realms, always culminated in music. The
hours spent in these daily meetings are too recent for me to be able to talk about them. It
was an exchange of ideas in the highest sense, without any pressure to voice opinions,
without any self-satisfaction, without any trace of envy or malice; and the recognition of
any creativity that betrayed talent and ability was unqualified and enthusiastic."[13]

Very quickly a cordial relationship developed between Busoni and Weill. Wladimir
Vogel recalls, "Kurt was a modest, rather quiet listener, who greatly respected Busoni and

was in turn esteemed by him."[14] And the music critic Rudolf Kastner wrote: "One afternoon Busoni introduced me to a small, quiet man about twenty years of age. Behind glasses two eyes shine, flicker. In conversation he showed himself to be an extraordinarily purposeful, serious person of strong character. Busoni spoke of him in his absence with special warmth. Indeed he 'tended' him like a fatherly, loving gardener who transfers all his love to one flower or one tree."[15]

The letters from Kurt Weill from the years 1921–24 that are preserved in Busoni's literary estate show how strongly the pupil returned his teacher's tender affection: "Esteemed, dear Master," he already writes toward the end of the first month of instruction in January 1921, "please take for granted that I, with all that I have, am at your disposal for your work, your life."[16] And seven months later he writes to his brother, "I am leading a wonderful life divided between productive work and priceless exchange of ideas with Busoni, who really has taken me to his heart."[17]

The first important composition of Weill's during his studies with Busoni was written between April and June 1921, a one-movement work for orchestra, now known as his First Symphony. The impetus was an encounter in November 1920 with the writer Johannes R. Becher, who told Weill about the expressionist-pacifist play he had just finished writing, *Arbeiter, Bauern, Soldaten: Der Aufbruch eines Volkes zu Gott* (Workers, Peasants, and Soldiers: The Awakening of a People to God). Weill wrote immediately to his brother about it, saying, "Furthermore, I have prospects of a composition commission for a play of J. R. Becher's. It's a great piece! 'Aufbruch eines Volkes zu Gott,' ecstatic suspense; the most important young composers are scrambling for it, since Becher is considered to have the greatest future among young writers."[18] A few days later Becher sent the manuscript to Weill. It is now impossible to tell whether the two of them perhaps envisioned an oratorio setting—which certainly would have suited the text—but the result instead was a one-movement symphony.

This symphony comes across as a youthful work by a composer of extraordinary ability. The title page of the score carries an epigraph from Becher's play of 1920, whose social-utopian text, influenced by Strindberg's religiosity, conjures up the vision of a people glorifying God and setting out for a land of social justice. The idea and the expressionistic, feverish diction of the stage work reflected the twenty-one-year-old Weill's own view of the world, and he constructed a symphonic conception upon it—formally influenced, no doubt, by Schönberg's Chamber Symphony, op. 9. It shows an expressive art that is already quite independent and mature; one can hear the influence of Liszt and Richard Strauss in its treatment of themes and motifs and of Gustav Mahler in its musical expression, but none of these overshadows the originality of Weill's achievement. In spite of the epigraph on the title page, this work is "programmatic" only insofar as it attempts to express through musical means the religious and revolutionary themes of Becher's play.

The symphony is written for a relatively small orchestra by comparison with Weill's own later orchestral works or those of Liszt and Strauss. This allows Weill to create in places transparent solo combinations that more closely resemble chamber music than a large symphony. Three main divisions (exposition, development, and recapitulation)

Portrait of Kurt Weill drawn by Busoni's son Raffaelo in 1925.

underpin the work, but it is also "pieced together" out of many small sections, each with its own thematic character. Weill's use of continuing thematic transformation ties the individual, quite diverse sections of differing character into a unified cyclical structure. The finale is a three-verse chorale variation, which provides a counterpart to Becher's *Aufbruch eines Volkes zu Gott*. Here Weill expresses his deep religious sensibilities, which he will often bring into his music, in their pure form.

Heinrich Strobel, who knew this work in manuscript form, wrote: "A first contact with the trends of the day, which will become decisive for later works, is evident here. The musical will piles up melodic appoggiaturas. Rhythmic elements erupt that had been lost in the chaos of sound and of musico-dramatic intensification. The construction is much more concise."[19]

When Weill presented the work in class at the end of June in a piano reduction for four hands, Busoni reacted quite critically. He did not approve of the expressionist idiom and the web of nonmusical ties to the intellectual movements of the day; only the chorale variation of the finale did he find worthy. The master also decided that Weill needed a more thorough grounding in counterpoint and arranged for appropriate instruction by Philipp Jarnach, who had come to Berlin from Zurich in the middle of 1921. So for a good year, through the end of 1922, Weill was also a pupil of Jarnach's.

In light of Busoni's criticism, Weill did not release the symphony for performance. The score, which disappeared in 1933, did not resurface until 1957, when the work was premiered, thirty-six years after its composition, in Hamburg.

Weill's material circumstances throughout his time as a student were extremely modest. Although the academy had waived tuition, his uncle's stipend did not suffice to support him. "My shirts are falling apart," he wrote to his father shortly before Christmas of 1920. "Will I be getting Hanukkah carp? I have a very immodest request: Could you all perhaps send me a little bottle of sherry, just to warm me through a bit?"[20] Starting in January 1921, this pupil of Busoni's had a regular source of extra income playing the piano for guests in a Berlin pub. Hans W. Heinsheimer, later head of the stage division of Vienna's Universal Edition, gives a vivid description of Weill's appearances: "He was forced to support himself by playing the piano in an obscure *Bierkeller* from evening until dawn. His earnings depended upon the generosity of the patrons, who were expected to drop their contributions on a plate conspicuously displayed on the piano. To encourage donations, Weill would break into an exorcising crescendo whenever he perceived a prosperous-looking party preparing to depart."[21]

Weill's financial situation finally improved somewhat at the end of 1922; now a certified master pupil of Busoni's, he could begin taking pupils of his own, often sent to him by Philipp Jarnach. These included the composer Nikos Skalkottas, who had come to Berlin from Greece; the pianist Claudio Arrau; and Maurice Abravanel (a Swiss citizen born in Greece), who later became one of the foremost conductors of Weill's music. Abravanel remembers his instruction from Weill at a time when inflation was skyrocketing in Germany:

> In '22 and '23 Kurt did not have a penny to his name, he was traveling all over Berlin to give lessons simply because he needed the money. I remember him coming to me and saying, "A White Russian girl, sixteen, gives me hell because I am twenty minutes late for her lesson. You know how difficult it is with a streetcar to be on time." That was the day when I decided I would go to him for my lessons. . . . But the basic thing with Kurt was music. Even though he did not have a penny, he said to me, "You know, on Good Friday at the St. Thomas Church in Leipzig, they do the *St. Matthew Passion*. And I am taking the train and going there. Would you go, too?" And I didn't have a penny either. But somehow we got the money to take the railroad to Leipzig. And we went to hear the *St. Matthew*.[22]

Of great importance for Kurt Weill's integration into the intellectual and musical life of Berlin was his participation in the Novembergruppe, starting in 1922. This was one of the most influential and most active artists' organizations in Berlin, founded in November 1918 and in existence through 1932. The group first came into being as a meeting point for visual artists and soon counted some 120 members. Starting in 1922, it also included musicians, and in January a separate division for them was formed within the group. The office was in the house of the group's director, Hugo Graetz, at Potsdamer Straße 113, where Weill was a frequent guest.

The Novembergruppe had begun its work of renewing art and politics in January 1919, but after just a few years the artistic concerns had come so much to the fore that a group of politically conscious, engaged members split off, formulating their position in an "Open Letter to the Novembergruppe," which stated: "For us our affirmation of the Revolution, to the new society, is not a matter of paying lip service, and so we want to take our acknowledged task seriously: to work together to form a new human society, the society of workers!"[23] The letter was signed by Otto Dix, George Grosz, Raoul Haus-mann, Rudolf Schlichter, and others. Significantly, there were no musicians among those who left the Novembergruppe for political reasons; for them a discussion of the new possibilities and forms for art was more important than throwing themselves into the political struggles of the day. Weill was no exception.

The numerous activities of the group afforded its members many opportunities for stimulating encounters with artists of other genres and for discussions and debates, as well as for the presentation of newly finished works.

The musical division was founded and presided over by Heinz Tiessen and Max Butting; this work was taken over by Hans Heinz Stuckenschmidt in 1924. In addition to these three and Weill, the other active members of this division were Philipp Jarnach, Wladimir Vogel, Felix Petyrek, Jascha Horenstein, George Antheil, Stefan Wolpe, and, starting in 1925, Hanns Eisler.

There were regularly scheduled concerts in the Kleiner Saal of the Vox house, in the Grotrian-Steinweg-Saal on Potsdamer Straße, and in the Meistersaal on Köthener Straße; and from time to time chamber music evenings were held in the director's apartment. Max Butting writes:

> The concerts took place in the Kleiner Saal of the Vox house. That, too, was done on purpose, because it meant that the hall was always overflowing, and the press always made much of how well the concerts were attended. If we had taken even a medium-sized concert hall, with the same audience there might well have been reports about the half-empty space. We also sought out the very best performers. A call to visual artists resulted in our having drawings, watercolors, and small sculptures of theirs at our disposal, and most of the performers took great pleasure in being asked to select one of them as an honorarium; furthermore, the artists were not likely to stay away from the concerts if they knew that the performers were taking home their own works. So we always had an audience, largely made up of artists, that took a lively interest in the concerts. We made sure we were the first to perform any works of chamber music which had been premiered outside Berlin and had been spoken of highly in the Berlin press. I remember that we were the first to perform Hanns Eisler's Piano Sonata, op. 1,

Portrait of Kurt Weill drawn by Max Dungert, a member of the Novembergruppe, toward the end of 1922, the year Weill joined.

and Hindemith's Second String Quartet in Berlin, that the Amar Quartet first played with us; and all this gave the podium of the Novembergruppe prestige and dignity. Since we didn't need to follow anything other than our artistic principle of bringing new works forward for discussion, we became a first important center for new music. What with the influence of the Berlin press throughout Germany and the ample attention given by the press to each concert, the activities of the Novembergruppe had quite a far-reaching influence.[24]

Let us listen to one other voice to gain an authentic sense of the atmosphere which—along with the instruction from Busoni and Jarnach—shaped Weill's artistic personality as it matured and developed. Hans Heinz Stuckenschmidt relates:

It must have been in 1922 that I rang Hugo Graetz's doorbell with greetings from Hirsch and, once inside his apartment, gazed with awe at the wet canvases of many artists whose work I knew. Soon thereafter I was taken in as a member. At the meetings I got to know Heinz Tiessen, Max Butting, and Kurt Weill. I first met Stefan Wolpe at the Bauhaus in Weimar in the summer of 1923. I attended the group's concerts whenever I came from Hamburg to Berlin. They took place in small halls like the Schwechten-Saal, the Künstlerhaus on Bellevuestraße, and the Grotrian-Steinweg-Saal. But they were packed with an audience for whom visual art, literature, and architecture predominated over music. That distinguished them, for example, from the performances of the Melos Circle and of the International Society for Contemporary Music, whose specialists kept more to themselves and whose resonance was correspondingly smaller. . . . In spite of its political name, the practical politics of the group did not play much of a role. But it was taken for granted that we would ask the politically active Viennese Schönberg pupil Eisler to join our circle. Wladimir Vogel, who had come to Berlin from Moscow imbued with the aura of a revolutionary musician, belonged to the circle of Ferruccio Busoni, whom we admired but whose calls for a classicist order we did not understand. Weill was more farsighted in this matter and defended Busoni's aesthetics in many discussions. It was he who suggested asking Philipp Jarnach to become a member. . . . In the often passionate discussions during group meetings on Achenbachstraße the most explosive topic was the situation of modern art in Soviet Russia. Vogel always held back in such discussions, but Eisler and Weill stood completely on the side of socialist aesthetics, which preferred to forgo the technical and intellectual achievements of the European avant-garde in favor of a widespread impact.[25]

Stuckenschmidt's reminiscences after forty years cannot be taken entirely at face value; to equate Eisler's and Weill's aesthetic views would be a crude simplification. Whereas Eisler was already busy formulating a concrete agenda of music for the working class and was about to start composing along these lines when he came in contact with the Novembergruppe, Weill's renewal efforts were restricted to the art forms of music and theater.

Weill turned to both areas in 1922, with three compositions and also his first Berlin performances. But first Busoni commissioned him to make a piano reduction of his Divertimento for Flute and Orchestra, op. 52, composed in 1920 and first performed on 13 January 1921 in Berlin. Both this reduction and the score were published in 1922 by Breitkopf & Härtel in Leipzig. At this time Weill also wrote his *Divertimento für kleines Orchester mit Männerchor* (Divertimento for Small Orchestra with Male Chorus), consisting of six movements, the last of which included a choral setting of a text by Jens Peter Jacobsen, the Danish writer whose verses were the basis for Schönberg's *Gurrelieder*. This last movement was first heard in a "concert with compositions by the pupils from the Staatsakademie in the master class of Prof. Dr. Ferruccio Busoni" on 7 December 1922. The concert, performed by the Berlin Philharmonic Orchestra and the chorus of the Kaiser-Wilhelm-Gedächtniskirche, took place in the venerable Berliner Singakademie and also included works by Geiser, Balmer, Blum, and Vogel. The conductor was Heinz Unger, who premiered the entire Divertimento somewhat later, on 10 April 1923, in a Philharmonic concert. Unfortunately, the score is only partially preserved, as is the score of the next work.

Kurt Weill had already made his debut with the Berlin Philharmonic a month earlier, when Alexander Sero and the Philharmonic Orchestra premiered his *Sinfonia sacra:*

104782

FERRUCCIO BUSONI

DIVERTIMENTO

FÜR FLÖTE UND KLEINES ORCHESTER

OP. 52

AUSGABE FÜR FLÖTE UND KLAVIER

BEARBEITET VON KURT WEILL

Eigentum der Verleger für alle Länder

BREITKOPF & HÄRTEL

LEIPZIG · BERLIN

E. B. 5305

**Title page of Weill's arrangement for flute and piano of Busoni's
Divertimento for Flute and Small Orchestra, op. 52, which was
published in Leipzig in 1922.**

Fantasia, Passacaglia und Hymnus für Orchester, dedicated to Philipp Janarch "in grati-
tude." It must have been a proud moment for Weill, who had worked along the lines of his
First Symphony in both these orchestral works. Deep religious bonds are again evident,
as is Busoni's influence. Heinrich Strobel notes:

> The transformation is slowly accomplished from a state of pathetic excitement to
> freely swinging, absolute melody. A sense of the formal, of the terseness and organic
> organization of the structure, is awakened. The spirit of the suite and polyphony—
> both essential elements of Busoni's work—break through, provide support for a flow
> that presses on toward a grouping of sections reminiscent of fantasy. Here one can see
> most clearly the dramatic tendencies even of his works written for the concert
> hall. . . . The real problem: blending the dramatic expressive will that runs in his
> blood with the new musical language that is more and more clearly marked in each
> new work. In time it will lead him to the theater.[26]

Konzertdirektion Hermann Wolff und Jules Sachs
Berlin W. 9   Linkstrasse 42

Preis 40,— Mk.

Sing-Akademie

Donnerstag, den 7. Dezember 1922, abends 7½ Uhr

KONZERT

mit

Kompositionen der Staatsakademischen
∴ Schüler aus der Meisterklasse ∴
Prof. Dr. Ferruccio Busoni

Ausführende:

Das Berliner Philharmonische Orchester
Der Chor der Kaiser Wilhelm Gedächtnis-Kirche

Dirigenten:

Dr. H. Unger und die Komponisten

PROGRAMM

1. **Walther Geiser:**
Ouverture zu einem Lustspiel

2. **Kurt Weill:**
Letzter Satz aus dem „Divertimento"

3. **Robert Blum:**
Drei kurze Stücke für Orchester
Ouverture, Intermezzo, Rondo

4. **Luc Balmer:**
Letzter Teil einer Symphonie (c-moll, d-moll)
Thema, Gegenthema, Recitativo, Reprise, Finale

5. **Wladimir Vogel:**
Symphonischer Vorgang (in einem Satz)

KONZERTFLÜGEL: BECHSTEIN

Während der Vorträge bleiben die Saaltüren geschlossen

Program from a concert of compositions written by members of Busoni's master class at Berlin's venerable Sing-Akademie, 7 December 1922. It includes the last movement, with chorus, of Weill's Divertimento for Small Orchestra with Male Chorus.

An opportunity for such work opened up as early as the late summer of 1922, when Weill—probably again through Jarnach's mediation—received a commission to compose a ballet pantomime.

The Russian choreographer Wladimir Boritsch had brought with him to Berlin a libretto he himself had written called *Die Zaubernacht* (The Magic Night), which was to be performed as a ballet pantomime for children during Advent at the Theater am Kurfürstendamm. Weill's score for nine instrumentalists and solo soprano stands at the beginning of his work for musical theater; although it received little notice at the time, it is of great significance for the composer's further development.

Weill himself remarked about the music: "I wrote the pantomime *Die Zaubernacht* for a Russian troupe at the Theater am Kurfürstendamm. I have learned two things from the concentrated intensity of Russian theater art: that the stage has its own musical form, which develops organically out of the flow of the plot, and that important events can truly be expressed only through the simplest, least conspicuous means. An orchestra of nine, a singer, two dancers, and a few children—that was the entire apparatus of this dream dance."[27]

The premiere of *Die Zaubernacht* took place on 18 November 1922 at the Theater am Kurfürstendamm. George Weller conducted the performance, Franz Ludwig Hörth was the director, and Elfriede Marherr-Wagner from the Staatsoper Unter den Linden sang the solo. The story of a magical fairy who can bring toys to life, set to Weill's simple, pointed music, offered the two solo dancers and the members of the Mary Zimmermann ballet school every expressive opportunity. The premiere's audience included Busoni, who wanted to assess his pupil's work, and the expressionist playwright Georg Kaiser, who would soon become an important partner for Weill.

Since the performances (there were three in all) took place in the afternoon, the Berlin press took little notice of *Die Zaubernacht*. Only three papers ran even short reviews— but these are very revealing, showing even in 1922 the same political tendencies that a decade later would characterize the *Kulturkampf* of the Weimar Republic's final years. Whereas the *Berliner Börsen-Courier,* a liberal paper that was always open to innovation in art, welcomed Weill's music as "interesting in its thematic structure, its fresh colorfulness, its liveliness, and its illustrative power which matches, furthers, and deepens each changing mood" and reported an "enthusiastic reception among the youngsters in the parquet,"[28] the arch-conservative *Germania* formed quite a different opinion. *Germania* reported that "Kurt Weill's orchestral sounds with their unmelodic dominants and paraphrases were rejected as too affected by small ears" and then pronounced the following verdict: "When it comes to ideas about the artistic education of children, we still have to

Announcement in the Berlin press of various performances, including (*bottom*) the premiere of *Die Zaubernacht* on 18 November 1922 at three o'clock in the afternoon.

**Program from a concert given in Dessau on 14 June 1923, which
included the premiere of Weill's Orchestral Suite, op. 9.**

keep the church in the village!"[29] (This is the very same language that the Nazis would use
ten years later to attack *Der Jasager!*)

Heinrich Strobel recognized the potential of this theater musician when he wrote, "If,
driven by his talent, he now should come to the theater, then the centrality of music in the
dance play or the opera play would be self-evident. It will take only a decisive poetic
stimulus, and the stream of music, powerfully gripped by dramatic content, will pour
itself out into the theater."[30] Three years passed, however, before Weill's development
took him to the opera stage.

In 1923 he arranged this music as an orchestral suite and dedicated it to his first
teacher, Albert Bing, who gave the premiere on 14 June 1923 in Dessau. Following its
publication by Universal Edition at the end of 1925 under the title *Quodlibet. Eine
Unterhaltungsmusik. Vier Stücke aus einem Kindertheater für großes Orchester* (Quod-

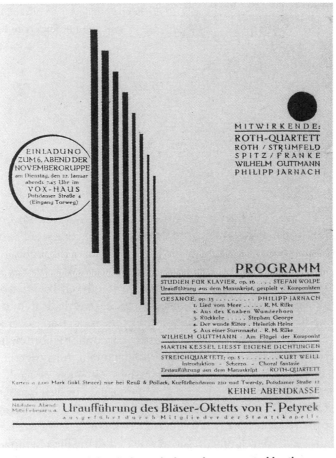

Program of the sixth musical evening presented by the Novembergruppe, on 22 January 1924. It included the Berlin premiere of Weill's String Quartet, op. 8, written the previous year.

libet. Light Music. Four Pieces from a Children's Play for Symphony Orchestra), the suite was performed numerous times by such prominent conductors as Felix Weingartner (Vienna, 1927), Alexander von Zemlinsky (Prague, 1927), and Jascha Horenstein (Berlin, 1929).

Die Zaubernacht was also the first work of Weill's to be performed in the United States; at the end of 1924 it appeared in New York as *Magic Night*. The Berlin production of *Die Zaubernacht* brought one further meeting whose significance Weill could not yet suspect. Among the young dancers who auditioned was Lotte Lenya,[31] then twenty-four years old, who had just come from Zurich with her teacher. She remembers: "When I was called to the stage, the producer said, 'Miss Lenya, I would like to introduce you to our composer, Kurt Weill,' and I said, 'Where is he?' The producer indicated that he was sitting in the orchestra pit, but I couldn't see him. I only heard a soft voice say, 'Very glad

Envelope of a letter to Busoni, 22 June 1923,
sent from Frankfurt to Berlin.

to meet you, Miss Lenya,' but I never actually saw him. So that was our first meeting."[32]

In 1923, that last year of his studies with Busoni, Weill composed two works which soon spread his reputation as a young avant-garde composer throughout Germany: the String Quartet, op. 8, and the song cycle *Frauentanz: Sieben Gedichte des Mittelalters für Sopran und fünf Instrumente,* op. 10 (Women's Dance: Seven Poems from the Middle Ages for Soprano and Five Instruments). The string quartet, dedicated to Weill's father, consists again of a single movement in three sections: introduction, scherzo, and fantasy on a chorale tune. The quartet is related to the First Symphony both in its treatment of harmonic material and in its overall structure, which again joins together a number of individual, self-contained sections in cyclical fashion. It must be said, however, that Weill's reworking of existing material in the final fantasy is not well handled; the chorale passages, played by an entire orchestra in the symphony, are less convincing when played by the considerably reduced forces of a quartet. Nonetheless, the string quartet is an important work in Weill's development. Closely related to the First Symphony and full of the expressionistic idiom of the Divertimento and the *Sinfonia sacra,* it shows Weill's new fondness for pure melodic invention and a reduction in contrapuntal complexity. Religious symbolism can still be found, but it is not paid nearly as close attention as in earlier compositions. Everything now is pressing on to the expressivity of vocal composition.

The premiere of the String Quartet, op. 8, took place on 21 June 1923 during the Frankfurt Chamber Music Festival. The famous Hindemith–Amar Quartet interpreted the work in the presence of the composer, who wrote to Busoni, "I'm hearing my quartet today for the first time because the Hindemith people are very overburdened. Strangely enough, the final movement—both in my eyes and in yours the most mature—seems to find the least resonance among the four gentlemen. I am afraid that Hindemith has already danced too far into the land of the fox-trot."[33]

The festival's audience, however, was paying less attention to this quartet by the still relatively unknown Weill than to such works as Hindemith's *Marienleben,* Busoni's *Fantasia contrappuntistica,* and Schönberg's *Lieder aus dem Buch der hängenden Gärten* (Songs from the Book of the Hanging Gardens). The high point—and in its effect on the development of German music almost impossible to overestimate—was unquestionably the German premiere of Stravinsky's *L'Histoire du Soldat* with Hermann Scherchen as conductor, Paul Hindemith as solo violinist, and Carl Ebert as narrator. Weill's first impressions of this work, which was to have a strong influence on his later theater compositions (as well as on the concept of "epic theater"), are interesting. His initial report to Busoni sounds somewhat reserved: "Then there was an experiment that made people sit up: Stravinsky's *L'Histoire du Soldat*. It is a kind of 'folk piece with song and dance,' something between pantomime, melodrama, and burlesque; the music is, insofar as this genre allows, masterfully written, and even the pandering to the taste of the street is bearable because it suits the material."[34]

Only two months later Kurt Weill and Wladimir Vogel accompanied Busoni to the Bauhaus Festival in Weimar, where in August 1923 the second German performance of *L'Histoire du Soldat* took place, again conducted by Hermann Scherchen. Stravinsky had also come from Paris. His meeting with Busoni in Weimar, where he must also have met Weill, he later described as follows: "I made the acquaintance of Ferruccio Busoni, whom I had never met before and who had always been described to me as an irreconcilable opponent of my music. I was therefore very much impressed by the sincere emotion that I saw he was feeling while my music was being played, which was confirmed by him that same evening. I was all the more touched by this appreciation, since it came from a very great musician, whose work and mentality were fundamentally opposed to the spirit of my art. It was my first and last sight of him; he died a year later."[35] Weill and Stravinsky later met in the United States on numerous occasions.

Two and a half years after his first encounter with *L'Histoire du Soldat* in Frankfurt, Weill's opinion of it had changed markedly: "What Stravinsky attempted in his *Soldier's Tale* undoubtedly can be appraised as the intermediary genre with the most certain future. Standing on the boundary between play, pantomime, and opera, this piece still displays such a strong predominance of operatic elements that it perhaps can become the foundation for a certain course of new opera."[36]

The String Quartet, op. 8, premiered in Frankfurt am Main in 1923, was first performed in Berlin in a concert of the Novembergruppe on 22 January 1924; in December of the same year it was heard in Paris, and from 1925 on it was performed by various quartets elsewhere.

Having finished the string quartet in March 1923, Weill turned in June and July to the song cycle *Frauentanz: Sieben Gedichte des Mittelalters für Sopran und fünf Instrumente*, op. 10. In the wind quintet he substituted a viola for the oboe, an instrument he did not particularly care for.

The cycle consists of seven songs based on *Minnesang* texts. Each song is a miniature of between twenty-seven and seventy-eight measures; the performance time of the entire cycle is only about ten minutes. Nonetheless, *Frauentanz* is an important work of Weill's and at the time enjoyed considerable success. Comparisons with the fairy's aria, the only vocal number in the ballet pantomime *Zaubernacht*, are in order. Like that aria, the songs of the *Frauentanz* are written for soprano voice and are provided with a rhythmically animated homophonic accompaniment. The text is set to music without any word repetitions. A clear declamation and a direct presentation of the words preclude extensive polyphony. The small instrumental ensemble is further divided up in the seven songs;

**Emil Hertzka, director of Universal Edition in Vienna, during a
trip to Italy in 1922. On the recommendation of Busoni, Universal
offered Weill a contract, which he signed on 22 April 1924.**

only the first and fourth songs make use of all the instruments. All the songs are marked
by continuous metrical variation, which allows Weill not only to capture precisely the
linguistic rhythm of the text but also to introduce complex rhythms in the accompaniment. Although a dance indication is given only once, in the first song, which Weill marks
"andantino, quasi tempo di menuetto," the rhythmic vitality of the songs is so pronounced that the entire cycle has a dance quality to it. At the same time the music presents
the text without illustrative effects or psychological characterization, making its own
independent contribution. The lyricism of a song composer gradually won out over the

polyphony of an instrumental composer. Kurt Weill had taken a further step along the road to the theater.

When Philipp Jarnach made special mention of Weill's latest work in a letter to Busoni, the latter responded with a very perceptive evaluation of his twenty-three-year-old pupil:

> I don't know Weill's *Frauentanz*. Considering his reserved vein and painstaking efforts, this youngster's productivity is surprising. He has any amount of "ideas"—as you say—but they are concealed or inferred, so that only "the likes of us" can discover and admire them. He—Weill—does not seem to be conscious of when he has arrived at the right place; instead, he passes over it as if over sand and rocks between which beautiful, individual flowers grow, which he neither tramples nor plucks, and over which he does not linger. His wealth is great, his selectivity at present inactive. One envies him and would like to help.—But he will come to the right thing of his own accord! — The eternal question: is he still developing, or has he already reached his peak?[37]

In October 1923 Weill reported to Busoni: "The seven songs with wind accompaniment, which I have gathered under the title *Frauentanz,* have been generally well received. Especially Jarnach thinks they are the best thing he's yet seen of mine. I put the thought of an intermezzo out of my head after writing four different pieces for it. In case it is performed I am looking for an appropriate singer."[38] Eventually he found Nora Pisling-Boas, who premiered the *Frauentanz* in February 1924 in a concert directed by Fritz Stiedry at the Preußische Akademie der Künste in Berlin.

But the composition's real breakthrough came with a performance during the Second Chamber Music Festival of the International Society for Contemporary Music (ISCM) in Salzburg in August 1924, sung by the Viennese soprano Lotte Leonard and conducted by Philipp Jarnach. "Through the most minimal means and in the most compressed form ultimate expressivity is achieved. For all his harmonic richness, Weill circumnavigates the shoals of Schönbergian interval copying where so many others founder. He creates his own melodic arcs and imbues the contents of the poems with music."[39] On 18 April 1927 the Berlin radio aired the song cycle, with the solo sung once again by Nora Pisling-Boas.

The last work which Weill completed in 1923 under the tutelage of Busoni shows him to be on a par with his teacher both intellectually and in his mastery of musical craftsmanship. His *Recordare: Klagelieder Jeremiae V. Kapitel,* op. 11 (Recordare: Lamentations of Jeremiah, Chapter 5) is a large a cappella choral cycle for four-part mixed chorus and two-part boys' choir based on Old Testament texts. Weill shows himself to be a master of polyphonic song techniques that extend back as far as the Renaissance.

When he showed this work to Hermann Scherchen at the end of 1923, Scherchen, one of the most active conductors of those years, told him he thought the cycle was technically so difficult as to be practically impossible to perform, even with unlimited rehearsal time. Not until 1971 did its premiere at the Holland Festival prove that this demanding piece of twentieth-century choral literature can indeed be sung.

In the meantime, Weill's studies with Busoni were drawing to a close. Just as the pupil had made the piano reduction of a work of his teacher's in 1922, so now in 1923 did the

KURT WEILL

STREICHQUARTETT Nr. 1

1ᵉʳ Quatuor à cordes   String Quartet I

PARTIES   STIMMEN   PARTS

Op. 8

UNIVERSAL-EDITION
No. 7700

Title page of the first printed edition of a Weill
composition, his first String Quartet, op. 8,
published by Universal in 1924.

master produce a version of the third song from Weill's *Frauentanz* for voice and piano. This also speaks for the close relationship that had developed between the two. Ferruccio Busoni did one further thing for his pupil's future. In July 1923 he recommended Weill to the director of what was then the most renowned publisher of contemporary music, Vienna's Universal Edition. He wrote to Dr. Emil Hertzka: "I have given my pupil Kurt Weill a letter addressed to you which you should receive shortly. It concerns Weill's string quartet, a work of exceptional quality with both power and originality. I can hardly think of another piece by a twenty-three-year-old that is so attractive and worthwhile.—It is 'modern' through and through without any unpleasant features. I have emphatically emphasized in the letter that you should seize this talent without delay. Furthermore (and this is why it is so important), Weill is a man who thinks and reads, a man of the most upright character."[40]

For several months there was no reply from Vienna, and in October 1923 Weill wrote to Busoni: "As far as the publisher goes, I am still wavering between trying Breitkopf, whose distinguished, solid style does quite appeal to me, and mounting a new attack on Universal Edition."[41] A few months later, however, he could report, "I had an encouraging telegram from Hertzka: 'Am keenly interested in taking on your works, request suggestions as to conditions.' Although I am very skeptical about publishing, I nonetheless want . . . to try to come to an oral agreement with Hertzka."[42]

An agreement was soon reached, and in April 1924 Universal concluded a ten-year contract with Weill granting the publisher the rights to all his compositions while stipulating that Weill would receive from the publisher a regular monthly income, later to be increased by anticipated royalties.

In December 1923 Weill's three-year period of study with Busoni came to an end. He received a diploma from the Preußische Akademie der Künste and bade farewell to his teacher, with whom he remained in close contact until Busoni's early death on 27 July 1924. In the years that followed he honored him in a number of articles and essays. In one place the grateful pupil writes, "And if Busoni had not left us his compositions and writings, his Bach edition, and the memory of his unforgettable piano-playing, then his personal influence alone would be a bequest to future generations."[43]

II

Berlin

Georg Kaiser, one of Germany's leading dramatists, in 1925, the year after Weill first met him.

Facing page 53: The two leads in the premiere of *Der Protagonist*, Kurt Taucher and Elisabeth Stünzner.

One-Act Operas

Thanks to the Dresden conductor and opera manager Fritz Busch, in 1924 Weill was able to make the acquaintance of one of Germany's leading dramatic writers, Georg Kaiser. In November 1923 Busoni's master pupils had attended a performance of their teacher's *Arlecchino* at Dresden's Semperoper. Afterward Fritz Busch—always on the lookout for new works—conversed with Weill, "whom Busoni had recommended to me"[1] and whose Berlin ballet composition he had heard about. Now Busch encouraged him to write something similar for Dresden. As a librettist Busch suggested his friend Georg Kaiser, and he arranged for the two to meet. Pleased by this offer of support from such prominent quarters, Weill agreed to the project.

With a total of forty-five completed plays, Georg Kaiser was the most prolific stage writer in the German language between 1910 and 1930, and he was without question the most frequently performed contemporary author of the Weimar Republic. Bertolt Brecht, who was twenty years his junior, acknowledged without envy in 1928, "Asked if I consider Georg Kaiser's drama to be decisively important, if I consider the state of European theater to be changed by him, I must answer yes."[2]

At the time of his meeting with Weill, the forty-six-year-old Kaiser was at the peak of his fame; his play *Gas* had marked a pinnacle of expressionist drama. In the 1921–22 season no fewer than seven plays of his were premiered, unleashing speculation among some critics that a whole group of playwrights might be hiding behind Kaiser's name. Kurt Weill, then only twenty-three, could have been Kaiser's son.

It was in early January 1924 that Weill first went to Grünheide bei Erkner, on the outskirts of Berlin, to visit Kaiser in his house by the shores of the Peetzsee. He must have felt somewhat apprehensive about meeting Germany's "number-one playwright." But it turned out that Kaiser had seen *Die Zaubernacht* in 1922 and thought well of it. And Weill's apprehensions soon gave way to delight when Kaiser said he would like to work with the young composer.

This was quite uncharacteristic for Kaiser—and a distinction for Weill. Kaiser used hardly any musical material at all in his plays, whose structure did not call for songs or choruses; a few exceptions, such as the revue *Zwei Krawatten* (Two Neckties), only prove the rule. So Kaiser did not particularly care what kind of music a theater might come up with in staging his plays. From 1912 on, he had consistently declined to rework his plays into opera librettos (at that time Fritz Stiedry had made a singspiel out of *Europa,* and Kaiser had forbidden its performance). Not until 1939, when he was in exile, did he agree to let Caspar Neher and Rudolf Wagner-Régeny rework his play *Die Bürger von Calais* (The Citizens of Calais) into an opera. Posthumously the suitability of Kaiser's texts for musical theater has been shown by Gottfried von Einem's *Das Floß der Medusa* (Medusa's Raft) and Robert Hanell's *Die Spieldose* (The Music Box).

The only exception to Kaiser's musical abstinence, the only composer he ever really collaborated with, was Kurt Weill. This association lasted nearly a decade, until 1933.

It began with Busch's ballet commission for Dresden. In January and February 1924 Weill became a frequent guest in Grünheide. "I was very pleased and happy when Georg Kaiser offered to write a full-length ballet libretto for me. We began the work together. In ten weeks [it was only six—author] nearly three-quarters of the work was done. The score for the overture and the first two acts was completed—and then we got stuck. We had grown beyond the bounds of the material. The silence of these figures was torturing us, and we had to break free from the constraints of pantomime. It had to become an opera."[3]

It is not entirely clear whether Kaiser's play *Der Protagonist,* written in 1920 and first performed in Breslau in 1922, was from the very beginning the basis for the planned

Kurt Weill in 1925.

ballet-pantomime. In mid-February, the two took a break from their work. Kaiser was busy with other projects, and Weill left for a trip to Switzerland and Italy. Not until the summer of 1924 did they resume work on what was now an opera project for *Der Protagonist.*

First, Weill traveled to Davos to see his distant cousin Nelly Frank. He had met Nelly in late 1922 at his brother Hans's wedding, and in the course of the following year a more than friendly relationship had developed between the two—regardless of the fact that she was married. Kurt Weill spent March 1924 in Milan, Florence, Bologna, and Rome. At Milan's La Scala he attended an opera performance with Arturo Toscanini conducting. "That alone makes the whole trip worthwhile," he reported to Busoni; "I didn't know that it was possible to 'play an orchestra' with such freedom, with such capricious rubati."[4] Toward the end of his trip he wrote to his teacher that "these couple of weeks of southern sun have caused things that were long lying dormant within me to unfold; at least I feel a strong drive to activity and am filled with plans."[5]

Back in Berlin by the end of March, Weill wrote his Concerto for Violin and Wind Orchestra, op. 12, in April and May. This work consists of three movements, with the second itself containing three parts: (1) andante con moto, (2) notturno–cadenza–serenata, (3) allegro molto un poco agitato. Although this mirrors precisely the formal structure of Mahler's Seventh Symphony, in it musical language the concerto bears a resemblance to Stravinsky, especially to *L'Histoire du Soldat*, the Symphony for Wind Instruments, and the Octet. Aside from such possible associations—and Weill himself often emphasized his affinity with Stravinsky—the concerto is by no means derivative; with its unique combination of Busoni-inspired clarity and purity of sound within a thoroughly polyphonic framework, it is entirely Weill's own creation. This concerto was the last purely instrumental work that he wrote in Germany; not until he was in exile did he again undertake a similar project, with his Second Symphony.

The instrumental concerto's traditional dramatic confrontation of solo instrument with orchestral accompaniment is fully played out in the angular first movement but comes to rest in the light-filled second movement. Each section of the third movement allows the violin's cantabile melodic line to rise above the rhythmically more animated accompaniment. The free atonality that Weill employs here stems from a creative and imaginative impulse that obeys only his inner ear. Nowhere is the sharpness of his inner ear more apparent than in the concerto's orchestration.[6] Weill never made the Vienna school's leap into twelve-tone music. The clarity and diversity of sound that Weill achieves with a limited set of instruments (ten wind instruments, percussion, and basses) is remarkable.

The Concerto for Violin and Wind Orchestra was premiered on 11 June 1925 in Paris with the violinist Marcel Darrieux and the conductor Walter Straram; but, like the song cycle *Frauentanz*, it first achieved a real breakthrough only when it was performed with triumphant success by Stefan Frenkel at an ISCM festival, in Zurich in June 1926. Adolf Weißmann wrote: "Kurt Weill's *Concerto for Violin and Wind Orchestra* was the most remarkable piece of the evening, because here the unusualness of the sound is linked with an originality of conception. One may be reminded of Stravinsky. But I believe that Weill is absolutely standing on his own two feet, with his strong contrasts between the soloist and the orchestra, in which the bass is the only string instrument."[7]

The German premiere of the violin concerto took place on 29 October 1925 in Weill's native Dessau. It was here that Stefan Frenkel first played the work which he was to perform more than twenty times in various European musical centers between 1925 and 1930.

Let us return, however, to the year 1924, when the interruption of his work with Kaiser had given Weill time to write the violin concerto. From June on, he was again a frequent guest in Grünheide, discussing the reworking of *Der Protagonist* into an opera. In the meantime Kaiser, his wife Margarethe, and Weill had developed a warm friendship. These weeks were troubled, however, by the news of Busoni's rapidly deteriorating

Program from a concert given in Dessau in October 1925 which
included the first German performance of Weill's Violin
Concerto, op. 12.

health; it was clear that death was not far off. Weill wrote to his sister: "Busoni is deathly
ill, and none of us knows where to turn. To suffer oneself would not be so hard as to see
such an individual suffer so terribly. When I am not with him I have to throw myself into
my work so as to forget somewhat the sight of his suffering. Last week I was again—
unfortunately under rainy conditions—in Grünheide with the Kaisers, who have become
dear friends to me and are perhaps the only ones who will be able to replace for me a part
of what I am losing in Busoni."[8]

But, as so often in life, in this summer of 1924 the pain of Busoni's suffering and death
(he died on 27 July) was mingled with the joy of a new, decisive encounter in Weill's life.

At this time a young actress and dancer who had come to Berlin from Zurich was
enjoying the hospitality of the Kaisers. Born in 1898 in Vienna as Karoline Wilhelmine
Blamauer, at age eighteen she had already taken the stage name Lotte Lenya, under which

```
                              EIGHTEENTH PAIR
        Friday Afternoon                        Saturday Evening
           March 28                                 March 29
                                  1930


                    CINCINNATI
              SYMPHONY ORCHESTRA
                   FRITZ REINER, Conductor


   MENDELSSOHN                Overture "To the Fairy Tale
                                   of the Fair Melusina"


   KURT WEILL            Concerto for Violin and Wind-Orchestra
                              (First Time in America)
                     I.   Andante con moto
                    II.   Nocturne, Cadenza, Serenata
                   III.   Allegro molto, un poco agitato
                          EMIL HEERMANN


   BOSSI                  Intermezzi Goldoniani for String-Orchestra
                     I.   Prelude and Minuet
                    II.   Gagliarda
                   III.   Serenatina*
                    IV.   Burlesca
                *Viola d'amore played by Vladimir Bakaleinikoff


                            INTERMISSION

   WAGNER                  "Der Venusberg" (Paris Version)
                                   from "Tannhäuser"


   BERLIOZ                    "Hungarian March" from
                                "The Damnation of Faust"


       The Baldwin is the official piano of the Cincinnati Symphony Orchestra

       If necessary to leave before the end of the concert, please do so
                  during an interval between the numbers
```

Program from a concert in Cincinnati in March
1930 which included the first American
performance of Weill's Violin Concerto, op. 12.

she was later to achieve fame. This young woman, who came from a proletarian family and had had a difficult childhood, knew what poverty was. As a six-year-old girl she was already working in the circus as an acrobat and a tightrope walker. Decades later, as a famous singer, she would still reply when asked which artists she especially admired: "Circus people. In the circus you must be totally aware of your performance—a slip can mean disaster—and your effect. You cannot cheat or lie when you are on a tightrope."[9] Upon completing the Mittelschule, Karoline went to Zurich, where she took instruction in acting and ballet. Starting in 1912, she worked first as an apprentice and then as a dancer at the local theater. But very soon she resolved to hang up her dancing shoes and become an actress. Since Zurich offered few opportunities for this, in 1920 she went to Berlin and took a position with Otto Kirchner's "Shakespeare Stage," an insignificant suburban troupe, where through 1923 she played any number of roles both small and large and learned her trade from the ground up. Similarities to Weill's experience in Lüdenscheid are self-evident.

**The sixteen-year-old Karoline Blamauer (Lotte Lenya) as a ballet
pupil at Zurich's Stadttheater in 1914.**

In 1923 Lotte Lenya met the Kaisers, who liked the young woman and invited her to
spend her summer vacation with them in Grünheide. She did this again the next year, and
it was there, in July 1924, that she and Kurt Weill met. Lenya later reminisced:

One Sunday morning, Kaiser said: "Oh, Lenya, I am expecting a young composer . . .
would you mind picking him up at the station?" Well, the shortest way was to row a
boat across the lake. But before I left, I asked Kaiser how would I recognize him, and
he said, "Oh, they all look alike." What he meant was that at that time, most musicians wore a certain style of black-brimmed hat which was very easy to recognize.
Anyway, I went to the station, and there he was . . . just a little taller than I, with a blue
suit, very neat and correct, with very thick glasses, and, of course, the black hat. I said,
"Are you Mr. Weill?" and he said, "Yes," and then I invited him to enter our "trans-
portation." So we sat down, and *I* rowed—in typical German fashion—the woman
does all the work. And while I was rowing, he looked at me and after a while he said,

**Kurt Weill, Lotte Lenya, Margarethe Kaiser, and her son Anselm
in the garden of the Kaisers' house on the Peetzee in Grünheide
bei Berlin, in the summer of 1924. It was at the Kaisers' that
Kurt and Lotte first met.**

"You know, Miss Lenya, we met before." I said, "Oh, really? Where?" And then he reminded me of that ballet audition. We were together from that point on.[10]

A description by Hans W. Heinscheimer gives us an idea of how the twenty-four-year-old Weill might have looked to Lotte Lenya: "[a] small, balding young man with eager, burning eyes, quiet in his manner, deliberate and always soft-spoken, dressed more like a candidate for a degree in divinity than a young composer in the flamboyant Berlin of 1923, sucking a conservative pipe with the absent-minded absorption of an instructor in higher mathematics."[11]

Kurt Weill and Lotte Lenya rapidly took a liking to each other. Two distinctive individuals had met, both still in search of their true artistic paths, each full of respect and love for the other. In May 1925 they moved together into a boarding house on the Luisenplatz in Charlottenburg. Weill wrote to his parents at this point that he was feeling increasingly free and secure in his compositional work. "Of course living with Lenya has a lot to do with that. It has helped me a great deal. It is indeed the only way I can abide having another person beside me: two different artistic interests next to each other, each encouraged along its way by the other. How long will this last? Quite long, I hope."[12]

The wish to fall in love "to the point of madness," which Weill had expressed in 1919, was now fulfilled. On 28 January 1926 he married Lotte Lenya; the letters preserved from

Opening page of the theater magazine *Der neue Weg* for 1 November 1925, with the beginning of one of Weill's first published essays, on Busoni and the new music.

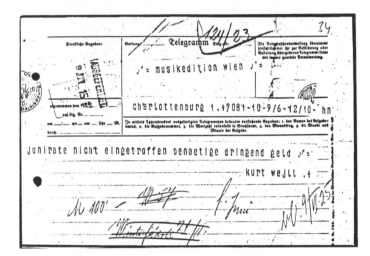

Telegram from Weill to his publisher in Vienna, June 1925, saying, "June payment not received. Money urgently needed."

these years are touching documents of his deep affection for her. Weill constantly invents new terms of endearment for her—from "Pummilein" (Little Roly-Poly) to "Rehbeinchen" (Little Deer's Foot)—and mostly he signs himself "Your Weillili."

Their financial situation was at first quite modest; so in January 1925 Kurt Weill was only too glad to accept an offer to become a regular contributor to the weekly radio program guide *Der deutsche Rundfunk*. For four years he wrote previews of the following week's musical and theatrical broadcasts (called *Sendespiel*, the early form of the *Hörspiel*), as well as reviews of what had been aired during the previous week. By 1929 he had written nearly four hundred such articles, in which he frequently showed himself to be a sharp-minded critic with a polished style. A number of these reviews and essays are of

**Kurt Weill and Lotte Lenya on the day of their wedding,
28 January 1926, in the grounds of Charlottenburg Palace.**

enduring value. Along with the welcome extra income, it was Weill's great interest in this new mass medium, which had been available in Germany for just two years, that led him to take on such extremely time-consuming work, requiring many evenings of listening. He shared this interest with many other composers and writers—one need only think of the theoretical and practical contributions made by Hindemith, Brecht, or Benjamin. Weill was particularly intrigued by the question of which new areas of composition might now be opened up by the potentially explosive dissemination of music through radio. At first he only wrote about this question, but starting in 1928 he followed through with his own compositional efforts.

Their marriage certificate, dated 28 January 1926, issued by the
registry office of Berlin-Charlottenburg.

In September 1924 Weill finished composing two orchestral song cycles, each with
three songs: *Das Stundenbuch: Orchesterlieder nach Texten von Rilke,* op. 13 (The Book
of Hours: Orchestral Songs Based on Texts of Rilke, op. 13). This work, preserved only in
fragments, was first performed on 22 January 1925 in the Berlin Philharmonie, with the
baritone Manfred Lewandowsky as soloist and Heinz Unger conducting.

By the end of 1924 Georg Kaiser had made enough progress on his libretto for Weill to
be able to start composing *Der Protagonist* as a one-act opera, in early 1925. In the
meantime Weill had considered *Kulissen* (Curtains) as a possible title, but Fritz Busch
rejected this. By April 1925 the score was done. When Weill went to Dresden on 21 May
1925 to take part in the posthumous premiere of Busoni's opera *Doktor Faustus* (Philipp
Jarnach had completed the score), he was able to tell Busch that the commissioned work
was now ready and awaited performance. To his brother he wrote, "I was in Dresden
again and this time spent the whole day with Busch—a worthwhile acquaintance in every
respect."[13]

Busch now planned the premiere of *Der Protagonist* for the late fall of 1925. In mid-
September Weill expected a visit from the director Josef Gielen: "On Sunday my Dresden
director is visiting me for a thorough consultation. . . . You all know how wearing the
rehearsal of an orchestral work is for the composer. How will it be for a stage work? All
that can help will be a good share of nerve and nonchalance—both of which I have
acquired over time."[14]

But the premiere had to be postponed for a few months, because the Dresden helden-
tenor Kurt Taucher—only he could sing the title role of the protagonist—had taken on an
American tour. Naturally, Weill was disappointed, but, as he wrote to his parents, "the

fact of its acceptance, the most valuable part of the whole business, is still there."[15] And another time he wrote them, "I don't think I can describe to you what it means to put together an opera of nearly an hour's length in two and a half months."[16]

The aspiring young composer wrote in December 1925: "Last week I was asked to participate in a musical tea at the Stresemanns'; when his office called, I told them they should ask Jarnach, that he was the only young composer with a dress coat. But yesterday I went to a ball hosted by the editor of the *Börsencourier,* and this evening I'm going with Kaiser to the premiere of Alban Berg's *Wozzeck,* a very modern opera. There was already a scandal at the public dress rehearsal." Thinking ahead to the premiere of his own first opera, Weill closes the letter saying, "In three months it will be my turn———."[17]

The big day finally came on 27 March 1926, at Dresden's venerable Staatsoper. It brought Weill the greatest artistic success and the stormiest applause he had yet experienced—with a work for musical theater!

Fritz Busch himself conducted the premiere of *Der Protagonist,* Josef Gielen directed it, and Kurt Taucher sang the title role. The one-act opera was presented along with Alfredo Casella's *Der große Krug* (The Large Jug). The success of the premiere was extraordinary: the audience in Dresden applauded for twenty minutes, there were more than forty curtain calls, and Kurt Weill and Georg Kaiser had to bow repeatedly. "We were so poor that Kurt had to borrow a tuxedo to appear at the opening of his first really big success," Lotte Lenya later recalled.[18] The press reacted with unanimous high approval and hailed Weill's development as "leading the way to a new kind of opera."[19] *Der*

Envelope of a letter from Weill to Lenya dated 23 July 1926, six months after their marriage. He playfully addresses her as "wife of a note cruncher."

Painting of Lotte Lenya by Ludwig Meidner, 1925.

Protagonist played at fifteen different German opera houses and launched Weill as a composer of opera.

Der Protagonist, set in Elizabethan England, is the tragicomic story of an actor who cannot distinguish between reality and fantasy. In a village inn preparations are under way for an evening performance by a troupe of actors at the ducal court. The protagonist's sister, held in highest esteem by her loving brother, meets her lover, who does not want to hear anything about her brother. Then news comes that the duke is expecting some foreign guests, so the actors are asked to present a pantomime so as to avoid any linguistic problems. Immediately the troupe starts rehearsing a coarse story of a wife who has been cheated on and a rather loose monk. After the rehearsal the sister takes advantage of the happy mood to tell her brother about her lover, and the protagonist asks her to bring the young man over so that he can meet him. Again the duke's steward intervenes and demands a different pantomime, since the duke's guests are to include a bishop, making the story of the loose monk inappropriate. The protagonist replaces the figure of the monk with a depraved aristocrat, and now the whole story takes a tragic turn as the protagonist in the role of the husband pursues the depraved aristocrat with a drawn knife. In this scene the sister appears with her lover. No longer in control of his senses, confusing fantasy with reality, the protagonist hurls himself at the girl and stabs her. Suddenly he comes to himself and throws himself off the stage, saying, "Go, tell the duke, your master, that he must protect me from prosecution until this evening. Otherwise he will rob me of my best role, which no longer distinguishes between real and played madness."

In front of the stage entrance of the Semperoper in Dresden the night of the premiere of *Der Protagonist,* 27 March 1926. *Left to right:* Kurt Weill, the conductor Fritz Busch, the manager Alfred Reucker, and the director Josef Gielen.

Musically *Der Protagonist* constitutes the apex of Weill's early work, combining linear polyphony, atonal material, and penetrating chromaticism. The two dancelike pantomimes—originally the work was to be a ballet!—are the opera's high point. First, a small onstage orchestra of eight wind instruments seems to comment on the action (in the first, light pantomime), then the accompaniment comes from the orchestra pit (for the second, tragic pantomime). The two orchestras relate to each other in a most intelligent fashion; and there are hints of what was to develop into Weill's characteristic toccata style.

Although there is much about this opera, which Weill dedicated to Lotte Lenya, that is reminiscent of Busoni's *Arlecchino,* the critics all agreed that, as Oskar Bie put it, "This is the pupil stepping beyond the master Busoni."[20] Weill's reaction to this comment was: "What do you say to the fabulous press? Bie's review that I sent you, is as he himself says, the best he has ever written about opera. . . . It is quite exciting to become world famous overnight! I don't even mind the few bad reviews; if the press were unanimously favorable, the demands on me would grow beyond all bounds. As it is, my telephone is ringing incessantly. And always the same honest enthusiasm. Who would have thought it?"[21]

Program from the premiere of Der Protagonist.

Under the title "Kaiser Transformed into Opera" Rudolf Kastner wrote: "Kurt Weill, one of the most respected talents among the new tunesters working in Berlin, has now with a single stroke—borne aloft by a performance under Fritz Busch that is outstanding in its artistic conscientiousness and the flexibility of all its participants—proved himself in his new one-act opera to be a creative potential for musical drama of the first rank. This evening Kurt Weill has entered the first rank of our great hopes."[22]

Weill's status with his publisher also changed with the success of the Dresden premiere. Heinsheimer later reminisced about the change that came over Emil Hertzka, the all-powerful head of Universal, after the premiere:

The next day we met Kurt in the dining room of the Bellevue Hotel for lunch. The Bellevue offered two luncheons: a simple two marks' one and a fancier one, including fish as well as meat in the fare, for three marks. All these days before the opening night we had shared lunch with Kurt, and every day Hertzka had ordered three luncheons without fish. Kurt had never said a word, and who was I to clamor for fish?

This time, however, Hertzka called the waiter, asked for a menu, and handed it smilingly to Kurt Weill.

"What would you like to eat, Mr. Weill?" he asked.

Then I knew that Kurt Weill was a composer to be reckoned with in the future.[23]

During the summer months of 1925, the time between the completion of *Der Protagonist* and its premiere, Weill met another writer with whom he would collaborate on two projects. One day in the Romanisches Café, a meeting place for artists and literary people, Kaiser introduced the composer to Yvan Goll, then thirty-four years old. Born in France in 1891, Goll had grown up in the bilingual region of Alsace-Lorraine, and in 1919 he had joined the circle of the surrealists in Paris. He lived there with his wife, Claire Goll, but was often in Berlin for extended periods. In the mid-twenties Goll's lyric poetry, which mixes social protest with grotesque visions of reality, for a time became a synonym for *Neue Sachlichkeit* (New Objectivity) in literature. Established by about 1923 as a stylistic direction in the visual arts, "Neue Sachlichkeit" became a motto in the years following the end of inflation in November 1923. A fascination with technology marked this period; people were excited about such American influences as jazz and the revue; a new

Title pages of the libretto of the play, published in Potsdam by
Gustav Kiepenheuer Verlag in 1921, and of the opera, published
in Vienna by Universal Edition in 1925.

Advertisement for the opera score by Universal in May 1926.

"modern feeling for life," accompanied by shorter dresses and bobbed hair, was spreading. All the arts tried to reflect this development; in musical theater the term *Zeitoper* (Contemporary Opera) came into use. Nearly all manifestations of Neue Sachlichkeit besieged the opera stage, and some enjoyed sensational success: jazz (Ernst Křenek's *Jonny spielt auf* [Johnny Strikes up the Band]), radio (Walter Goehr's *Malpopita*), film (Wilhelm Grosz's *Achtung, Aufnahme!* [Action, Camera!]), technology (Max Brand's *Maschinist Hopkins* [Machine-Minder Hopkins]), politics (George Antheil's *Transatlan-*

Family reunion in Kleinsteinberg bei Leipzig in Weill's parents'
garden. *Back row, left to right:* not known, father Albert Weill,
Nathan Weill, Kurt Weill. *Front row, left to right:* Helene Weill
(wife of Nathan), her child Hannelore, mother Emma Weill,
Lotte Lenya, Eva Sohn (daughter of Weill's sister, Ruth Sohn).

tic), boxing (Ernst Křenek's *Schwergewicht oder die Ehre der Nation* [Heavyweight: The Nation's Honor]), and modern forms of marriage (Paul Hindemith's *Neues vom Tage* [Today's News]).

Weill's first work with Goll was the cantata *Der neue Orpheus* (The New Orpheus) for soprano, violin, and orchestra. In this work, which lasts a good fifteen minutes and is dedicated to the singer Lotte Leonard, Orpheus descends to the "red-light district of life" (*Ackerstraße des Lebens*) to find his Eurydice in the guise of a prostitute not far from the Silesian train station. Goll's lyrics, written in 1918, took the form of saucy parody—for example:

> Orpheus, who does not know him? A meter seventy-eight tall,
>   sixty-eight kilos;
> Brown eyes, narrow forehead, a stiff hat, Catholic and
>   sentimental, by virtue of democracy and profession a
>   musician. . . .

> On Wednesday between 12:30 and 1:30, as a shy piano teacher,
> He liberates a girl from her mother's greediness.
> In the evening variety show, between the Yankee girl and the
>   snake charmer, his couplet about human love
>   is the third number.

Photograph of Yvan Goll, 1930. Weill first met Goll in Berlin in the summer of 1925 and subsequently set several of his texts.

> In all the subscription concerts with Gustav Mahler he makes
> hearts shudder terribly.

Weill set Goll's collagelike poetry to music that is a mixture of concerto, cantata, opera, and cabaret song. The solo violin is set apart distinctly from the small orchestra, which includes no other violins. A clear tonal structure suggests that Weill is beginning to look to popular music. The long poem describing Orpheus's activities, which consists of seven sections, is composed as a set of variations. But the music does not yet make independent commentaries, nor do the soprano passages give any hint of the song style which Weill will later adopt.

Right after completing the score in September 1925, he composed the one-act opera *Royal Palace*, on a libretto by Goll involving a story of "modern" marriage set in an ultramodern luxury hotel—Weill's contribution to *Zeitoper*. To his parents he wrote: "I am now going through the years in which an artist is always sitting on a powder keg, when unused energy has to be discharged explosively, when a heightened oversensitivity produces a constant state of suspense, of excitement. Now it has seized me again. I am buried in this new opera. I must master an expressive form that is still new to me. And I am finding, happily—as I did with *Der neue Orpheus*—that I am gradually moving

Kurt Weill composing, 1926.

forward to 'me,' that my music is becoming much more secure, much more fluid, free, and simple."[24]

By January 1926 the score of *Royal Palace* was completed. It is the first work of Weill's to include popular dance forms and jazz elements, as well as features of the revue and theatrical effects—it is thus a milestone work for Weill. The harmonic and contrapuntal vocabulary has been simplified: the composer is on his way to a musical Neue Sachlichkeit. Unfortunately, Goll's libretto was so weak that *Royal Palace* was not a great success.

The story is of an elegant young woman by the name of Dejanira who appears, surrounded by three men (her husband, yesterday's lover, and tomorrow's suitor), in the "Royal Palace," a luxury hotel on an Italian lake. The men compete with one another to entertain Dejanira. First the husband arranges an extravagant, exotic dinner during which the entire hotel staff dances to jazz rhythms; then he sends Dejanira by airplane on a short dream trip through all the European capitals. Yesterday's lover arranges a fantastical ballet for her—"The Heaven of Our Nights"—with the moon and the stars as the main characters. Finally, tomorrow's suitor presents Dejanira with "Fantasy," a futuristic play of machines, wheels, and constructions that move in the most ludicrous colors and forms. But Dejanira laughs at all three: "Miserable competitors! Pathetic lovers! You understand your saint but poorly. . . . Like children with building blocks you picked up fragments from a foreign world and laid them before me as if I were a wooden queen. . . . None of you has recognized me. I am free again from all of you!" she says and leaps into the lake. Then there is a gigantic tango finale in which the three men stand on the shore and for the last ten minutes (20 percent of the whole performance!) do nothing but sing syllabic rearrangements of the name Dejanira (Janirade, Rajedina, Nirajade). In the orchestra Weill not only experiments with the saxophone and car horn; in the opera's four entertainment scenes (the exotic meal, the European trip, the star ballet, and the play of machines) jazz band orchestration as well as revue sound are heard from the orchestra pit. Tango rhythm, which Weill will use again in many forms, also makes its first appearance here. *Royal Palace* marks a turning point in Weill's work. Here he first tried out all the means that he would soon master completely.

Whereas the initiative for the premiere of *Der Protagonist* had come from the Dresden theater, Weill himself handled the negotiations for *Royal Palace*. In the years that followed, he dedicated considerable energy to this important aspect, seeing to it that his works were not only composed but performed. He was continually seeking contacts with producers, directors, and conductors—usually with success, much to the satisfaction of his Vienna publisher. For *Royal Palace* he had no lesser goal than a premiere at Berlin's Staatsoper. In May 1926 he reported to Universal: "I have just come from a long meeting with Kleiber and Hörth. Both were extremely pleased with *Royal Palace,* which I played for them, and they are absolutely determined to perform it."[25]

After the run-through Weill summed up his feelings in a letter to his parents: "*Royal Palace* is to be the first big premiere after the renovation of the Staatsoper. Sometimes I am a little fearful about how fast it is all going—the Berlin Staatsoper already, there's nowhere higher to aim for than that. But all this is not affecting my work, and I am further than ever now from making concessions. I only need peace and quiet for my work—otherwise you can have all the fame."[26]

The premiere of *Royal Palace*—and of *Der neue Orpheus*—took place on Weill's twenty-seventh birthday, 2 March 1927, in the Berlin Staatsoper. Weill's two works were combined with Manuel de Falla's *Maestro Pedro's Puppet Play*. Erich Kleiber, who had pushed through the premiere of Alban Berg's *Wozzeck* in 1925, conducted. The director was Franz Ludwig Hörth, who had staged Weill's *Zaubernacht* in 1922 and had in the meantime become director of the Staatsoper. In *Royal Palace* he incorporated film for the first time.

This was the new medium's introduction to the opera stage. Hörth reports: "In Weill's one-act tragic revue *Royal Palace* I added film to give the plot a new element of suspense. . . . What could make more sense than to show the grand trip through the most beautiful cities on earth on film? I took the main actors to the German Lufthansa at the airport, where they got on an airplane in costume and flew away. These episodes were filmed and a few other shots were taken in front of the Palast-Hotel on Potsdamer Platz; they were then rounded out with some good clips of international cities, and then the whole sequence was inserted into the opera as a cinematic intermezzo."[27]

Scene from the premiere of *Royal Palace* at Berlin's Staatsoper, on Weill's twenty-seventh birthday, 2 March 1927. It was the first of Weill's works to incorporate dance forms and jazz elements, and the production at the Staatsoper used film for the first time.

But in spite of all the effort expended on its staging, the performance was not a success, and it ran for a mere seven evenings. *Royal Palace* was performed only one other time before 1933 (in Essen in 1929), whereas *Der neue Orpheus* was heard several times in concert. Weill's excursion into pure Zeitoper had not succeeded. The problem of the genre overall was pinpointed by Alban Berg when he wrote in 1927: "The use of contemporary materials, such as cinema, revue, or jazz, ensures only that a work will be contemporary. But this cannot be called real progress. Before we can say that opera as an art form has truly developed further, it will take more than merely pulling in the latest developments and anything that happens to be popular at the moment."[28] Only a little later, in March 1928, Kurt Weill was similarly critical of attempts at pure Zeitoper (including *Royal Palace*), although he did consider it an important transitional phase for later developments:

> This word *Zeitoper* . . . was just as hastily coined as it was incorrectly employed. . . . The *Zeitstück*, as we have come to know it in recent years, moved superficial manifestations of life in our time onto center stage. People took the "tempo of the twentieth century," combined it with the much-praised "rhythm of our time" and, for the rest, limited themselves to the representation of sentiments of past generations. . . . Only now, after the hitherto existing *Zeittheater* has freed the material, have we reached the unintentionality, the self-evident level where we can represent the world view that we see—each perhaps in his own way—no longer as a photograph, but as a mirror reflection."[29]

Kurt Weill himself was to make significant contributions to that effort.

Cast list from the second performance of *Royal Palace* on 5
March 1927 (identical to the cast of the premiere).

Let us now return to the year 1926, by the beginning of which Weill had finished composing *Royal Palace*. The young Weill–Lenya couple made their home in two rooms in the Pension Hassforth; one room contained Weill's piano, where he composed. The usual horrible pictures hung on the walls, causing the Weills to call their boarding house "Grieneisen," after a well-known Berlin undertaker. Lotte Lenya had this to report about Weill's method of composition:

Kurt always sat down at his desk at 9:00, completely absorbed and working like a happy child. This daily routine never varied unless he had rehearsals to go to. At that time I didn't have much to do at the theater. I sat at the table, Weill came downstairs for breakfast, and then he went back to his music. He resurfaced for lunch, and then he went back to his music again. After a few days I said to him, "This is a terrible life for

**Kurt Weill's study in the Pension Hassforth, where the couple
lived from May 1925 until October 1928. This photograph was
taken in 1953, when Lotte Lenya paid a return visit to the
pension and found the room, including the piano at which Weill
composed, just as they had left it.**

me—I only see you at mealtime." He looked at me through his thick glasses and said,
"But Lenya, you know that you come right after my music." For Weill there really was
nothing but his music. Other composers had hobbies; Schönberg and Gershwin
painted, for example. I think that for Weill music was his hobby as well as his profession.[30]

Perhaps it is appropriate at this point to add a testimony of Weill's to the warmth of his
relationship with Lotte Lenya:

She is a terrible housewife but a very good actress. She can't read music, but when she
sings, people listen as if they were hearing Caruso. (By the way, I pity every composer
whose wife can read music.) She doesn't get involved in my work (this is one of her best
qualities). But she would be very upset if I were not interested in her work. She always
has a few male friends, which she justifies by saying that she doesn't get along well
with women. (But maybe she doesn't get along so well with women because she
always has male friends.) She married me because she wanted to learn to shudder, and
she says this wish has been more than fulfilled. My wife is named Lotte Lenya.[31]

In June and July of 1926 the two went on a belated honeymoon; in January there had not been enough money. They traveled via Zurich and northern Italy to the French Riviera, where they relaxed in Cannes for a few weeks.

Back in Berlin in July, Weill received a commission—no doubt in part because of his work on the radio magazine—to compose the music for a radio production of Christian Dietrich Grabbe's play *Herzog Theodor von Gothland*. This was Weill's first work for radio, and he scored it for a large orchestra and chorus. As a contemporary critic noted, the relationship between text and music was especially significant. A full year later, the composer would call such a use "epic"; but the first signs of this are already evident here, in 1926. "Kurt Weill's music treads completely new paths. . . . In this work of expressive power the music does not try to accompany. Drama and music meet in the only possible way; the result is a synthesis of lasting significance for both the text and the music."[32] The play was broadcast on 1 September 1926, with Bruno Seidler-Winkler conducting Weill's music. The actors included Werner Krauss and Theodor Loos.

Toward the end of March 1926 Weill met the young music critic Felix Joachimson, the lyricist of many cabaret chansons of those years, who suggested a collaboration. They quickly developed an intensive working relationship, and Joachimson was a frequent guest in Weill's and Lenya's home in the Pension Hassforth. Later he gave an authentic description of Weill's method of composition:

> Kurt Weill composed at his desk. He literally "wrote" his music. Sometimes, he would get up and double-check a complicated chord on the piano. But his musical ideas were not conceived or developed on musical instruments. The inner sound didn't need instrumental ratification. It reverberated in the written notes.
>
> Ideas for orchestrating came to him immediately. He used to sketch them briefly. But the real job of orchestrating started after the first act of creating was finished. He always orchestrated himself. He wouldn't have left it to anyone else. He loved it. And he considered orchestrating fifty percent of composing.
>
> In spite of his classical training, Kurt Weill didn't play the piano very well. He used to make fun of it himself but he never realized that his playing didn't sound as he imagined it did. Nevertheless, he could demonstrate convincingly a new melody or a whole score. He used to play the orchestra part with utmost precision, adding the vocal parts with a hoarse, soft voice. It was an exercise in aspirating rather than singing but it was effective.[33]

Weill's and Joachimson's plans for a play were not to result in much success. They worked on a libretto entitled *Na und?* (So What?), a story of contemporary Berlin, which Weill expanded into a "comic opera." On 4 April 1927 he wrote to his publisher: "It is the first attempt in opera to illuminate the essence of our era from within and not by means of obvious superficial props. The theme of this opera: the tendency of modern man to talk and act at cross-purposes. The title *Na und?* is therefore the summary expression of the content. It is the sort of comic opera that hasn't been developed since *Der Rosen-kavalier* and is just what the theaters are looking for—not grotesque or burlesque, but jaunty and musical. The musical form: seventeen closed numbers, in between a bit of recitative or spoken dialogue with piano or chamber music scoring."[34]

Among the few sketches that have been preserved is a three-verse "Niggersong," a fox-trot with the characteristic cantilenas that were soon to mark Weill's song style. Joachimson's lyrics reflect the atmosphere of the fascination with jazz that then prevailed in Berlin:

> Du Lady Lily You, my husband
> Du Lady Lily You, die jazzband
> Von dem Nigger Ging-Gong
> Spielt ein Nigger Sing-Song
> Für Dich.[35]

Upon reading through the work, Universal's director Hertzka wrote to Weill that he could not conceal the fact "that the first impression is not good."[36] He said he would need to have Weill play it for him. Weill immediately went to Vienna and presented *Na und?* to his publisher on 10 April 1927.

Hans W. Heinsheimer, director of the stage division, was likewise opposed to the work and recalls:

> Weill played the entire opera [for us], softly singing with a veiled, pleasant, expressive voice, playing the piano in a dry, matter-of-fact, unflourished manner. Hertzka and I followed with the libretto. We did not like anything about the work. We did not like the libretto, which was by a little-known German playwright and musician who had never written a libretto before, and as we read on we ardently wished he had let it go at that. We loathed the title of the opera which seemed to reflect the worst asphalt cynicism of Berlin. . . . The music seemed handicapped and weighted down by the story and the lyrics. As the composer played on, one could sense an aura of despair creep into the room.[37]

Hertzka told Weill that the libretto was too weak for the work to be successful, and that there could be no question of publishing it. Back in Berlin, Weill took the work to Hans Curjel, the designated stage director of Berlin's Krolloper, to get a second expert opinion. Curjel came to the same conclusion: "I told him that I didn't think it worked—from the standpoint of either the text or the music. But I conceded that I might have deceived myself, and we agreed to lock it up in my desk for four weeks. This way, Weill also had some distance from his own work when he picked it up again in a month's time. And that is just what happened: after a few days Weill called me to say that he now had the same impression of it and had decided never to allow this opera to be performed."[38]

Weill had little time for great disappointment, since he was working hard during those weeks of March and April 1927 on another project. After the first successful run of *Der Protagonist* (productions in Erfurt and Nuremberg had followed the one in Dresden), a number of theaters were asking Weill for another one-act opera that could be paired with it.

Kurt Weill was also—along with Paul Hindemith, Darius Milhaud, and Ernst Toch—one of the composers to receive a commission from the directors of the German Chamber Music Festival in Baden-Baden for a short opera to be performed in July. He sought to win over Georg Kaiser again as librettist. Contact between the two had never actually broken off—Weill had dedicated *Royal Palace* to him—and they met again in March 1927. Kaiser agreed not to rework one of his older plays this time but to write an original libretto. A close collaboration over the ensuing months produced *Der Zar läßt sich photographieren* (The Czar Has His Picture Taken), an opera buffa. While they were working on it, Weill and Kaiser considered calling it *Photographie und Liebe* (Photography and Love) and even *Der Zar läßt sich . . .* (The Czar Has . . .) before settling on the final title. The story of this one-act opera is as original as it is theatrical.

An imaginary czar comes to the studio of the Parisian fashion photographer Angèle to be privately photographed. But there are conspirators on his trail who replace Angèle with one of their accomplices and install a pistol in the camera, which is set to go off as soon as the shutter is released. The false Angèle and the czar find that they are attracted to each other, and the potentate proposes an exchange of roles: he would like to take the pretty young woman's picture before she takes his. In the course of their playful skirmish the czar learns from a bodyguard that he is the intended victim of a conspiracy and that the police are already on their way to the studio. The false Angèle continues to play the part of a lover. She puts on a record of tango music while the czar awaits her on the divan; but before anything further can happen, the police arrive, arrest the conspirators, and the real Angèle returns. Somewhat puzzled over the change in the photographer's appearance, his majesty finally has his picture taken.

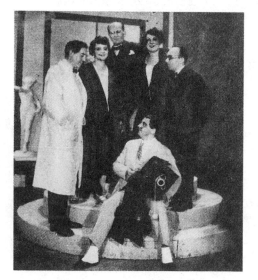

Dress rehearsal for the premiere of *Der Zar läßt sich photographieren,* based on an original libretto by Georg Kaiser, 17 February 1928, at Leipzig's Neues Theater. Joining the actors are the director Walther Brügmann (*left*), the conductor Gustav Brecher (*back center*), and Kurt Weill (*right*).

Scene from the highly successful premiere of *Der Zar läßt sich photographieren* in Leipzig, 18 February 1928.

Weill's part in this story is quite obvious. Not long before beginning this work, he had discussed in detail a broadcast of Lortzing's *Zar und Zimmermann* (Czar and Carpenter), the story of Czar Peter the First's attempt to flee from public service into private life. Kaiser and Weill's czar makes a similar attempt in Paris. The influences of the 1920s also more likely came from Weill than from Kaiser. Photography was then a popular art form; both Weill and Lenya were acquainted with the Berlin star photographers Lotte Jacobi and Elli Marcus and had numerous portraits done by them. The gramophone and its central role in the play are indicative of the fascination of the time with records, which, thanks to the invention of the electric microphone, were just entering the marketplace with higher-quality sound recordings. Finally, the unmistakable suggestion of pulp fiction points to one of Kaiser's favorite topics at the time, and a serious background shows through—political assassinations and murders were constantly in the news in the Weimar Republic.

It soon became apparent to Weill that *Der Zar* could not be performed in Baden-Baden. On 23 March 1927 he wrote to his publisher: "We have worked out a scenario, and it is now perfectly clear that the material would be too much for Baden-Baden. It will be a work of about three-quarters of an hour, which cannot be done without a real orchestra and stage apparatus. Quite honestly, I would have been sorry to have wasted the

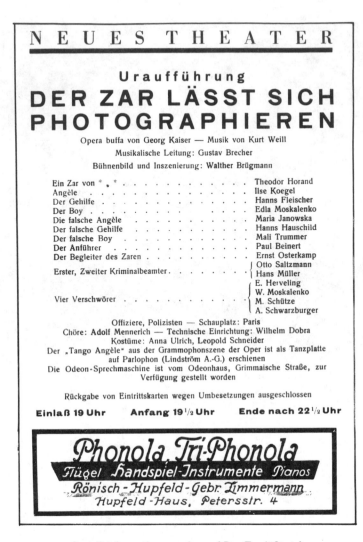

Cast list from the premiere of *Der Zar läßt sich photographieren.*

work on the snobbishness of a music festival."[39] While he was now working on a new project for Baden-Baden—which would ultimately result in the songspiel *Mahagonny*—he continued work on *Der Zar läßt sich photographieren.* On 20 April Weill reported to his publisher that he had just received the last page of Kaiser's libretto, and on 4 August he wrote, "I have finished the composition of the new Kaiser one-act and am busy at work on the full score."[40]

The designation *opera buffa* points to a tradition that Weill returned to again and again: to Mozart as master of the genre, to Lortzing's comic operas, and to Offenbach's *opéra bouffe.* Certain elements appear in this score that will soon become characteristic of Weill's musical theater—the appropriation of popular dance forms (the fox-trot at the first appearance of the czar, the tango in the gramophone scene); jazz instrumentation in the orchestra (here, at first, "only" by means of a record in the "Tango Angèle"); and a commenting role for the chorus, which often interrupts the action onstage from the orchestra pit. The structure of the music is marked by rhythmic and melodic ostinato figures. This is Weill's last theater score to set the entire text of a libretto to music; later he will turn more and more often to the "number principle," allowing him to work with small, self-contained musical forms.

A detailed study of Weill's stylistic development in the twenties has yet to be undertaken. But it is quite evident that his innovations in musical language are always intimately linked with the dramatic structure of a work. Weill proceeds dualistically. In *Der Protagonist,* because of the intermixture of opera and pantomime, expressionist and neoclassical stylistic elements are found side by side; in *Royal Palace* and *Der Zar,* by contrast, atonal passages are clearly set off from tonal passages. The latter primarily serve the dramatic function of introducing elements of popular music, which, though taken over as a prefabricated musical language, is nonetheless made to seem thoroughly foreign. A comparison with the later *Mahagonny* songspiel and opera clearly shows that toward the end of the twenties the "foreign," or "wrong," notes gradually disappear, giving way to a classical shaping. *Der Zar,* with its tango adaptation, stands, as it were, at the gateway to this development.

Weill wrote about his score:

> Just as I had created new musical possibilities in *Der Protagonist* by inventing a musical frame, by juxtaposing the eight winds in the orchestra, and by expanding the pantomimes vocally, so also I made adaptations to this new text. I tried to forge a link

Der „**Tango Angèle**" aus der Oper: „Der Zar läßt sich photographieren", komp. von Kurt Weill, ist **nur** auf **Parlophon**-(Beka)Musikplatten erschienen! Zu haben im Odeon-Parlophon-Musikhaus, Grimmaische Str. 9/11 (neben Schneider) Fernruf: 19767

Advertisement for the Parlophon record of the "Tango Angèle" in the program of the Leipzig premiere.

The first record with music by Kurt Weill, released in February 1928.

between the stage and the audience by adding a men's chorus, for which I myself wrote the texts, to the orchestra. In many places I extended the dialogue to make room for small ensemble movements—arias, buffo duet, and the like. Finally, I believed that the kind of inner intensification that the final flight scene called for could be achieved only through a complete transformation of the sound color. Thus I came to add the gramophone scene, in which I let a mechanical instrument and a dancelike musical style help advance the plot. I was able to reserve a saxophone and jazz sound for this "Tango Angèle" (as I called it). After careful study of the gramophone I then worked out a special instrumentation of this self-contained dance piece for the gramophone record and had it recorded by Lindström AG.[41]

The recording took place on 11 January 1928, with the Dobbri saxophone orchestra. The record of "Tango Angèle"—the first recording of Weill's music—was on hand for the premiere of *Der Zar läßt sich photographieren*. It became part of the performance material distributed to theaters by Universal.

The one-act opera was premiered on 18 February 1928 in Leipzig's Neues Theater. Unfortunately the opera's management had not agreed to pairing it with *Der Protagonist;* instead it was added as a second piece following Nicola Spinelli's short opera *A Basso Porto.*

The director was Walther Brügmann, and Gustav Brecher conducted. The premiere was judged to be a success by all. The critics noted: "Unless we deceive ourselves, the German stage has been given an excellent complementary work to *Der Protagonist,*"[42] and "Even if this opera is to be considered a transition and does not yet represent the goal of new opera, it goes a long way toward smoothing out the path to the new opera form. What Weill, supported by Kaiser, has achieved here in textual-musical unity leaves the contemporary opera repertoire far behind."[43]

Again it was Weill himself who conducted the negotiations for the first joint performance of *Der Protagonist* and *Der Zar.* His former pupil and friend Maurice Abravanel had been musical director of the Reußisches Theater in Gera since 1927. In 1928 this theater was merged with the Altenburger Bühne. Weill knew Gera's prince apparent, Reuß, who as a dramaturg was a staunch proponent of contemporary works. Weill had already talked to him in December 1927 about a joint production of his two one-act

Scene from a performance by the Städtische Oper of Berlin-Charlottenburg of *Der Zar läßt sich photographieren,* in May 1928, with Joseph Burgwinkel as the czar and Maria Janowska as Angèle.

Landestheater Altenburg

Mittwoch, den 4. April 1928

30. Vorstellung im Mittwochs-Anrecht

Zum ersten Mal:

Der Protagonist

Ein Akt Oper von Georg Kaiser. Musik von Kurt Weill
Inszenierung: Rudolf Otto Hartmann
Musikalische Leitung: Maurice de Abravanel
Bühnenbild und Kostüme: Vera Braun

Personen:

Protagonist . . . . Heinz Edeler
Schwester . . . . Elly Nowak
Der junge Herr . . . . Rolf Scharf
Der Hausmeister des Herzogs . . . . Josef Heckhausen
Der Wirt . . . . Kurt Jüttner
1. Schauspieler . . . . Max Kerner
2. Schauspieler . . . . Erich Bürger
3. Schauspieler . . . . Käte Benad

Die acht Musikanten des Herzogs: Richard Bischof, Hans Dörste,
Paul Herbert, Paul Limbach, Kurt Löpitz, Paul Möbus, Otto Ulrich,
Arthur Wunderlich
Zeit der Handlung: Das England Shakespeares
Bühneninspektion: Theo Leidsbach

— Pause —

Hierauf:

Zum ersten Mal:

Der Zar läßt sich photographieren

Opera buffa in einem Akt von Georg Kaiser
Musik von Kurt Weill
Inszenierung: Rudolf Otto Hartmann
Musikalische Leitung: Maurice de Abravanel
Bühnenbild und Kostüme: Vera Braun

Personen:

Ein Zar von . . * . . . . Rolf Scharf
Angéle . . . . Bergljot Brandsberg-Dahl
Der Gehilfe . . . . Josef Heckhausen
Der Boy . . . . Maria Stumpf
Die falsche Angéle . . . . Kirstine Bredsten
Der falsche Gehilfe . . . . Alexander Helfmann
Der falsche Boy . . . . Gertrud Wilde
Der Anführer . . . . Walter Hageböcker
Der Begleiter des Zaren . . . . Kurt Jüttner
Erster Kriminalbeamter . . . . Albertus Kinkel
Zweiter Kriminalbeamter . . . . Heinz Wagner

Verschwörer, Offiziere, Polizisten
Bühneninspektion: Theo Leidsbach

Einlaß 19 Uhr   Anfang 19¹/₂ Uhr   Ende ungefähr 22¹/₄ Uhr

**Program from the first joint production of the two one-act
works *Der Protagonist* and *Der Zar läßt sich photographieren* at
Altenburg's Landestheater, 4 April 1928.**

operas, and on 2 April 1928, a good seven weeks after the Leipzig premiere of *Der Zar,* this production opened as a double bill. Weill himself was present for the occasion, and a few days later he wrote a letter expressing his appreciation of Abravanel's and the entire Altenburg ensemble's commitment to his works.

In October 1928 Walther Brügmann staged *Der Protagonist* and *Der Zar* at Berlin's Städtische Oper, with Robert Denzler conducting. Oskar Bie wrote: "Time will sort this all through. But one thing is already clear, that Kurt Weill is now showing a special gift, independent, serious, and developed into a firmer discipline than in the still unreflective era of *Royal Palace.*"[44]

By 1933 *Der Zar*—often paired with Stravinsky's *Oedipus Rex*—had been performed at more than sixty German and European opera houses and had thus become, after *Die Dreigroschenoper,* Weill's greatest theatrical success. After coming out as a record, the "Tango Angèle" was published by Universal as a single piano–vocal sheet. The composer had achieved his first "hit" with a piece of music that spoke to wide circles beyond opera audiences and quickly became popular.

Kurt Weill had thus reached a turning point in the middle of 1927, when the score to *Der Zar* was completed. The critical situation in which the composer found himself has been very aptly described by Theodor W. Adorno. Adorno, then twenty-four years old, had just completed his study of composition with Alban Berg and of philosophy at the University in Frankfurt and had begun his editorial work at Vienna's *Anbruch,* the

Advertisement by Universal Edition on the occasion of the thirty-fifth production of *Der Zar*, in March 1931.

journal most committed at the time to contemporary music. Some of the most incisive critical essays on Weill would come from Adorno in the years that followed.

In June 1928 the two met for the first time in Frankfurt am Main on the occasion of the city's premiere of *Der Protagonist* and *Der Zar;* numerous further meetings ensued until 1933. Adorno wrote: "In *Der Zar,* which very evidently represents technical progress over *Der Protagonist,* the music occasionally runs the danger of sinking into the scenery to reemerge only as *Gebrauchsmusik.* . . . But anyone who can learn as much from himself as Weill will be all the more likely to avoid all that as his sound judgment leads him to distance himself energetically from conventional theater."[45]

Weill had now reached this point. The musical groundwork had been laid for his efforts to open up the boundaries of traditional musical theater and create a new kind of opera. All that he needed now was to meet a writer who would be able to bring the same determination and ability to the literary material. This meeting took place in April 1927, while Weill was working on the score of *Der Zar;* his new collaborator was named Bertolt Brecht.

(1 9 2 7 – 3 0)

Collaboration with Brecht

When Weill and Brecht met in Berlin, the Weimar Republic was just approaching the high point of its "golden" years between 1925 and 1929. These years were characterized by a tumultuous growth in technology and industry; the penetration of a new functional aesthetics into the spheres of architecture and design; a polished, glittering entertainment industry; and, in the area of "serious" art, multifaceted attempts to counter the crisis in traditional genres and institutions with new forms. At the same time, the first political polarizations were appearing, which—unleashed by the repercussions of the world economic crisis in Germany—would start erupting with all their force in 1929. Berlin had long since become the unrivaled mecca of art and politics in Germany, and the Brecht–Weill team would soon join the ranks of its leading figures.

Kurt Weill and Bertolt Brecht had most likely already met in March 1927 in the context of their radio work. Weill often went to the studio of Funkstunde Berlin, where a radio version of Brecht's *Mann ist Mann* was produced on 10 March 1927, in which the author himself participated. Weill reviewed the broadcast almost euphorically: "A writer, a real writer, has presented a solution to a significant portion of all the questions raised by broadcast theater with a bold stroke and a wonderful sensibility."[1]

At the time, finding the one-act *Zar* written with Georg Kaiser unsuited to the purpose, Weill was searching for a libretto for the Baden-Baden festival's commission for a short opera. His extensive correspondence with Universal Edition allows a fairly exact reconstruction of the beginning of his collaboration with Brecht. On 23 March Weill declared: "I won't write a short opera for Baden-Baden, since I now have enough one-act works. Instead, I plan to take a passage from a classical tragedy (*Antigone, Lear,* or the like) and write a short vocal scene of at most fifteen minutes." A month later, on the heels of his disappointment over the rejection of *Na und?*, he decided he would prefer not to participate at all in Baden-Baden, even though he was being pressed by the festival management. On 25 April he wrote: "In the meantime Burkard has written and telegraphed several times, but I will remain with my refusal." Then, only seven days later, on 2 May, a surprising turnaround: "In haste, a note that I have changed my mind about Baden-Baden. I have suddenly had a very good idea, on which I am working at the moment. Title: *Mahagonny*–a songspiel on texts by Brecht. I hope to finish this short work by the middle of May."

Since Brecht's collection of poetry entitled *Die Hauspostille* (Domestic Breviary), which contained as its "fourth reading" five *Mahagonnygesänge* (Mahagonny Songs), had just been published by Propyläen-Verlag, it is safe to assume that Weill's inspiration was the result of having read this book. Lotte Lenya reports that Weill immediately sought out Brecht and that friends directed him to the writer's local haunt. "We met him first in a very famous theatre restaurant in Berlin called 'Schlichter.'"[2] It must have been toward the end of April 1927, in the Lutherstraße pub run by Max Schlichter (brother of the painter Rudolf Schlichter), that the two first sat across from each other to discuss a joint production. Evidently the spark of shared aspirations and the sense that they would be able to work together became apparent very quickly; they immediately embarked on an extremely intensive collaboration that was to last nearly four years.

It was a meeting between two personalities who differed fundamentally in their cultural backgrounds and in the artistic paths they had followed up to that point. Nearly the same age, they were brought together at this time essentially by their desire to break open the forms of institutionalized theater and opera and seek new paths that would reflect the social reality of their time. Brecht, born in 1898 in Augsburg, had, like Weill, reached a turning point in his career. With his first plays, *Baal* and *Trommeln in der Nacht* (Drumming in the Night), he had emerged on the German stage as a natural talent, and in 1922

Portrait photograph of Kurt Weill by Lotte Jacobi, 1927.

Bertolt Brecht in 1927, when he and Kurt Weill first met.

he had been honored with the Kleist Prize. In his work with Lion Feuchtwanger and later in his play *Mann ist Mann,* premiered in 1926, he had continued his search for a new formal language that would reflect his conception of the theater. This search, as his biographer Werner Mittenzwei has written, led him into a cul-de-sac of uncompleted projects and sketches. "He got into even greater trouble when he took up material that he wanted to use to show not only how we live from commerce but also how the whole system of buying and selling works."[3] This was the beginning, in October 1926, of Brecht's theoretical appropriation of Marxism. Contemporaneous with his collaboration with Weill, it would become an important factor in the eventual parting of ways in 1930.

When they first met, of course, none of this was yet evident. In 1927 Brecht was primarily interested in renewing conventional theater, which he attacked vehemently and denounced as "an old, mismanaged, broken-down circus robbed of its magic, with its effeminate tenors and masculine prima donnas, its rinsed-out lingerie and bellowing pipes."[4] Opera, he thought, was particularly in need of reform. His intentions coincided with Weill's.

Unlike Brecht's later lifelong working friendship with Hanns Eisler, which rested on a deep accord on nearly all questions of worldview and aesthetics, the relationship between Brecht and Weill—"two such dissimilar yet strikingly complementary minds," as David Drew has put it so aptly[5]—was confined almost entirely to their joint projects. Once this foundation was gone and the two had drifted away from their once congruent positions, the relationship was destined to fall apart.

Music had always played a large role in Brecht's plays and poems. Among the decisive influences of his youth were the folk ballads (*Bänkellieder* and *Moritaten*) he heard sung at annual street fairs, as well as Frank Wedekind's rebellious *Lieder zur Laute* (Lute Songs) and the enigmatic ballads of the Bavarian folk comedian Karl Valentin. Brecht himself played the guitar and made up melodies to a number of his poems. Songs already constituted a musical plane corresponding to the text in his first play *Baal,* and this continued in *Mann ist Mann*. At first he worked without benefit of a professional composer, however; in the few performances of Brecht's plays up to 1926, either his own melodies were used or the theaters produced stage music without his participation. Not until it became clear in November 1925 that the planned poetry volume *Die Hauspostille* would contain a musical supplement did Brecht call upon a specialist, the young Berlin cabaret composer Franz S. Bruinier, who helped edit the appendix and also set a few of Brecht's poems to music. But this relationship was not meant to last; once he met Weill, "Franz S. Bruinier disappeared from Brecht's field of vision."[6] Bruinier died in 1928 in Berlin at the age of only twenty-three.

The *Mahagonny* project, the first that Weill and Brecht turned to, offered them an opportunity to work with two of their favorite subjects: first, the "Moloch" of the large cities, which were expanding quickly in the wake of rapid industrialization and urbanization (Brecht's poetic cycle *Lesebuch für Städtebewohner* [Reader for City Dwellers] centers on this topic), and the dominant middle-class mores governing life in them; and, second, the fascination with America that at the time pervaded nearly all areas of art in different ways.

The origin of the name "Mahagonny" for Brecht's imaginary city is not altogether clear. He was already writing *Mahagonnygesänge* (Mahagonny Songs) in 1921; at this time a record with an instrumental version of the American shimmy *Komm nach Mahagonne* (Come to Mahagonny) had just appeared on the German market. This may well be the origin of the name. Gunter G. Sehm conjectures that, with his thorough knowledge of the Bible, Brecht may have derived the name from Magog, the biblical city surpassed only by Babylon in its sinfulness.[7] Arnolt Bronnen relates in his memoirs that the name came to Brecht when they jointly attended a Nazi demonstration in Munich's Zirkus Krone in 1923 and saw the SA Brown Shirts, leading Brecht to remark, "If Mahagonny is coming, I'm leaving."[8] But this was more likely written in response to the later uproar surrounding the *Mahagonny* opera.

Photograph of a rehearsal for the premiere of *Mahagonny,*
Weill's first collaborative venture with Brecht. The work was
performed in a boxing ring. *Left of the ring*: Kurt Weill and Paul
Hindemith. *Right of the ring*: Bertolt Brecht. *Center*: Lotte
Lenya and Irene Eden as Jessie and Bessie.

In Brecht's diary there is a listing of future projects from July 1924 that includes, in seventh place, the entry "Mahagonny opera . . . Mar."[9] "Mar" refers to Marianne Zoff, Brecht's first wife, who was an opera singer at Augsburg's Stadttheater. Brecht did not immediately pursue the project. But now, when Weill approached him with a plan to set the *Mahagonnygesänge* to music, they talked not only about the commission for Baden-Baden but, from the very beginning, about fleshing out the material into an opera.

First, the songspiel *Mahagonny* was written in a scant two weeks. Weill changed the order of the five poems from *Die Hauspostille* and songs on their texts, adding orchestral interludes as well as a prelude and a postlude, and he asked Brecht for a new text for the finale. The play, which lasts approximately thirty minutes, has the following sequence:

Part 1. Prologue
1. Off to Mahagonny—The four gold diggers Charlie, Billy, Bobby, and Jimmy are on their way to the dream city Mahagonny. 2. Alabama-Song—The two prostitutes Jessie and Bessie, the "sharks," are likewise on their way to Mahagonny.

Part 2. Life in Mahagonny
3. Those who stayed in Mahagonny—The four men sing the principle of Mahagonny.

4. Benares-Song—The four men and the two girls decide to leave Mahagonny for Benares. They learn that Benares has been destroyed by an earthquake and realize that they must stay in Mahagonny. 5. One morning in the middle of whiskey—The play of God in Mahagonny.

Part 3. Finale

6. But this whole Mahagonny—all six end the play with the following observation:

> But this whole Mahagonny
> Exists only because everything is so bad
> Because there is no rest
> And no harmony
> And because there is nothing
> You can hold on to.

Jessie comes to the edge of the stage:

> Mahagonny—it is nothing
> Mahagonny—it is nowhere
> Mahagonny—it is just a made-up word.[10]

In the songspiel, "Mahagonny" still stands as a more or less generalized counterpart to "large cities"; its unmistakably negative expansion into a capitalistic "city of nets" did not take place until the opera.

Weill introduces three radical innovations into his music here, at the beginning of his collaboration with Brecht: a new orchestral configuration of ten musicians (two violins, two clarinets, two trumpets, alto saxophone, piano, and percussion); a new kind of song style derived from elements of popular music (including jazz and popular hits), which makes its appearance here for the first time as a Weill song style; and the use of self-contained, independent numbers. The orchestral interludes, which tie the songs together, are still composed in the harmonic style of *Der Zar* and *Royal Palace*.

Weill was able to write to his publisher by 14 May 1927: "I have almost finished composing the piece and am working on the score." Lotte Lenya later reported Brecht's reaction when she first sang the "Alabama-Song" for him: "I sang the Alabama song, and Brecht listened with that deep courtesy and patience that I was to learn never failed him with women and actors. 'Not so Egyptian,' he said, turning my palms upward, extending my arms in direct appeal to the moon of Alabama. 'Now, let's really work.'"[11]

How deeply Weill and Brecht were enmeshed in their opera project is shown in a contemporaneous project that closely resembles the *Mahagonny* opera in its intentions and basic features: the first plans for a *Ruhrepos* (Epic of the Ruhr). In 1927 Rudolf Schulz-Dornburg, opera director of Essen's Städtische Bühnen, had first suggested a festival for the Ruhr area which would open the theater to a wider segment of the population, especially to workers. He asked Weill to compose an "industrial opera." Weill was immediately taken "by the plan for a new kind of musico-dramatical work for the Ruhr"[12] and in turn suggested Brecht as the lyricist—a further indication of how closely the two were already working together after just a few weeks. From Brecht came the suggestion that his acquaintance Carl Koch, who experimented in film, be brought in. The city of Essen approved the production team, commissioned a detailed prospectus, and invited Weill, Brecht, and Koch to come for local studies. In the early summer of 1927 the trio traveled to Essen. But because of local political squabbles, the project was eventually called off. All that remains is the prospectus by Brecht, Weill, and Koch, "one of the very earliest textual sketches for epic musical theater,"[13] which shows the far-reaching intentions of its authors. Here Brecht wrote: "The *Ruhrepos* should be a document of contemporary history along the lines of the Orbis Pictus of the seventeenth century, reflecting this century's view of the world in simple pictures. Songs are written and composed to elucidate large placards [*Tafeln*] depicting mines, types of people, machines, etc. Slide and film projections show the actual documents that are treated by the poetry and the music."[14] Weill remarked about the musical intentions of the project: "The music of the *Ruhrepos* condenses all the expressive means of absolute and dramatic music into a new unity. Rather than creating mood paintings or naturalistic sound accompaniments, it gives precision to the tensions in the poetry and the scene with its expression, its dynamics, and its tempo."[15]

One can only agree with Albrecht Dümling when he writes: "Everything indicates that, had the city of Essen financed it, the *Ruhrepos* would have become a masterpiece. Never again was a comparable artistic treatise of a landscape conceived. It clearly pointed the way to the *Mahagonny* opera."[16]

A month after their return from Essen, Weill and Brecht traveled to Baden-Baden for the premiere of the songspiel *Mahagonny*. Here their team was joined by Brecht's childhood friend, the stage designer Caspar Neher, whom Weill was soon also calling "Cas." From then until 1933 he was to play an important part in Weill's work, both as a designer of important performances and as a librettist. Born in 1897, Caspar Neher was already one of the most sought-after stage designers in Germany by this time. Especially with his projections, which employed a flowing watercolor technique, he made a significant contribution to the development of scenography.

The premiere of *Mahagonny* at the German Chamber Music Festival in Baden-Baden took place in the large concert hall of the Kurhaus as part of an evening of short operas. The concert opened with the "musical fairy tale" *Die Prinzessin auf der Erbse* (The Princess and the Pea) by Ernst Toch and was followed by the eight-minute "opéra minute" *Europa* by Darius Milhaud, Brecht and Weill's "songspiel," and finally Paul Hindemith's "sketch" *Hin und zurück* (Forward and Back).

All four compositions had consciously rejected the designation *opera*. After Milhaud's "opéra minute" a boxing ring was constructed on the stage, and here *Mahagonny* was presented for the first time. A large backdrop was erected for Neher's projections, and the small orchestra, conducted by Ernst Mehlich, sat on the stage, to the side of the boxing ring. The roles of the four men and of Bessie were taken by opera singers, but Lotte Lenya sang the part of Jessie. Her great career as interpreter of Brecht–Weill songs began

DEUTSCHE KAMMERMUSIK
BADEN-BADEN 1927

15.–17. Juli 1927

Veranstaltet von der Stadt Baden-Baden

Künstlerische Leitung:

Heinrich Burkard   Josef Haas   Paul Hindemith

Mahagonny

Ein Songspiel nach Texten von Bert Brecht
von Kurt Weill

Personen:

Jessie	Lotte Lenja
Bessie	Iréne Eden
Charlie	Erik Wirl
Billy	Georg Ripperger
Bobby	Karl Giebel
Jimmy	Gerhard Pechner

Dirigent: Ernst Mehlich

Regie: Bert Brecht

Bühnenbilder: Caspar Neher

Kostüme entworfen von Caspar Neher, ausgeführt von Emilie Walut-Franz Droll

Musik. Einstudierung: Otto Besag

Orchesterbesetzung: 2 Violinen, 2 Klar., 2 Tromp. Saxophon, Posaune,
Klavier, Schlagzeug.

Kurt Weill, geb. 2.3.1900 in Dessau, badischer Abstammung. 1918 Hochschule in Berlin.
1919 — 1920 Theaterkapellmeister. 1921 Schüler Busonis. Weill lebt in Berlin.
Werke u. a. Streichquartett op. 8. Quodlibet op. 9. Frauentanz Op. 10. „Recordare"
(a capella-Chorwerk) op. 11. Violinkonzert op. 12. „Der neue Orpheus" op 15.
Opern: „Der Protagonist," „Royal Palace."
In seinen neueren Werken bewegt sich Weill in der Richtung jener Künstler
aller Kunstgebiete, die die Liquidation der gesellschaftlichen Künste voraus-
sagen. Das kleine epische Stück „Mahagonny" zieht lediglich die Konse-
quenz aus dem unaufhaltsamen Verfall der bestehenden Gesellschaftsschichten
Er wendet sich bereits an ein Publikum, das im Theater naiv seinen Spass
verlangt.

**Program from the premiere of the songspiel *Mahagonny* in
Baden-Baden, 17 July 1927.**

On the steps to the entrance of the Kurhaus, during the Baden-
Baden Chamber Music Festival in 1927. *Front row, left to right:*
Lotte Lenya, Leipzig opera director Walther Brügmann, and
Essen dramaturg Hannes Küpper. *Middle row, left to right:*
Bertolt Brecht and the festival director, Heinrich Burkard.
Back row, left to right: Kurt Weill, Frau Brügmann, and the
Mahagonny actors Irene Eden, Georg Ripperger, the
Kapellmeister Ernst Wolff, and, *standing,* Karl Giebel.

that evening with her rendition of the "Alabama-Song." Brecht directed, assisted by Hans Curjel, who had been named dramaturg of Berlin's Krolloper.

The thirty-five minutes of the performance sufficed to polarize the middle-class festival audience, which had come to Baden-Baden to hear forward-looking music but was now confronted with an aggressive story of money-grubbers and whores that turned every value of the bourgeois ethic on its head. By the time the performers hoisted signs with anti-capitalistic slogans in the finale, the commotion was complete. As some members of the audience gave vent vociferously to their indignation, the singers responded by blowing whistles that Brecht had slipped to them just before the performance in anticipation of the audience's reaction. On Lotte Lenya's sign, which she held up high, unperturbed by the tumult around her, were written the words "For Weill!" The program commented that "in his more recent works Weill has been moving in the direction of those artists in all spheres who are predicting the liquidation of the social arts. The little epic play *Mahagonny* simply draws the consequences of the irreversible demise of the existing social classes."[17]

The reaction from the press was mixed; only a few critics understood that the door had been opened to a whole new kind of musical theater. Heinrich Strobel wrote:

> The sensation of the opera evening was *Mahagonny*. It begins as a revue. This includes the music, which is quite original in its blending of jazz, cabaret songs, and lyric elements. Refined *Gebrauchsmusik*. Gradually a social and political message makes its way into what starts out as a purely musical play. A plot starts forming. In close concert with this, music grows out of dance into drama. The last song, a protest against the existing world order in the guise of a revue, rears itself up in a steep dramatic curve. This goes beyond *Der Protagonist* in its intensity of expression. One is swept away by it. It once again betrays Weill's eminent gift for theater, his capacity for dramatic concentration.[18]

Universal Edition published the libretto of the songspiel in 1927 (containing only the lyrics to the songs, not the stage directions); a piano–vocal reduction was planned but not actually published. Not until 1963 was the songspiel published in David Drew's reconstruction (score and piano–vocal reduction). Since Weill himself showed no special interest in performing it in the course of expanding it into an opera (in 1930 he said it was "nothing more than a stylistic study for the opera"[19]), the songspiel was produced only once more in his lifetime, in November 1932, as part of an evening of contemporary opera in Hamburg. Hans Curjel organized a couple of concert performances, in Paris in December 1932 and in Rome in December 1933. Lotte Lenya participated in both performances. The "Alabama-Song" was published by Universal in February 1928 as a single sheet for voice and piano, and in April it was recorded by Electrola in an instrumental version with the orchestra of Marek Weber; the record label read "*Mahasong–Kurt Weill.*"

MAHAGONNY

SONGSPIEL NACH TEXTEN VON BERT BRECHT

MUSIK VON
KURT WEILL

GESANGSTEXTE
ENTNOMMEN AUS BRECHTS „HAUSPOSTILLE"
(PROPYLAEN-VERLAG BERLIN 1927,
COPYRIGHT 1927 BY PROPYLAEN-VERLAG G. M. B. H., BERLIN)
MIT BEWILLIGUNG DES VERLAGES

Nr. 8917
AUFFÜHRUNGSRECHT VORBEHALTEN. DROITS D'EXÉCUTION RÉSERVÉS
UNIVERSAL-EDITION A. G.
WIEN   COPYRIGHT 1927 BY UNIVERSAL-EDITION   LEIPZIG

Title page of the libretto of *Mahagonny* published by
Universal in 1927.

Those July days in Baden-Baden brought Weill and Brecht a whole string of encounters and contacts that proved important for subsequent ventures. This was where they met Walther Brügmann, the opera director from Leipzig, and entered into conversations with the radio managers Ernst Hardt (from Werag in Cologne) and Hans Flesch (from Funkstunde Berlin). Otto Klemperer, soon to become director of Berlin's Krolloper when it split off from the Staatsoper, also seemed impressed by *Mahagonny:* "Even Klemperer couldn't stop singing 'Oh Moon of Alabama.' "[20] And Kurt Weill met Darius Milhaud, who had come to direct his "opéra minute." A cordial friendship later developed between the two when they were both in France.

While Lotte Lenya stayed in Baden-Baden for a few days after 17 July at Hertzka's invitation, Weill and Brecht returned immediately to Berlin to continue work on the opera. This work sparked a revealing exchange of letters in August. Emil Hertzka, who evidently still heard the reactions of the Baden-Baden reception ringing in his ears, made no secret of his misgivings about Weill's new opera plan:

> We would scarcely be in a position to place with the large stages an opera in the style of the *Mahagonny* songs, with daring passages. . . . For this reason I would like to urge you to make clear to Brecht that an opera libretto is not like a prose play . . . and that you would be ill served indeed if you produced a full-length work that was musically thoroughly effective and attractive, but which as a result of its text was simply unperformable in a large number of cities. Naturally, these remarks are not in any way directed against Mr. Brecht but are only intended to urge you, as an opera composer, to exercise the greatest caution.[21]

Weill responded with what amounts to a statement of principle:

> The reason I am drawn to Brecht is, first of all, the strong interaction of my music with his poetry, which surprised all those in Baden-Baden who were competent to judge. But further I am convinced that the close collaboration of two equally productive individuals can lead to something fundamentally new. There can certainly be no doubt that at present a completely new form of stage work is evolving, one that is directed to a different and much larger audience and whose appeal will be unusually broad. This movement, whose strongest force in the spoken drama is Brecht, hasn't had any effect upon opera to date (except in *Mahagonny*), although music is one of its most essential elements. In long discussions with Brecht I have become convinced that his idea of an operatic text largely coincides with my own. The piece we are going to create won't exploit topical themes, which will be dated in a year, but rather will reflect the true tenor of our times. For that reason it will have an impact far beyond its own age. The task is to create the new genre which gives appropriate expression to the

Record of "Alabama-Song," the song that launched Lotte Lenya's career as interpreter of Brecht–Weill songs, in an instrumental arrangement. The record was released in April 1928, and the label refers to the songspiel as *Mahasong* rather than *Mahagonny*.

completely transformed manifestation of life in our time. You were able to observe in Baden-Baden that this art, in spite of its novelty, can have a sensational effect. I would be very happy to elaborate these possibilities for you on the basis of our drafts.[22]

By the end of 1927 Brecht and Weill had completed a first draft of the libretto; it is not clear at what point they settled on the title *Aufstieg und Fall der Stadt Mahagonny* (Rise and Fall of the City of Mahagonny). In November Weill wrote to his publisher: "I am working with Brecht every day on the libretto, which is being shaped entirely according to my instructions. This kind of collaboration, in which a libretto is actually formed according to purely musical considerations, opens up entirely new prospects. I have already begun the composition."[23] A few days later he wrote: "We have now finished the second act of the libretto and hope to have a rough draft of the whole opera by the beginning of December."[24] On 8 December Weill sent his publisher a prospectus which, taking Hertzka's misgivings into account, emphasizes that "we have succeeded in laying a solid foundation for a genuinely popular success, mainly through the extremely exciting plot, the 'popular numbers,' as well as in the revue scenes (Mahagonny Idyll, Boxing Match, Trip to the Bilbao, Courtroom Scene)." But, he stresses emphatically, this work ushers in "a totally new operatic style with real potential for development."[25] Hertzka again expressed misgivings, particularly about the plot, which he hoped would be more "symbolically conceived"; but he nonetheless responded, "Of course even in this form I'll accept the work with great interest."[26] Once again, at Christmastime of 1927, Weill wrote him a key letter:

> I never expected that you would find *Mahagonny* even in this form "lacking in plot." If you consider that in Baden-Baden I succeeded in holding the audience in rapt attention for twenty-five minutes *without a trace of plot* I would think that an opera with a plot so logical and direct and with such a wealth of exciting individual incidents would seem enough. If I have worked with Brecht day after day for three months on shaping this libretto, then my own, this time very substantial share of the work was directed almost entirely toward achieving the most logical, straightforward and easily comprehendible plot possible. . . . However, in the operatic style I am establishing here, music has a much more fundamental role than in the purely story-line opera, since I am replacing the earlier bravura aria with a new kind of popular song.[27]

After this the correspondence shows no further evidence of misgivings on the part of the publisher, and Weill continued his work into the new year, 1928. "*Mahagonny* continues to make great progress," he wrote in March to Vienna. "I am counting on having the composition finished by May."[28] This was not to happen, however, thanks to a momentous interruption.

Even in the preceding months Weill had written a number of other compositions alongside the opera. Shortly after the premiere of the songspiel, in September 1927, he had set to music another poem from Brecht's *Hauspostille,* the long ballad "Vom Tod im Wald" (Death in the Woods). Scored—unconventionally—for bass voice and ten wind instruments, the ballad was premiered on 23 November 1927, in a concert of the Berlin Philharmonic (with Heinrich Hermanns, bass, under the direction of Eugen Lang). The

**Kurt Weill and Lotte Lenya at a party in the
spring of 1928 (cropped photograph from a
personal album of Lenya's).**

dark colors of the wind writing corresponded to Brecht's lyrics. Lotte Lenya once called
"Vom Tod im Wald" her favorite work of Weill's and spoke of the music's "marvelous,
mysterious quality."[29]

Weill was also increasingly in demand as a composer of stage music. In October 1927
he wrote the music for Victor Barnowsky's production of Strindberg's *Gustav III,* which
was premiered on 29 October 1927 at the Theater an der Königgrätzer Straße. Walter
Goehr directed the twelve-member orchestra. In 1975 David Drew arranged the suite
Bastille-Musik from the surviving material of this work. In April 1928 Weill again wrote
purely orchestral music, this time for a performance of Bronnen's play *Die Katalaunische
Schlacht* (The Battle of Catalonia) at Berlin's Staatliches Schauspielhaus under Hilpert's
direction; the premiere took place on 25 April 1928. At the same time Kurt Weill also
became associated with the political theater of Erwin Piscator. For Leo Lania's play
Konjunktur (Economic Upturn)—a portrayal of the oil industry's battles for oil-drilling
rights—he wrote music that climaxed in a "petroleum song" called "Die Muschel von
Margate" (Margate's Shell), clearly a takeoff on the well-known emblem of Royal Dutch
Shell. The song's text was written by Felix Gasbarra, who, like Lania, belonged to
Piscator's dramaturg collective group. Erwin Piscator directed the play, and the musical
director was Edmund Meisel; the premiere took place on 8 April 1928. Tilla Durieux
sang "Die Muschel von Margate." Drew also arranged a suite from this material, which
he entitled *Öl-Musik*. Piscator's theater work always involved his collective group, which
became a meeting ground both for its permanent members and for artists working on a
particular production. Weill's work on *Konjunktur* brought the composer into contact
with Brecht, who was preparing the dramatization of *Schweik* with Lania; Hanns Eisler,

Manuscript of the first page of the petroleum song, "Die Muschel von Margate," of 1928. Weill wrote the song for the Piscator production of the play *Konjunktur,* by Leo Lania. The lyrics were written by Piscator's dramaturg, Felix Gasbarra.

who was to write the music for Mehring's *Der Kaufmann von Berlin* (The Merchant of Berlin); George Grosz, who was working on a number of sets for Piscator; and other progressive theater people.

The next piece of work that Weill took on, from the end of April through mid-September 1928, was also of a collective nature. Elisabeth Hauptmann, Brecht's well-read colleague, had heard of the enormous success that a revival of the old English *Beggar's Opera* by John Gay, with music by John Christopher Pepusch, had enjoyed in London's Lyric Theatre. She made a rough translation of Gay's text for Brecht, and he added it to his long list of current projects.

Around the same time a young Berlin actor named Ernst Josef Aufricht, who had come into a substantial inheritance and had decided to seek his fortune as a theater director, had just rented the Theater am Schiffbauerdamm and was looking for a play for the opening night of "Direction Aufricht" on 31 August 1928. After many unsuccessful attempts with various publishers and playwrights, he went one day, probably around the beginning of April 1928, to the Café Schlichter, as he reports in his memoirs:

On the walls hung pictures for sale by the painter Rudolf Schlichter. There was

Ernst Josef Aufricht, whose Theater am Schiffbauerdamm saw the premiere of *Die Dreigroschenoper;* photograph taken in 1930.

someone sitting in a second room. It was Brecht. I didn't know him personally, though I did know his literary experiments for the stage, and thought highly of his poetry. . . . We [Aufricht was probably accompanied by at least his deputy, Heinrich Fischer] sat down at his table and posed the vital question. He began to relate to us a plot he was working on at the time. He noticed, however, that we were not interested, since we asked for the bill. "There is always a minor work of mine. You can have six of the seven scenes tomorrow. It's an adaptation of John Gay's *Beggar's Opera*. I have given it the title *Gesindel* [Scum]." . . . The story smelled of theatre. We agreed to collect the manuscript the next day in the Spichernstraße.[30]

After consulting Erich Engel, who was to direct the opening night performance, Aufricht accepted the project and signed a contract with Brecht, even though the playwright had only a few preliminary fragments to show them. Brecht stipulated that Weill be involved in the project, but not a note had been written when the contract was signed. So now the work had to be done with lightning speed so that the rehearsals and premiere could be guaranteed for the end of August. Brecht was fascinated by this old story; and the milieu of beggars, whores, and thieves seemed extraordinarily well suited to a formulation of his critique of bourgeois conventions.

With their *Beggar's Opera* of 1728 Gay and Pepusch had founded the new genre of the "ballad opera," in sharp opposition to the fossilized Italian courtly opera of the time and also to Handel's operas. Along with its profane contents, it brought street songs, ballads, and *Bänkelgesänge* to the opera stage. It also brought a biting satire of the Whigs'

**Kurt Weill and Lotte Lenya in Le Lavandou on the French Riviera
during the writing of *Die Dreigroschenoper*, in May 1928.**

mismanagement of England under Prime Minister Robert Walpole and of an upper class living in luxury and decadence. The play's enormous success spawned dozens of imitations, and the "ballad opera" became the most successful type of play in eighteenth-century England.

Brecht shifted the plot to the Victorian period of the nineteenth century. Gay's "disguised critique of public wrongs" gave way to Brecht's "open critique of disguised wrongs," as Werner Hecht has put it. "It is no longer aimed at the cream of society but at the so-called normal bourgeois existence."[31] To this end the main characters and their relationships with one another are changed around: the petty thief turns into the beggars' king, Peachum, who deals in misery; the prison director Lockit turns into Brown, chief of police in London. Whereas the gangster and thief are business partners being pursued by Lockit in Gay's version, Brecht's Macheath is an accomplice of the chief of police. The whole wedding scene in the stable in Soho is new, as is the whorehouse at Turnbridge; Gay has Macheath receive ladies in the hotel.

During the month of April Brecht wrote a first draft of the text (incorporating poems by François Villon and Rudyard Kipling), entitling it *Die Ludenoper* (The Pimps' Opera). This draft differs in fundamental respects from the later version. In many scenes it adheres very closely to its model, and it shows few signs of any input from Weill, with whom Brecht had had only preliminary discussions. A number of songs are indicated simply by an anticipated title, without lyrics; in other cases the lyrics did not make their way even into the final version. Nonetheless *Die Ludenoper*, which was no more than a first step toward the later play, was published in May 1928 as a stage copy by the publisher Felix Bloch Erben. Since Aufricht was now pressing for greater speed—rehearsals were to start at the beginning of August—Weill and Brecht, together with their wives, left Berlin in mid-May for a few weeks of uninterrupted work in the south of France. Here, in Le Lavandou on the Riviera, large parts of *Die Dreigroschenoper* were written in a period of intensive collaboration. Lotte Lenya later described the atmosphere: "The two men wrote and rewrote furiously, night and day, with only hurried swims in between."[32] By mid-June Weill was back in Berlin working under great pressure to complete the composition, as well as to produce a piano reduction for the rehearsals. On July 22 he wrote to his publisher: "In the next few days you will be receiving . . . the piano reduction of my *Beggar's Opera*. I would ask you not to reproduce this piano reduction quite yet, as the arrangement of the various numbers is not yet fixed and two numbers are still missing. . . . Rehearsals begin on 10 August."

The cast that was lined up promised an outstanding performance, but then one catastrophe followed another. First Carola Neher, who was slated to play Polly, had to be replaced, because her husband, the poet Klabund, was dying in Davos, Switzerland. Then a new Mister Peachum was required, and Erich Ponto came from Dresden to Berlin. Before the first music rehearsal Weill played the piece on the piano. Aufricht later described the scene: "The small, gentle man with glasses, who had a soft metallic voice that expressed exactly what he wanted to say, began to play and sing. I believe we were all put off at first, but then Vambery [a dramaturg of Aufricht's—author] whispered in my ear, 'The music has as great a chance of success as the play.' The longer Weill played, the more my bias against it receded. In spite of its strangeness this music had something naive, and at the same time refined and exciting, about it."[33]

A number of disputes arose during the rehearsals. At one point Rosa Valetti criticized some of the texts, and then another actor thought his role was too small; so Brecht was constantly making changes. One day the lead, Harald Paulsen, who had previously played mostly in operettas and was an idol of Berlin's female theater audience, insisted on wearing a frightful blue bow tie with his suit. Brecht saved the day: "Let's leave him as he is, oversweet and charming. Weill and I will introduce him with a *Moritat* that tells of his

Die Ludenoper

The Beggar's Opera

ein altenglisches Balladenstück

von

JOHN GAY

Übersetzt v. ELISABETH HAUPTMANN

Deutsche Bearbeitung

von

BERT BRECHT

Musik von

KURT WEILL

Uraufführung im Theater am Schiffbauerdamm
unter der neuen Direktion von
Ernst Josef Aufricht
im September 1928
Musikverlag: Universal-Edition, Wien

Announcement by Brecht's publisher, Felix Bloch Erben, June
1928, of Weill's score, published by Universal Edition. At this
time the work went by the title *Die Ludenoper*. It was only
during the course of rehearsals that the title *Die
Dreigroschenoper* was adopted.

gruesome and disgraceful deeds. The effect made by the light-blue bow will be all the
more curious."[34]

Thus the "Moritat von Mackie Messer" (Mack the Knife) was born practically overnight. A number of friends and acquaintances wandered in and out of the theater during
rehearsals, including Karl Kraus and Lion Feuchtwanger. The latter is said to have
suggested changing the title from *Des Bettlers Oper* (The Beggar's Opera) to the more

**Bertolt Brecht and Kurt Weill in conversation in the courtyard
of the Theater am Schiffbauerdamm in Berlin during rehearsals
of *Die Dreigroschenoper* in August 1928.**

Weill and Lenya in 1929.

effective *Die Dreigroschenoper* (The Threepenny Opera)—a suggestion that Brecht and Weill readily accepted.

Orchestral rehearsals began on 25 August. Top-notch musicians had been found in Theo Mackeben as musical director and the seven-member Lewis Ruth Band (whose leader, Ludwig Rüth, coined this fashionable name).

As the premiere approached, the tensions and conflicts mounted. Caspar Neher insisted on various details of the set, Weill defended musical passages that Engel wanted to omit, Brecht talked Engel into certain details of direction—in short, the atmosphere was charged with foreboding. Everyone had lost confidence in this strange play's prospects for success. Aufricht, anticipating a rather short run for *Die Dreigroschenoper*, was already secretly looking around for a new work to stage.

On the afternoon of the premiere, when the programs arrived in the theater, even Weill, who usually radiated great calm, lost his cool. His wife, who was playing the role of Jenny, was not listed in the cast of characters. An insert was quickly printed up.

Finally the evening of 31 August 1928 arrived, a date that was to go down in the history of twentieth-century theater. Up until the "Kanonensong" (Cannon Song) the audience was rather reserved. But then came a breakthrough. The audience grew increasingly excited; approving murmurs and applause swelled to a crescendo. By the end, the

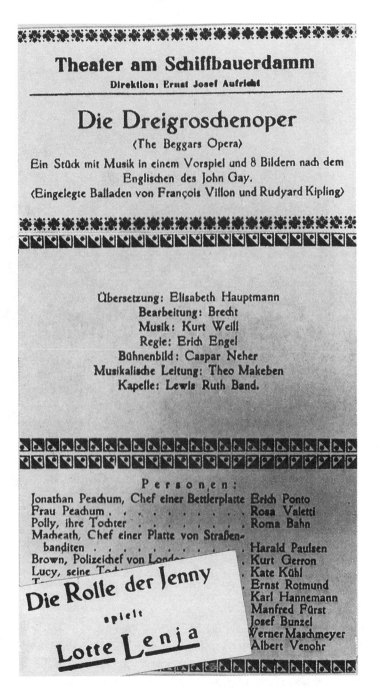

Theater am Schiffbauerdamm

Direktion: Ernst Josef Aufricht

Die Dreigroschenoper

⟨The Beggars Opera⟩

Ein Stück mit Musik in einem Vorspiel und 8 Bildern nach dem
Englischen des John Gay.
⟨Eingelegte Balladen von François Villon und Rudyard Kipling⟩

Übersetzung: Elisabeth Hauptmann
Bearbeitung: Brecht
Musik: Kurt Weill
Regie: Erich Engel
Bühnenbild: Caspar Neher
Musikalische Leitung: Theo Makeben
Kapelle: Lewis Ruth Band.

P e r s o n e n :

Jonathan Peachum, Chef einer Bettlerplatte	Erich Ponto
Frau Peachum	Rosa Valetti
Polly, ihre Tochter	Roma Bahn
Macheath, Chef einer Platte von Straßen-	
banditen	Harald Paulsen
Brown, Polizeichef von Londo~	Kurt Gerron
Lucy, seine To~	Kate Kühl
T~	Ernst Rotmund
	Karl Hannemann
	Manfred Fürst
	Josef Bunzel
	Werner Maschmeyer
	Albert Venohr

Die Rolle der Jenny

spielt

Lotte Lenja

Program from the premiere of *Die Dreigroschenoper*, on 31
August 1928 at Berlin's Theater am Schiffbauerdamm, with the
insert listing Lotte Lenya, whose name had been omitted.

Scene from the premiere of *Die Dreigroschenoper* with, *left to right,* Rosa Valetti as Mrs. Peachum, Harald Paulsen as Macheath, and Roma Bahn as Polly.

triumphant success in which no one had believed had become a reality. What had happened? Let us listen to the composer:

> What we were aiming to create was the prototype of opera [*Urform der Oper*]. With every musical work for the stage the question arises: how is music, particularly song, at all possible in the theatre? Here the question was resolved in the most primitive way possible. I had a realistic plot, so I had to set the music against it, since I do not consider music capable of realistic effects. Hence the action was either interrupted, in order to introduce music, or it was deliberately driven to a point where there was no alternative but to sing. . . . This return to a primitive form of opera entailed a far-reaching simplification of musical language. . . . At first this appeared to be a limitation. As work progressed, however, it proved to be an enormous enrichment.[35]

A scene from the 1929 production of *Die Dreigroschenoper* in
Oldenburg with Maria Martinsen as Jenny.

Weill's music fits Brecht's *Dreigroschen* art language, which includes powerful elements of Luther's German as well as worn-out colloquial clichés and criminal jargon, like
a hand in a glove. The score incorporates Baroque elements, which it uses in the parodying finales to attack the institution of opera; shabby flourishes from light music; ballads;
and *Moritat* forms—all blended with Weill's own great melodies. It frequently includes a
characteristic, almost skidding, progression by half steps.

"The harmonies, the fatal diminished seventh chords, the chromatic alterations of
diatonic melodic steps, the expressivo that expresses nothing, they sound false to us—in
which case, Weill must make the chords he draws on false, add to the triads a tone . . .
must distort the melodic steps . . . or, in the most artful passages of the score, must shift
the modulatory balance to such an extent that the harmonic proportions become over-
turned." Thus Adorno aptly described the characteristics of Weill's music.[36]

The overture, a grand fugue in the Baroque style, with intentionally wrong—even
cheap—harmonies that nonetheless make the listener shudder, makes it clear from the
very start that something new is afoot. The orchestra plays not in the pit but in the recesses

Theo Mackeben, music director of the premiere of *Die Dreigroschenoper*; photograph taken in 1930.

of the stage. A change in lighting precedes each musical number; thus a "song lighting" marks the separation of the elements of theater and song. The overture is followed by the "Moritat von Mackie Messer." Sixteen measures are all Weill needs to convey the two-sidedness of this character through simple harmonic means—the added sixth chord, a few secondary triads, suspensions, and the intentionally wrong fourths in the bass in the third and fourth measures. With its characteristic descending seventh shortly before the end, the "Moritat" betrays artful refinement under the guise of simplicity.

The first act opens in Peachum's beggar's shop. Jonathan Jeremiah Peachum sings his "Morgenchoral" (Morning Hymn); originally, before the "Moritat" was inserted, this was the play's first song number. Taken straight from Pepusch, it is an early indication that this work involves the adaptation of older music. In the course of scene 1 the Peachums realize that their daughter, Polly, has spent the night with Macheath. They sing the "Anstatt-Daß-Song" (No, They Can't Song), whose music lays bare the parents' true feelings, revealing their supposedly great concern to be quite small indeed.

Scene 2 depicts the wedding of the gang leader, Macheath, and Polly, daughter of the beggar king, in an empty stable in Soho. First the members of the beggars' gang serenade their leader with the "Hochzeitslied für ärmere Leute" (Wedding Song for Poor People); this is followed in rapid succession by two of the opera's most important musical numbers. The bride, Polly, sings her song "Seeräuber-Jenny" (Pirate Jenny) to entertain the

The Lewis Ruth Band in the dummy organ designed by Caspar Neher for the premiere of *Die Dreigroschenoper*.

party. This Brecht–Weillian "maiden's prayer" expresses the hopes, wishes, and fantasies of a small "cleaning girl from a four-penny bar"; but in reality it is much more than this—both an apotheosis and a dismantling of a petit bourgeois dream world. Ernst Bloch wrote about this song:

> Even the impudent minor mode, which mediates between *chanson* and funeral march, is appealing; so are the prettily incisive seconds at the question "Kill?," the ephemeral arpeggios at the words "ship" and "sails," and the triad sounded by the organ at the word "me" as the ship disappears. . . . Small flowers grow out of the stalest operetta glitter, out of ribald turn-of-the-century vaudeville songs, out of the glory of American jazz products, copied and preformed by hand. A new folk moon breaks through all the tearjerkers in the skies of servant girls and picture postcards. An unspeakable theology was contained in this sentimental mush; how instructive it is to set it in aspic.[37]

Soon Brown, the chief of police, appears at the wedding party of his old friend Macheath. Remembering the old days, the two sing the "Kanonensong" (Cannon Song). Weill's pounding, strident music, whose threatening tone makes the aggressiveness of these two characters palpable, suddenly transforms the scene into one of foreboding. At the end of it Macheath and Polly bid each other farewell; Weill gives their kitschily romantic love song "Siehst Du den Mond über Soho?" (Do You See the Moon over Soho?) an almost narcotic setting. The use of winds and a bandoneon (a kind of concertina), playing a third above the vocal line, makes the sham atmosphere, the falseness of Macheath's parting words, painfully clear.

The next scene returns to Peachum's outfitting shop, where Polly tells of her wedding and sings the "Barbara-Song." Weill's song style here is marked by a highly differentiated treatment of the verses and the refrain. The rapid-fire verse, with its melody confined to a narrow range of notes, is followed by the famous, lazily sensual refrain "Ja, da muß man sich doch einfach hinlegen" (Yes, you just have to lay yourself down), with its little melodic ripples, a subtle transformation of the text following the first "Yes," and a saxophone like melted butter. The act ends with the "Erste Dreigroschenfinale" (First Threepenny Finale) in which the Peachums (of all families!) bemoan the "cruelty of all human relationships."

The second act opens in the stable, where the young couple has set up housekeeping. Since Peachum has sworn to turn Macheath over to the police, Macheath leaves his wife, Polly, in charge of the gangsters and flees from the police into the moor of Highgate. In an interlude Mrs. Peachum, suspecting that Macheath will show up in a brothel, appears with the prostitute Jenny, to whom she promises money in exchange for turning in Macheath. Then the two sing the "Ballade von der sexuellen Hörigkeit" (Ballad of Sexual Obsession), which was omitted from the Berlin premiere. The ballad's lilting 3/4 meter and accordion accompaniment form a crass antithesis to the text.

In spite of the police threats, Macheath does turn up at the brothel at Turnbridge in the next scene, because it is "his Thursday." Jenny betrays him, and he is arrested; but first the two sing the "Zuhälterballade" (Ballad of Immoral Earnings), another of the opera's best musical numbers. The sublime ballad is based on a tango, Weill's favorite popular dance. The music reflects the bittersweetness of erotic relations but at the same time introduces little harmonic estrangements betraying businesslike calculation.

The following scene shows Macheath sitting handcuffed in a cell in the Old Bailey, where he sings the "Ballade vom angenehmen Leben" (Ballad of Good Living) with its provocative closing line, "Nur wer im Wohlstand lebt, lebt angenehm" (The only comfortable life is a life of wealth). Then Lucy, the daughter of Brown, the chief of police, appears and claims to have been made pregnant by Macheath. She encounters Polly in front of the prison cell, and the two sing the "Eifersuchtsduett" (Jealousy Duet), a wonderful parody of traditional opera clichés, right up to the final measures, in which the two voices swing up into higher and higher bel canto ranges and then suddenly fall into the sentimental "Mackie und ich, wir lebten wie die Tauben" (Mack and I, we lived like doves), which they sing in thirds. Weill had even more operatic parodies in mind for this scene; he had planned a "Lucy's Aria," but it proved too demanding for the actors (even Kate Kühl, who played Lucy in the premiere, was not able to master the music), so Weill left it out.

Macheath escapes from jail with the help of his old friend Tiger Brown, and Peachum threatens Brown that if Macheath is not hanged soon, the coronation procession scheduled for the following Sunday will be seriously endangered by a throng of beggars. Meanwhile Macheath and Jenny, the prostitute, sing the "Zweite Dreigroschenfinale" (Second Threepenny Finale).

The third act brings us back to Peachum's outfitting shop, where preparations are in full swing for the beggar's demonstration at the coronation. Suddenly Brown shows up, ready to arrest the people surrounding Peachum; but Peachum indicates to him that there are hundreds more waiting outside, so it won't be of much use to arrest just a few. To drive his point home, he sings the "Lied von der Unzulänglichkeit menschlichen Strebens" (Song of the Insufficiency of Human Endeavor). Weill sets Brecht's famous lines "Der

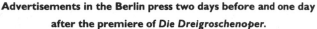

Advertisements in the Berlin press two days before and one day
after the premiere of *Die Dreigroschenoper*.

Mensch lebt durch den Kopf" (Man lives by his head) to a monotonously repeating melody, reminiscent of the opening ballad; it, too, could almost come from a hurdy-gurdy.

Now Brown is forced to arrest Macheath. Jenny, who has betrayed him again, stands in front of the curtain and sings the "Salomon-Song" (which was left out of the premiere because of time constraints). Accompanied, like the Moritat, by a hurdy-gurdy, the song describes the fall of great men, from Caesar to Macheath. Weill's use of a rather shabby waltz melody as the basis of the musical commentary is his way of honoring the "great ones of this world."

The final scene in the Old Bailey shows Macheath on death row. Preparations are being made for his execution, and he sings the "Ballade, in der Macheath jedermann Abbitte leistet" (Ballad in which Macheath Asks Forgiveness from Everyone), in which Weill employs grand musical means, in places with echoes of choral invocations.

The procession to the gallows is already under way when the parodying of opera reaches its high point. A placard is lowered onto the stage (announcing the appearance of the messenger on horseback), and the "Dritte Dreigroschenfinale" (Third Threepenny Finale) begins. The queen pardons Macheath on the occasion of her coronation, bestows on him a castle and a lifetime pension, and elevates him to the nobility. Here Weill makes musical reference to the style of Handel's opera finales. This *deus ex machina* type of solution is accomplished in the interplay of chorus and recitative; then all the performers assemble for the final song, a grand chorale that once again takes up the style of the overture. Thus the musical arc of the piece is closed.

The immediate reaction of the Berlin press to the premiere was not uniformly positive. The conservative papers spoke of "literary necrophilia" (*Neue Preußische Kreuzzeitung*, 1 September 1928) and of a "political horror ballad" (*Deutsche Zeitung*, 2 September 1928). Even some of the liberal bourgeois critics gave voice to certain reservations, as, for example, Harry Kahn in the *Weltbühne* and Felix Hollaender in the *B. Z. am Mittag*. The critics from the Communist paper declared that the work contained "no trace of modern social or political satire" (*Die Rote Fahne*, 4 September 1928). The leading drama and

Caricatures by Erwin Goltz for the review of the premiere of *Die Dreigroschenoper* in the *12-Uhr-Blatt,* 1 September 1928.

music critics meanwhile emphasized what was new about *Die Dreigroschenoper* and discussed the revolutionization of the operetta industry that it was sparking. Hans Heinz Stuckenschmidt wrote: "Opera and operetta are blended in this singspiel into a mystical union; both, disturbingly close to ruin in recent times, have been given a fresh infusion of blood that will enable new growth. Historians of music and drama can rest assured that *Die Dreigroschenoper* has introduced to the stage an emerging art form of immeasurable importance and potential."[38]

For the first time the National Socialist press came out against a work of Brecht's and Weill's. When *Die Dreigroschenoper* was premiered in Munich, the *Völkischer Beobachter* wrote: "Some especially noxious cesspool they find in a corner of any big city is barely good enough for the celluloid romance of this two-bit culture and is otherwise really just a matter for the police to take care of as a part of street cleaning."[39] But in spite of such critical controversies and undisguised rejections and attacks, *Die Dreigroschenoper* was to begin its victory march within a few weeks of the premiere.

For Weill the premiere did not signal the completion of his work. The final version was only barely finished in time for the dress rehearsal, and the musicians played from handwritten parts that were being changed up until the very last minute; so now it was time to prepare final manuscripts of the orchestral material and the piano reduction. This took Weill nearly two weeks, since he had to secure the various texts from the actors. There were still whole new sections to be written, too, as they would be needed by other theaters. "In addition, some things that I had needed only to tell the local musicians about had to be fixed in writing for the printed edition."[40]

By the beginning of October 1928 Universal had published the piano reduction (without the "Ballade von der sexuellen Hörigkeit") and, in conjunction with the publisher Felix Bloch Erben, the stage copy of *Die Dreigroschenoper*. At the same time Gustav Kiepenheuer published a large print run of a collection of the most important lyrics called *Die Songs der Dreigroschenoper*. With Weill's agreement, Universal decided to publish a piano conductor's score that could be used to conduct the music from the piano rather than from a full score. The orchestral parts for seven musicians, who together were to play nineteen instruments, appeared at the same time. Since the *Dreigroschenoper* music is often heard to this day in reduced or "arranged" versions, I will give Weill's original instrumentation:

Ullstein published a collection of *Dreigroschen* songs for piano and voice in the popular high-print-run series "Musik für alle" in the spring of 1929. The cover shows a scene from the premiere with, *left to right*, Erich Ponto as Peachum, Roma Bahn as Polly, Harald Paulsen as Macheath, and Kurt Gerron as Tiger Brown.

alto saxophone in E-flat (flute, clarinet 1 in B-flat)
tenor saxophone in B-flat (soprano saxophone in B-flat/bassoon/clarinet 2 in B-flat)
trumpet 1 in C/trumpet 2 in B-flat
trombone/bass
timpani/percussion
banjo/guitar/bandoneon/cello
piano/harmonium

The following excerpt from a letter that Weill wrote to his publisher shortly after *The Threepenny Opera* had started experiencing a wave of success still retains its validity:

Beginning in October 1928, as *Die Dreigroschenoper* was starting its hit run, the first records appeared with songs from the show. Here, an advertisement from January 1929 for two Homocord recordings.

"Incidentally, I hear from Frankfurt that they already want to start making all kinds of orchestral reductions in the *Dreigroschenoper*. I consider that very dangerous and ask that you forbid Director Hellmer from making any changes in the music or instrumentation without my permission."[41]

The success of *Die Dreigroschenoper* in the theater and of its songs, which perfectly captured the spirit of the times, is still unparalleled in the twentieth century. In the Theater am Schiffbauerdamm it ran for the entire season of 1928–29 to a continually sold-out house with changing casts, since the original performers had other obligations and had not been able to foresee such a long run. Within a year after the premiere, fifty theaters had staged over four thousand performances. By 1932 it had been translated into eighteen languages and was celebrating triumphs all over Europe. The songs had an even greater impact. Berlin and Germany were seized by a veritable *Dreigroschen* fever: Weill's melodies were sung and danced to everywhere. Universal was running its presses at full speed, publishing piano–vocal sheets of the most important songs, arrangements (by Jerzy Fitelberg) for salon and jazz orchestra, and an edition for violin and piano (by Stefan Frenkel) that proved too difficult and had to be followed by a simplified version. Ullstein published a collection of *Dreigroschen* songs for piano and voice in its popular, high-print-run series "Musik für alle" (Music for Everyone). Much as Weill was concerned that his music not be compromised in theatrical performances, he did not mind at all seeing his melodies reworked and disseminated in this manner. He agreed with his publisher, who wrote him: "The main purpose of such separate editions . . . is that the numbers be sold and played as often as possible."[42]

The record industry also contributed significantly to the mass dissemination of the *Dreigroschen* music. In Germany alone eight different record companies produced over twenty recordings between 1928 and 1930. Here, too, authentic performances were mixed with popular revisions. Harald Paulsen sang four songs for the Homocord label; Orchestrola released "Seeräuber-Jenny" and the "Barbara-Song" with Carola Neher, as well as a record on which Brecht himself sang the "Moritat" and the "Ballade von der Unzulänglichkeit menschlichen Strebens." Electrola issued a record entitled *Die Songs der Dreigroschenoper* with Carola Neher, Kurt Gerron, and Arthur Schröder, accompanied by the "Dreigroschenband," as the Lewis Ruth Band called itself on some recordings. The most comprehensive recording, now considered the most authentic—Telefunken's four records entitled *Aus der 3-Groschen-Oper*—includes some new con-

Advertisement for songs from *Die Dreigroschenoper* by
Universal Edition, February 1929.

necting texts written by Brecht in 1930 and spoken by Kurt Gerron. Lotte Lenya, Erika
Helmke, Willy Trenk-Trebitsch, and Erich Ponto also collaborated on this recording, and
Theo Mackeben conducted the Lewis Ruth Band. From the large number of arrangements, three records are worth mentioning: the "Barbara-Song" and the "Moritat" in
instrumental arrangements with the Haller-Revue jazz orchestra on the Parlophon label;
a "dance potpourri" from *Die Dreigroschenoper* with Marek Weber and his orchestra on

Cover of the piano reduction of *Die Dreigroschenoper* published by Universal Edition at the beginning of October 1928.

DIE
DREIGROSCHENOPER

(THE BEGGAR'S OPERA)

Ein Stück mit Musik in einem Vorspiel
und acht Bildern nach dem Englischen des John Gay
Übersetzt von Elisabeth Hauptmann

Deutsche Bearbeitung von

BERT BRECHT

Musik von

KURT WEILL

Die Uraufführung fand am 31. August 1928 im
Theater am Schiffbauerdamm in Berlin statt.

Alle Rechte, in-besondere das d.r Aufführung, der Radioübertragung, der Übersetzung
sowie die Verfilmungsrechte sind ebenso wie die Nachdruck-rechte vorbehalten. Aufführungsrechte jeder Art sind ausschließlich von dem Bühnenvertrieb Felix Bloch
Erben, Berlin-Wilmersdorf, Nikolsburgerplatz 3, zu erwerben. Die Vergebung der
Aufführungsrechte in Österreich und den Nachfolgestaaten erfolgt durch den Theater-
verlag Otto Eirich Ges. m. b. H., Wien, III. Lothring-rstraße 20.

ALLEINVERTRIEB DER BÜHNENMATERIALE, MUSIKALIEN UND
TEXTBÜCHER DURCH DIE
UNIVERSAL-EDITION A. G.
WIEN, L KARLSPLATZ 6
COPYRIGHT 1928 BY UNIVERSAL-EDITION A. G., WIEN — LEIPZIG

One of the numerous dance arrangements on records. This one, of the *Moritat,* was released in 1930.

Title page of the libretto of *Die Dreigro-schenoper* published by Universal in October 1928. In 1930 Brecht made substantial changes to the play (which he did not discuss with Weill) for the edition published by Gustav Kiepenheuer Verlag in 1931 as part of his *Versuche.* The text has appeared in this radically altered version in all subsequent Brecht editions. Only the libretto pictured here gives the original Weill–Brecht version.

Cover of a single piano–vocal sheet from 1929. Altogether six songs were published in this fashion.

Title page of Stefan Frenkel's arrangements of seven pieces from *Die Dreigroschenoper* for violin and piano, 1929. They proved too difficult for many amateurs, so the publisher released a "simplified edition" the same year.

the Electrola label; and instrumental versions of the "Kanonensong" and "Tangoballade" played by Paul Godwin and his jazz symphony on the Grammophon label.

While the popularity of Weill's music grew by leaps that no one could have foreseen, few critics understood what the work was all about. Adorno wrote in late 1929: "The success of *The Threepenny Opera*, comparable only to that of operetta, entices one into believing that here, with simple means, with utter comprehensibility, operetta has quite simply been exalted and made palatable for the requirements of the cognoscenti. . . . But a second look at the work reveals that all is not so. . . . It is *Gebrauchsmusik* which, because one is safe, may be enjoyed today as an enzyme, but which cannot be used to cover up what exists. Where it switches from interpretation to direct language it demands quite openly: '. . . for it is cold: Consider the darkness and the great coldness.' "[43]

Toward the end of 1928, when it was already becoming clear that the *Dreigroschen* songs were being subsumed into the realm of popular music, Weill wrote a suite arrangement for the concert hall entitled *Kleine Dreigroschenmusik für Blasorchester* (Little Threepenny Music for Wind Orchestra). This was premiered on 7 February 1929 in the

Record of the suite arrangement of the music
of *Die Dreigroschenoper* for the concert hall.
Otto Klemperer, who had conducted the
premiere, also conducted this first recording,
released in 1931.

For this recording (which takes up four records
altogether) Brecht wrote his own connecting
texts, which were spoken by Kurt Gerron.

Krolloper in a concert of the Preußische Staatskapelle under Otto Klemperer. Conducted
again by Klemperer with great success in Leningrad and Moscow in 1929, this work
rapidly became a favorite concert item; by 1930 it had been given more than sixty
performances.

Weill changed the orchestration for the *Kleine Dreigroschenmusik,* scoring it for a
large complement of winds—still, however, as with many other of his works, without
oboe. The suite consists of seven movements, which include instrumental arrangements
of a total of ten musical numbers from the opera. All the biting satire of the opera comes
through in the suite. Adorno noted: "It begins with a Handel overture from the perspective of a night café, with foreshortened and drawn-out cadenzas in the style of Stravinsky;
the trombone and tuba, too close to each other in sound, function as terrifyingly raw over-
basses. . . . And finally the potpourri itself. . . . That is all. Hardly a melody is missing;
they pass by in a throng that is so condensed that they sometimes get entangled in each
other; and as they gather for their demonstration march they hold on to each other—
mutilated, damaged, used up, and yet still rebellious."[44]

The *Kleine Dreigroschenmusik* underwent one further revision. In 1938 the suite was
reorchestrated in London, this time with strings added, and was premiered under the title
Judgement of Paris as a one-act ballet.

For Brecht and Weill, who had both lived on very modest means up till now, *Die
Dreigroschenoper* led to financial prosperity. Brecht bought a new car, and Weill and
Lenya moved into a modern apartment in Berlin's Westend neighborhood. In March
1932 they bought a house in the artists' suburb of Kleinmachnow.

One of three records released by Homocord in Prague in 1930 of songs from the production of *Die Dreigroschenoper* in Prague's Divadlo na Vinohradech.

In June 1933 the opera was performed in Hebrew at the Ohel Theatre in Tel Aviv; His Master's Voice in London subsequently produced the record pictured here, with Lea Deganith as Polly.

In 1928, the city of Berlin held a four-day festival (13–16 October) called "Berlin im Licht" (Berlin in Light), which celebrated both the ultramodern shop-window lighting and neon advertisements of the city center—now referred to by the English word "City" —and the city's illuminated monuments and commercial buildings. Heinz Tiessen, Max Butting, and Kurt Weill were all commissioned to write compositions for the various high points of the festival. Weill composed the "Berlin im Licht-Song" on a text he wrote jointly with Brecht, and it was performed in two different versions during the festival. On 15 October the instrumental version for wind orchestra was heard under the direction of Hermann Scherchen as part of a concert at the Wittenbergplatz. The next day, at the grand light ball in the Krolloper, the actor Paul Graetz sang the vocal version.

Immediately thereafter Weill wrote the stage music for Lion Feuchtwanger's play *Die Petroleuminseln* (The Petroleum Islands), which was premiered on 28 November 1928 in the Staatliches Schauspielhaus am Gendarmenmarkt. The play was directed by Jürgen Fehling, and Lotte Lenya played the role of Charmian Peruchacha alongside Eugen Klöpfer and Maria Koppenhöfer. As in *Konjunktur,* an "oil song" is at the heart of the composition: "Das Lied von den braunen Inseln" (The Song of the Brown Islands), with lyrics by Feuchtwanger. This performance, only a few months after the premiere of *Die Dreigroschenoper,* was Lotte Lenya's second big success in Berlin. "Fehling has taken a chance on this artist who was just discovered in the *Groschenoper,* and he has converted the doubters. Her Charmian *was* a mulatto, charming in a foreign kind of way, enchanting."[45] In rapid succession Lenya took on three more roles that made her popular in Berlin: Ismene in Sophocles' *Oedipus* (at the Staatliches Schauspielhaus am Gendarmen-

Program from the concert that included the premiere of the *Kleine Dreigroschenmusik für Blasorchester,* on 7 February 1929, at Berlin's Krolloper, conducted by Otto Klemperer.

markt, 4 January 1929, directed by Leopold Jessner), Alma in Marieluise Fleißer's *Pioniere in Ingolstadt* (Pioneers in Ingolstadt; at the Theater am Schiffbauerdamm, 30 March 1929, directed by Bertolt Brecht), and Ilse in Frank Wedekind's *Frühlings Erwachen* (Spring's Awakening; at the Volksbühne am Bülowplatz, 14 October 1929, directed by Karlheinz Martin).

Meanwhile Kurt Weill still had a hefty piece of work ahead of him at the end of 1928. The Reichs-Rundfunkgesellschaft (Imperial Radio Society) had commissioned radio compositions from a number of writers and composers, including Hindemith, Schreker, Hauer, and Weill. In November 1928 a press release noted: "The Frankfurt station has commissioned Bert Brecht to write a cantata. It will be entitled 'Memorial Tablets, Epitaphs, and Death Songs' and will treat, among other things, the deaths of the French aviators Nungesser and Coli as well as the lives of famous athletes. Kurt Weill will write the music for four singers and small orchestra."[46] Such a cantata did not come into being, but the themes suggested in this press release were subsequently developed in *Das Berliner Requiem, Der Lindberghflug,* and *Das Badener Lehrstück.*

Poster for the production of *Die Dreigroschenoper* by Karlheinz
Martin at Vienna's Raimund-Theater in June
1929. Harald Paulsen celebrated new triumphs as Macheath
in this production. Meanwhile, Hermann Thimig took over the
role in Berlin.

Table of contents of the *Kurt-Weill-Song-Album*
published by Universal Edition in 1929.
Included is the "Ballad of Sexual Obsession,"
judged to be too "coarse" to be sung at the
premiere of *Die Dreigroschenoper,* made
available here for the first time.

Cover of the song "Berlin im Licht,"
commissioned by the Berlin magistrates for a
festival of the same name in October 1928.

In November and December 1928 Weill composed *Das Berliner Requiem,* a cantata for tenor, baritone, male chorus, and wind orchestra. As texts he used poems Brecht had already written, which the two assembled together. Weill remarked regarding the purpose of this work: "For the first time radio poses for serious musicians of the present the task of creating works which can be taken up by as large a circle of listeners as possible. . . . We attempted to express what urban man of our era has to say about the phenomenon of death. . . . The overall impression of the performance must show if we were correct in our statement that we are dealing here with a serious, non-ironic work, a type of secular Requiem, and expression about death in the form of memorial tablets, epitaphs, and funeral dirges."[47] To his publisher he wrote, "I . . . believe that it is one of my best and most original pieces."[48]

The cantata opens with the "Großer Dankchoral" (Great Hymn of Thanksgiving). The second number is the "Ballade vom ertrunkenen Mädchen" (Ballad of the Drowned Girl), immediately followed by number three, "Marterl" (Memorial Tablet). In 1929 Weill exchanged this text of Brecht's for the "Grabschrift 1919" (Epitaph 1919), dedicated to Rosa Luxemburg. Numbers four and five are two "Berichte über den unbekann-

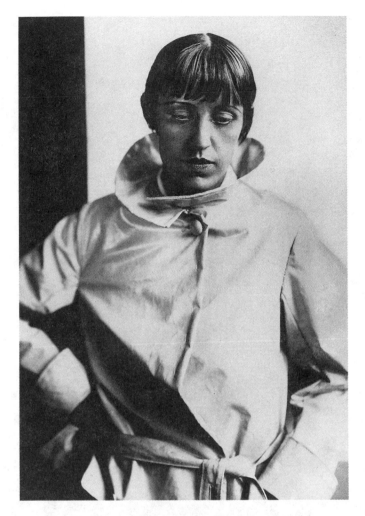

Lenya as Charmian Peruchacha in Lion Feuchtwanger's play *Die Petroleuminseln,* premiered on 28 November 1928 at the Staatliches Schauspielhaus am Gendarmenmarkt in Berlin, directed by Jürgen Fehling. Weill wrote the "Song of the Brown Islands" for this production, which was the occasion of Lenya's second big success in Berlin.

ten Soldaten" (Reports of the Unknown Soldier), and number 6 repeats the "Großer Dankchoral." Weill experimented at length with this work, undertaking numerous revisions. Settings of Brecht's poems "Vom Tod im Wald" (Death in the Woods), "Potsdam," and "Können einem toten Mann nicht helfen" (Can't Help a Dead Man) were originally to be included in the requiem as well, but Weill ended up leaving them out.

Lotte Lenya in the Weill family's first car, bought in 1930 on the
strength of the financial success of *Die Dreigroschenoper*.

Weill published "Lucy's Aria"—intended for the second act of *Die Dreigroschenoper* but omitted because even Kate Kühl, who played Lucy in the premiere, could not manage it—in the journal *Die Musik* in November 1932.

Das Berliner Requiem is unequivocal in its anti-militaristic message, and the 1928 festivities marking the tenth anniversary of the end of World War I and of the November Revolution doubtless influenced Weill's conception of the work. The pairing of the "Ballade vom ertrunkenen Mädchen" and the "Grabschrift" for "Red Rosa" pointed plainly to Rosa Luxemburg, whose body had been dredged up from the Landwehrkanal. The two "Berichte über den unbekannten Soldaten" were also clearly anti-war pieces.

After months of hesitation and political reservations on the part of the responsible parties in the radio company, *Das Berliner Requiem* was finally premiered and broadcast on 22 May 1929 in Frankfurt am Main. The conductor was Ludwig Rottenberg with the Orchester des Südwestdeutschen Rundfunks. Only this one performance was put on; the explosive work was not heard on Berlin's air waves. Furious, Weill decided to terminate the work he had been doing for the past four years for the journal *Der deutsche Rund-*

7. Jahrg. Heft 20   Der Deutsche Rundfunk   613

NOTIZ ZUM „BERLINER REQUIEM"
Von Kurt Weill

Szene aus der „Dreigroschenoper" von Brecht-Weill / Kanonensong
Scherenschnitte von Lotte Reiniger

Article about *Das Berliner Requiem* by Weill in *Der deutsche Rundfunk,* 17 May 1929. The silhouettes by Lotte Reiniger were made for the premiere of *Die Dreigroschenoper.*

funk. In connection with his work for *Das Berliner Requiem,* he wrote two a cappella choral pieces on texts by Brecht: "Zu Potsdam unter den Eichen" (At Potsdam under the Oaks), also arranged for piano and voice, and the "Legende vom toten Soldaten" (Legend of the Dead Soldier). Both were performed in November 1929 by Berlin's Schubert-Chor under the direction of Karl Rankl.

The next work the Brecht—Weill team turned to, this time along with Paul Hindemith, was also a radio experiment and an attempt to go in new directions, both in the use of music and in the transmission of music. The commission came once again from Baden-Baden, where the 1929 festival was to center on the technical mass media of film and radio. Brecht was represented by two works that belong to the phase of his didactic plays: *Lehrstück,* later called *Das Badener Lehrstück vom Einverständnis* (The Baden Didactic Play on Consent), with music by Paul Hindemith, and *Der Lindberghflug* (The Lindbergh

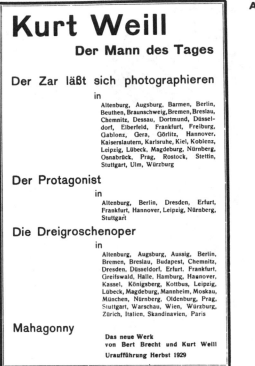

Advertisement of recent stage works by Weill, by Universal in the fall of 1929.

Flight), with music by Weill and Hindemith. The two composers had agreed which parts of the text each would set to music.

This work tells the story of the American aviator Charles Lindbergh's transatlantic flight in his single-engine *Spirit of St. Louis* in May 1927, an event that inspired many of his contemporaries as a great technical achievement. In Brecht's text, as Jan Knopf points out, this technical achievement is not the ultimate goal but "rather leads to a human self-understanding that the mastery of nature is also an expression of 'collective achievement.'"[49] Thus natural and technical phenomena (fog, ships, the engine) are articulated by the chorus as a kind of "collective essence."

Kurt Weill wrote his sections of the joint composition during April and May 1929. Even before the performance he decided that, independently of the immediate project, he would set the rest of the work to music. "The sections I have done (more than half) are so successful that I will compose the whole piece, that is, including the sections Hindemith is doing now. We could then publish a very nice volume: Three *Songspiele* by Weill and Brecht—(1) *Mahagonny* Songs (that is, the Baden-Baden version), (2) the *Berliner Requiem*, and (3) the *Lindberghflug*. I also plan to have these three works performed together in a new form between concert and theater."[50] Unfortunately this publishing and performing project of Weill's was never realized. But at least the "new form between

Sketch of Lotte Lenya by Benedikt Dolbin, 1929.

concert and theater" that he envisaged was achieved in the premiere of *Der Lindberghflug* in Baden-Baden.

Brecht had written to Hardt, manager of Cologne's radio network, who was underwriting the performance:

> I have been thinking about the radio broadcast of *The Flight of Lindbergh,* especially about the plan to open the dress rehearsal to the public. We could use this as an experiment. It could be shown, at least visually, how listeners could participate in radio art. . . . I would thus suggest the following small set for this demonstration. We put up a large screen, onto which the enclosed principles on the use of radio are projected throughout the entire play. The radio people (singers, musicians, speakers, etc.) sit in front of the screen on one side of the stage; on the other side a room is suggested by a folding screen, where a man in shirtsleeves sits on a chair in front of a

Kurt Weill in 1929, the year of _Der Lindberghflug_.

table with the score in his hand and hums, speaks, and sings the Lindbergh part. This is the listener. Since the audience will include a number of experts, it will probably be necessary to have a sign saying "Radio" for one side and another saying "Listener" for the other side.[51]

A surviving photograph from the dress rehearsal shows that Brecht's suggestions were followed.

This performance took place on 27 July 1929, again in the Grand Hall of Baden-Baden's Kurhaus. The director was Ernst Hardt, and the conductor was Hermann Scherchen. Even among large segments of the "expert audience" Brecht's radio experiment met with a lack of comprehension, and the project—like many of Weill's ideas about new applications of this medium—remained in the realm of utopia. The critics all agreed that musically _Der Lindberghflug_ was "the most important event of the whole festival,"[52] in

Octavo edition of Weill's a cappella choral piece "Zu Potsdam unter den Eichen" on a text by Brecht, published by Universal in 1930.

spite of the evident lack of homogeneity between Weill's and Hindemith's compositions—hardly surprising, considering the two composers' stylistic differences. Heinrich Strobel called attention to the differences between "Weill's songlike, clearly declamatory composition" and the "more descriptive, heavy music of Hindemith."[53] Hermann Scherchen performed the Baden-Baden version of this piece again on 18 March 1930 in the Berlin Philharmonie for a radio broadcast; this performance is documented on records. Neither Weill nor Hindemith submitted their Baden-Baden pastiche for publication, and it did not appear until 1982, as volume 6 of series 1 of the complete works of Hindemith.

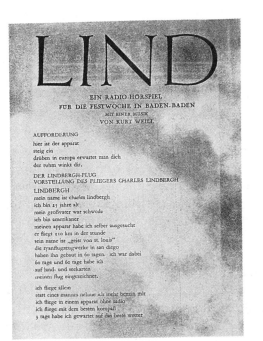

Opening spread of the first printing of Brecht's text for _Der Lindberghflug_ in the Ullstein magazine _Uhu_ in April 1929. Hindemith's participation in the project is not listed at this stage.

Weill realized his plan to compose the entire piece anew in the fall of 1929. _Der Lindberghflug_ now became a fifteen-part cantata for soloists, chorus, and orchestra. The part of the aviator is sung by the tenor solo, while the chorus (at times in conjunction with the baritone solo and the bass solo) presents the collective phenomena: America, Europe, fog, the ship. Part 10 of the cantata is a pure a cappella chorus; and part 14, "The Aviator's Landing," is an orchestral march, harmonically and melodically in Weill's best style. The other thirteen parts are composed for chorus (or soloists) and orchestra, with frequent dialogues between the aviator and the chorus. The musical inventory is very limited, and a simple musical language serves Weill's stated didactic purpose: "I consider it necessary to designate the practical goal for which vocal music is written beyond its use in the concert hall. Brecht's text _Der Lindberghflug_ is presented here in a musical version that is intended ultimately for performances in schools."[54] The score is still too complex for this purpose, however, and there is no evidence that the work was ever performed by amateur ensembles.

The premiere took place on 5 December 1929 at Berlin's Krolloper, along with Stravinsky's _Les Noces_ and Hindemith's cello concerto, _Kammermusik Nr. 3_. Otto Klemperer directed the Preußische Staatskapelle, Erik Wirl sang the part of Lindbergh, and Karl Rankl had prepared the chorus. The conservative press dismissed the work altogether; for example, the critic from the *Berliner Lokal-Anzeiger* entitled his report, "Symphony Concert or Kindergarten?" (6 December 1929). Even Alfred Einstein expressed some reservations: "The strong impact of Baden-Baden is not repeated here: it has all become a bit too sober, almost to the point of tedium; it lacks enthusiasm, heroicism, the appeal to the imagination."[55]

This was offset by a number of positive appraisals, however, including this one by Erich Urban: "I like this piece because it gives an artistic formulation of contemporary events, because the combining of voice and speech, the voice distribution, the conversations between people, nature, and things are unusual. Weill took care of this with his means; it has a lot going for it. The introduction of the aviator Lindbergh, the conversations with fog, snow storm, and engine, the lullaby (an enchanting blues song), the ghostlike fishers, and the apotheosis. Erik Wirl as Lindbergh is outstanding. Opera—operetta—opera."[56]

In 1930 Universal published the piano reduction and a bilingual score of *Der Lindberghflug* (George Antheil had translated Brecht's text into English). On 4 April 1931 Leopold Stokowski conducted the work for the first time in the United States with the Philadelphia Orchestra. Weill sent a copy of the piano reduction to Charles Lindbergh in the United States with a handwritten dedication, "Dedicated to Charles Lindbergh with great admiration by Kurt Weill."[57] Later, Lindbergh's political behavior—his sympathies with National Socialism beginning in 1935 and his opposition in 1941 to American involvement in the war—led Brecht to change the work's title to *Der Ozeanflug* (The Ocean Flight) and to remove Lindbergh's name from the text.

But let us now return to May 1929, when Weill was just completing the first version for Baden-Baden. The preceding months, since the premiere of *Die Dreigroschenoper*, had brought him success and recognition, but they had also been extraordinarily hectic and stressful. He urgently needed a rest. So in mid-May he set off for a lengthy stay at Saint-Cyr-sur-Mer on the French Riviera—already with plans for a new Brecht project, however. On 25 May Weill wrote: "After a lovely six-day auto trip I arrived here on Thursday. Brecht, who came along in his car, had an accident near Fulda, where we were to meet for a meal, and I had to have him taken back to Berlin with a broken kneecap. Unfortunately that has postponed all my plans, since we wanted to come here together to work. We wanted to write the song texts for *Happy End* and discuss new plans."[58]

Ernst Josef Aufricht wanted to build on the success of *Die Dreigroschenoper* in the 1929–30 season and had commissioned Brecht and Weill to write another similar work. The director Erich Engel, Caspar Neher, and the Lewis Ruth Band under Theo Mackeben

Advance announcement of the German Chamber Music Festival in Baden-Baden, July 1929.

**Kurt Weill in front of the Kurhaus in Baden-
Baden at the time of the festival, July 1929.**

**Sketch made by Benedikt Dolbin during a rehearsal of *Der
Lindberghflug* at Baden-Baden, 26 July 1929. *Left to right*: Kurt
Weill, Paul Hindemith, and the conductor, Hermann Scherchen.**

Open dress rehearsal of *Der Lindberghflug* at Baden-Baden, 27
July 1929. In the foreground we see the conductor, Hermann
Scherchen (*center*), and the co-director, Bertolt Brecht (*right*).
Projected on the screen at the back are Weill's principles
concerning the use of radio: "The individual participates in the
music (thus adhering to the principle that it is better to do than
to feel), by reading along with the music and humming missing
passages, or by following with the eyes in the book, or by
singing out loud along with others."

were also engaged again. The only problem was that Brecht had neither suitable material
nor a text that could be adapted. But Elisabeth Hauptmann had just read an American
short story about gangsters and the Salvation Army that held some promise, and this was
now adapted under the title *Happy End*. Hauptmann was given the pseudonym Dorothy
Lane—all very much in the contemporary style of German romanticism about America.
Brecht and Weill contributed only the songs.

 Happy End takes place in Chicago. The "lady in gray," head of the gangsters, and her
accomplice, Bill Cracker, owner of a dubious establishment, want to get rid of a member
of the band called "the governor." A division of the Salvation Army appears on the scene
under Lieutenant "Hallelujah Lilian." Lilian falls in love with Bill Cracker, while next
door a shot signifies the death of the governor. She rather drunkenly sings a sailors' song,
and the rest of the Salvation Army girls report her defection to the major, who throws her
out of the Salvation Army. She returns to Bill Cracker, who in the meantime has fallen out
of the lady in gray's good graces. He runs away from the gang and rushes into the local
Salvation Army headquarters right in the middle of a Christmas party, with the other

Caricatures of key participants in the Baden-Baden festival of July 1929, by Benedikt Dolbin.

Baden-Baden, 1929. *Left to right:* Kurt Weill; Ernst Hardt, manager of the Westdeutscher Rundfunk; Paul Hindemith; Hans Flesch, manager of Funkstunde Berlin; and Bertolt Brecht.

Advertisement in the Berlin press for a concert at Berlin's Krolloper on 5 December 1929. The program includes the premiere of the second version of *Der Lindberghflug,* composed by Weill alone.

gangsters hot on his heels. The police also appear and accuse Bill of murdering the governor. Lilian testifies that she was with him when the shot rang out—but then comes the happy ending. The governor appears, having only been grazed by the bullet; the lady in gray recognizes the major as the husband she had long believed to be dead; and Lilian persuades the entire gang to join the Salvation Army.

By contrast with the weakness of the plot, the songs are among Brecht and Weill's strongest. They were written mostly in July 1929 during a joint stay at Brecht's house in Unterschondorf am Ammersee. Weill then finished the score in Berlin, and it was completed by the time the orchestra started rehearsing on 25 August. The number of musicians and the instrumentation are similar to *Die Dreigroschenoper,* since the Lewis Ruth Band under Mackeben was again slated to play.

The music for *Happy End* is of two different kinds. The six Salvation Army songs are splendid parodies of conventional religious inspirational music. Written for unison high soprano, the parody lies in their "angelic" quality. The other six songs show Weill at the apex of his style and have far outlasted the play. The "Lied des Branntweinhändlers" (Song of the Brandy-Seller) and the "Lied von der harten Nuß" (Song of the Tough Nut) have not enjoyed quite as much popularity as the other four. The "Song von Mandelay" (Song of Mandelay) was reworked for the *Mahagonny* opera.

The "Matrosen-Song" (Sailors' Song), the "Bilbao-Song," and "Surabaya-Johnny" are the three that have become internationally renowned. They are all sung in Cracker's shabby establishment called "Bill's Ball House," and their mixture of romanticism, coarseness, eroticism, and fantasy makes them among the best of the Weill–Brecht songs. Brecht had written the words to "Surabaya-Johnny" in 1925 for Feuchtwanger's play *Kalkutta 4. Mai* (Calcutta, 4 May). Weill turned it into something similar to the "Barbara-Song" from *Die Dreigroschenoper.* The rather quickly sung verses, which tell of a girl who has fallen for a scoundrel and has followed him to obscure parts of India,

**Cover of the piano reduction of the second version of *Der
Lindberghflug*, published by Universal in the spring of 1930,
sporting a collage made up of photographs of Lindbergh's
departure and triumphant return to New York.**

lead after a long fermata into a refrain of devoted self-sacrifice: "Surabaya Johnny, warum
bist du so roh, Surabaya Johnny, o mein Gott und ich liebe dich so" (Surabaya Johnny,
why are you so cruel, Surabaya Johnny, oh my God and I love you so). This refrain starts
with the same four notes as the "Moritat von Mackie Messer," but in a different key. A
coincidence? Or was it Weill's intention to reuse this especially accessible phrase?

The "Matrosen-Song" also contains one of Weill's incomparable refrains: "Und das
Meer ist blau so blau" (And the sea is blue, so blue), full of romanticism, longing, and
nostalgia for an anarchical, untrammeled past, a past that is also conjured up in the
"Bilbao-Song" when the band imitates the "music of yesteryear" to the words "Alter

A rehearsal of *Happy End* at the Theater am Schiffbauerdamm
in August 1929. The players include (*first row, left to right*)
Theo Lingen, Erich Engel, Peter Lorre, Helene Weigel, Kurt
Gerron, Carola Neher, and Oskar Homolka.

Bilbao-Mond, wo noch die Liebe wohnt" (Old Bilbao moon, where love still flourishes). These gems of that song style have not been matched to this day; as typical products of their time, those hectic years of 1928–29, with all their conflicting trends, they probably could not be replicated.

The premiere of *Happy End* took place on 2 September 1929 in the Theater am Schiffbauerdamm. Carola Neher played the lead role of Lilian alongside a glittering cast of performers. (The program also listed the names of Peter Lorre, Oskar Homolka, Kurt Gerron, Theo Lingen, and Helene Weigel.)

Until intermission the evening went smoothly, and a new success seemed to be in the making. But in the second part, as the wind started going out of the plot and the audience became increasingly restless, the promise of success gave way to a complete fiasco, when Helene Weigel suddenly broke with her role (as the lady in gray), strode to the edge of the stage, and launched into a political attack on the audience. The play's failure was sealed with the scandal that followed, and Aufricht had to end *Happy End*'s run after only seven performances. The press almost uniformly came down harshly on the weak play and the transparently obvious attempt to repeat the success of *Die Dreigroschenoper* (Willy Haas wrote: "It smelled the whole time of profiteering"[59]), but the critics agreed that the songs had reached the high point of their style. The dyed-in-the-wool Brecht opponent Alfred Kerr, who was otherwise reticent with his musical judgments, remarked about Weill: "A jolly good fellow! With purpose. Do I need to assure you that he moved me?"[60]

The popularity of this doomed play's songs grew as rapidly as that of the play itself declined. Universal published single sheets of the "Bilbao-Song," the "Matrosen-Song," and "Surabaya-Johnny." Lotte Lenya sang the "Bilbao-Song" and "Surabaya-Johnny" for a recording by Orchestrola; the Lewis Ruth Band played four songs in an instrumental version for Electrola; and Theo Mackeben recorded "Surabaya-Johnny" and the "Bilbao-Song," likewise in instrumental versions, with the Ultraphon jazz orchestra under his frequently used recording pseudonym Red Roberts.

Kurt Weill himself saw clearly that he had reached a certain end point:

> From our standpoint the fact that my . . . music has become commercialized doesn't speak against it, but for it, and we would be falling back into our old mistakes if we were to deny certain music its importance and artistic value simply because it found its way to the masses. You are right: *I* cannot copy this song style indefinitely . . . and I have no intention of copying it. But we cannot deny that this style has set a precedent and that today more than half of the young composers of the most diverse backgrounds make their living from it. That's why it's very easy for the general public to overlook the fact that I myself, who defined this style only a year ago, have quietly continued on my own path.[61]

The last sentence of this letter presumably refers not only to the cantatas *Das Berliner Requiem* and *Der Lindberghflug* that Weill had written since *Die Dreigroschenoper* but also to the opera he had just completed. This opera, *Aufstieg und Fall der Stadt Mahagonny* (The Rise and Fall of the Town of Mahagonny), is the core and high point of Weill's work with Brecht. Its status as *opus magnum* derives not only from the long period the two spent working on it—from May 1927 to September 1929—but above all from the theory of epic theater and epic opera that emerged in the process, a theory that was to have a decisive influence on the further development of theater and opera in the twentieth century. Weill's share in the shaping of Brechtian theatrical theory has up to now received too little attention in the literature.

Brecht's development of a theory of epic theater (he first used this term in 1926) came out of a number of sociological works that appeared at the time. On the basis of attempts

Program from the premiere of *Happy End* at the Theater am Schiffbauerdamm on 2 September 1929.

Theater am Schiffbauerdamm
Direktion: Ernst Josef Aufricht

Happy End

Eine Magazingeschichte von D o r o t h y L a n e
Deutsche Bearbeitung: E l i s a b e t h H a u p t m a n n
Songs: B r e c h t und W e i l l
Regie: E r i c h E n g e l und Brecht
Musikal. Leitung: T h e o M a c k e b e n
Kapelle: L e w i s R u t h B a n d
Bühnenbilder: C a s p a r N e h e r
Techn. Leitung: H a n s S a c h s

P e r s o n e n :

Lilian Holliday, genannt „Hallelujah-Lilian"	Carola Neher
Bill Cracker, genannt „Ballhaus-Bill"	Oskar Homolka
Die Dame in Grau, genannt „Die Fliege"	Helene Weigel
Sam Worlitzer, genannt „Mammy"	Kurt Gerron
Jimmy Dexter, genannt „Reverend"	Theo Lingen
Dr. Nakamura, genannnt „Governor"	Peter Lorre
Johnny Dutch, genannt „Das Baby"	Albert Hoerrmann
Bob Merker, genannt „Professor"	Karlheinz Carell
Major der Heilsarmee	Paul Günther

Carola Neher as Lilian in *Happy End*.

to penetrate the mechanics of the bourgeois world of his time, to "get to the bottom" of things, he began to look at the function of theater in this world. His first recognition was that traditional forms of drama were no longer suited to representing the processes and life stories of this society. "If one sees that our contemporary world no longer fits into the drama, then the drama also no longer fits into the world."[62] A new form of theater must come to terms with a changed world. "How, then, should our large form be? Epic. It must report. It must also not believe that one can feel one's way into our world; it must not even want that. The material is monstrous, and our drama must acknowledge that."[63]

Caught in dead ends with his own projects, however, he urgently needed practical experiments on which the development of a theory could rest. Ever since his years in Augsburg with Marianne Zoff, he had felt challenged to think about the radical renewal of opera, the most conventional of all institutions of bourgeois artistic expression. His

Manuscript of the first page of the "Mandelay-Song" in the
version for *Happy End*, 1929. Weill later reworked this song for
Aufstieg und Fall der Stadt Mahagonny.

Berlin
(Berlin O – Stettin – Magdeburg)

8 nm. (20)

Programm der aktuellen Abteilung

Wovon man spricht

(Redner und Thema werden durch Rundfunk bekanntgegeben)

8.30 nm. (20.30)

Großstadt=Musik
Offenbach – Weill

Dirigenten:
Dr. Ernst Römer und Kurt Weill

Solisten:
Lotte Lenia (Diseuse), **Else Knepel** (Sopran), **Iso Golland** (Bariton)
Lewis Ruth Band

Evening program of the radio station Funkstunde Berlin, 21 September 1929. Kurt Weill conducts the Lewis Ruth Band, and Lotte Lenya sings his songs.

In late 1929 the Lewis Ruth Band recorded instrumental arrangements of four songs from *Happy End*, including "Surabaya-Johnny."

collaboration with Weill now gave him an opportunity to go beyond theoretical considerations and put them into practice. At the outset the two were of a similar mind, for Weill also saw clearly that the world could no longer be portrayed by the means of traditional musical theater. He wrote, in complete accordance with Brecht, "If the bounds of opera cannot accommodate such a rapprochement with the theatre of the times [*Zeittheater*], then its bounds must be broken."[64]

The two had begun their attack on the institution of opera by developing new forms of musical theater outside of opera: plays with music, songspiels, radio cantatas, radio didactic pieces. A school opera was to follow. As part of their aesthetics, along with developing new kinds of works, Brecht and Weill were constantly thinking about the new audience they wanted to reach. The differences between Weill's and Brecht's positions burst open after the completion and first performance of *Aufstieg und Fall der Stadt Mahagonny*, when they published separate theoretical reflections.

After Brecht presented his famous scheme distinguishing the processes of the old "dramatic" theater from those of the new "epic" theater, he came to what he felt was his most important thesis about epic opera: "When the epic theatre's methods begin to penetrate the opera the first result is a radical *separation of the elements*. The great struggle for supremacy between words, music and production—which always brings up the question 'which is the pretext for what': is the music the pretext for the events on the stage, or are these the pretext for the music? etc.—can simply be by-passed by radically separating the elements."[65]

Brecht and Weill had indeed made full use of this principle in *Die Dreigroschenoper* (where a change in lighting indicated the beginnings of songs, and the stage provided a caesura, after which the music "came into its own"), but this work was of a different type from opera. For opera Weill did not even want to allow the question of a "struggle for

A 1922 shimmy (one of four shellac recordings), the probable source of Brecht's imaginary city name "Mahagonny."

supremacy." In his remarks about *Aufstieg und Fall der Stadt Mahagonny,* he wrote: "The subject of this opera is the history of a city, its formation, its first crises, then the decisive turning point in its development, its time of glory, its decline. It is a set of 'morality-pictures of our time' projected on an exaggerated level. Corresponding to this subject, the purest form of epic theater, which is also the purest form of musical theater, could be selected. It is a series of twenty-one separate musical forms. Each of these forms is a closed scene, and each is introduced by an inscription in narrative form."[66] He further writes: "The epic form of theater is a stepwise *sequence of situations.* . . . The subject matter of the opera *Aufstieg und Fall der Stadt Mahagonny* made possible an *organization according to purely musical precepts.* For the form of the chronicle, which could be chosen here, is nothing other than a sequence of situations." And he concludes: "In staging this opera, it must be continually taken into consideration that *closed musical forms* are present here. Therefore, an essential task is to guarantee the purely musical flow."[67]

In his view of the renewal of opera Weill lays claim, if not to the primacy of music, then certainly to musical principles as the overarching element. He did not want to see the separation of elements in a Brechtian sense applied so radically to epic opera. This in turn led to irritation on the part of Brecht, who did not want to be thought of as an ordinary librettist. Hence the break that begins to make itself felt in these writings from 1930.

After two years of work Weill completed the first draft of the opera in April 1929, and in November Universal published the piano reduction and the libretto. Using all the means of traditional opera—from the overture and the bel canto aria to large ensembles and chorus scenes—*Aufstieg und Fall der Stadt Mahagonny* is nonetheless the great antithesis of traditional opera. A merciless mirror is held up to the bourgeois world, and the laws of capitalism that govern it are laid bare. In the story of Jim Mahoney, compara-

**General Music Director Gustav Brecher, who premiered
three of Weill's stage works in Leipzig, in 1930.**

ble to Christ's Passion and ending with the demise of both the man and the city, what Weill
calls the "morality-pictures of our time" are linked to a visionary, parable-like portrayal
of the epoch.

Weill told the tale as follows:

Two men and a woman, in flight from the authorities, break down in a desolate region.
They decide to found a city where the men who pass through from the Gold Coast
would be able to fulfill their needs. In the "Paradise City" that arises here, people lead
a contemplative idyllic life. But in the long run, that cannot satisfy the men from the
Gold Coast. Discontent reigns. Prices drop. During the night when a typhoon moves

Program from the premiere of *Aufstieg und Fall der Stadt Mahagonny*.

toward the city, Jim Mahoney discovers the new law of the city. The law states: "You can do anything." The typhoon curves away. People live on according to the new law. The city flourishes. Needs increase—and prices with them. For people are permitted everything—but only if they can pay for it. When his money runs out, Jim Mahoney himself is condemned to death. His execution is the occasion for a gigantic demonstration against the high cost of living, which announces the end of the city.[68]

In the opening scene the widow Begbick, who is being sought on a warrant for her arrest, and her two companions decide to found a city. This scene introduces narratively—or epically—the story that the audience will watch unfold through the course of the evening. Begbick and her companions sing an extended arioso that immediately turns the vocabulary of opera on its head. A largo movement follows as soon as Begbick has settled on a site for the center of the city, the "you-can-do-anything inn." This is the movement that had ended the songspiel, with its penetrating melodic line, "Aber dieses ganze Mahagonny" (But this whole Mahagonny). In the next scene Jenny and the six girls step out in front of the curtain and sing the "Alabama-Song." After scene 3, in which Fatty and Moses advertise Mahagonny, four lumberjacks appear. Singing the quartet "Auf nach Mahagonny" (Off to Mahagonny), which in places has parodistic echoes of Weber's *Der Freischütz,* they reach the city and are welcomed by Begbick. Jenny and Jim meet right after this, and Jenny sings "Ach, bedenken Sie, Herr Jakob Schmidt" (Oh, Think It Over, Mister Jack O'Brien). This song, which was not added until 1931 and was also known as the "Havanna-Song," is another Weill masterpiece.

But life in Mahagonny is boring, as is portrayed in a wonderful musical travesty in scene 9. The curtain opens with a grandiose virtuoso setting of the "Gebet einer Jungfrau" (Maiden's Prayer), after which one of the men says quietly, "Das ist die ewige Kunst!" (That is immortal art!). This is followed by Jim's nostalgic reminiscence of Alaska's deep woods, set to 3/4 time in a consciously distorted waltz rhythm. The kitsch of the bourgeois salon (in the maiden's prayer) and the kitsch of bourgeois opera (in the nostalgic aria) are turned inside out and simultaneously shattered. Next comes the hurricane scene, a dramatic trick to reach the turning point in the plot. Here Weill employs the means of traditional opera—an orchestral fugue in a hasty rhythm to symbolize the flight, a three-part chorus to portray the great terror. The pious horror of the men follows, and the fugue gives way to a chorale. Weill inserts Jenny's refrain from the "Alabama-Song" into the male chorale, and the music turns the men's resignation to fate inside out. This is followed by the melodically successful song "Denn wie man sich bettet, so liegt man" (For As You Make Your Bed, So Must You Lie in It), harmonically and rhythmically close to "song" style. The misanthropic brutality of the text is juxtaposed with a relaxed melodic line, and the music drives the sense of oppressiveness to an extreme, until the light is extinguished and the scene closes.

The second act shows Mahagonny at its high point. The scenes of this act are tied together by an ostinato refrain, "Erstens, vergeßt nicht, kommt das Fressen" (Don't forget, the most important thing is eating), one of the strongest musical inventions of the opera. Trivialities are presented: eating (Jack O'Brien feeds himself to death to an uncanny tune played on a zither), lovemaking (to the "Song von Mandelay"), boxing (a brisk march, its melody at times intentionally distorted, accompanies a deadly boxing match), drinking (Jenny and the drunken men play a scene of a grand sea voyage, for which Weill skillfully uses the trivial song "Des Seemanns Los" [The Sailor's Lot]). One of the most beautiful numbers of the whole work is placed between the "lovemaking" and the "fighting" scenes: Jim and Jenny sing the duet "Sieh jene Kraniche" (Crane Duet) on Brecht's famous poem. For a few minutes two simple people break out of the Mahagonny world; they cannot come to any good end. In the trial that opens the third act, Jim is sentenced to death for having failed to pay for three bottles of whiskey. During the court scene the music uses rhythmical accompanying figures to portray the hair-raising trial

Kurt Weill and his mother on 9 March 1930 on Leipzig's
Georgiring, on their way to the premiere of *Aufstieg und Fall der
Stadt Mahagonny* at the Neues Theater.

and judgment. Weill employs a two-measure cadential formula to mark the end of each part of the sentence. The "Benares-Song" returns once more, followed by the grand finale of the opera, in which Weill works the music from the preceding scenes into a suggestive montage. Parts of "An einem grauen Vormittag" (On a Gray Morning), of the "Spiel vom lieben Gott in Mahagonny" (Play of God in Mahagonny), of "Aber dieses ganze Mahagonny" from the opening song, of the "hurricane" choruses, of "Denn wie man sich bettet" are woven together into a dissonant collage that expresses musically what Neher's projections portray visually: chaos. The grandiose final song "Können uns und euch und niemand helfen" (Can't Help Us or You or Anyone) starts out largo, slows to a più largo, and finally to a molto largo; two fortissimo measures, which reinforce the warning, close the work.

It went without saying that Kurt Weill would want to have his opera premiered in Berlin. As early as April 1929 he played parts of it for Otto Klemperer, and in May Universal sent a proposed contract draft to Berlin's Krolloper. Everything seemed to be falling into place, but then Klemperer apparently began to have reservations. He asked Weill to play for him again at the beginning of July, in the presence of his director, Ernst Legal. Weill gave his publisher the following account of the outcome:

> The *Mahagonny* matter has taken a very surprising turn. After I had played the third act for Klemperer I left. Legal, who was extremely impressed, urged immediate categorical acceptance of the work. Klemperer expressed basic agreement. Two hours later Klemperer called me at my apartment to say that he wanted to come by to see me right away. He arrived in a state of absolute despair and declared with tears in his eyes that

A projection by Caspar Neher for the premiere.

he had now spent two hours wrestling with himself, but that it was impossible; he acknowledged the importance of the whole thing, he recognized the musical beauties, but the whole thing was foreign to him and incomprehensible.[69]

Upon hearing this, Universal contacted a number of opera house directors and eventually received a favorable reply from Leipzig's Gustav Brecher, which the publisher immediately conveyed to Weill, saying, "We are very happy after so many difficult and wearisome negotiations that we have now found the starting point for *Mahagonny*."[70] The contract with Leipzig contained compromises on both sides: "In consideration of the special character of the work the authors will be entitled to give advice on the staging." And, even more important, "This contract is predicated upon the immediate binding assurance by both authors that they will agree to undertake the discussed alterations in keeping with the misgivings of the Leipzig management."[71]

Thus the history of the opera began with forced changes even before its first performance. This continued through almost every staging until 1931; indeed, the performance material published in 1929 consists of a version that never actually made its way onto the stage. The "misgivings of the Leipzig management"—and not only of this management—concerned in particular the "Play of God in Mahagonny," the "lovemaking" scene, and the placards in the finale. The first had to be dropped altogether, and the other two had to be toned down. Even the name "Dreieinigkeitsmoses" (Trinity Moses) had to be changed for Leipzig; in the premiere this character was called "Virginia Moses."

As far as the names of the main characters were concerned, Brecht and Weill seem even in the final phase of their work to have had second thoughts; the performance material published in November 1929 already contained the following note:

> Since the human pleasures that can be had for money are in every place and time almost exactly the same, and since the pleasure city Mahagonny is thus in the broadest sense of the word international, the names of the protagonists can be changed to local ones. For German performances, for example, the following names would be suitable:
> for Fatty . . . Willy
> for Jim Mahoney . . . Johann Ackermann (or Hans)
> for Jack O'Brien . . . Jakob Schmidt
> for Bill . . . Sparbüchsenheinrich [Piggy Bank Heinrich] or Heinz
> for Joe . . . Josef Lettner, also called Alaska Wolf Joe.
> Any suggestion of Wild West or cowboy romanticism and any accentuation of a typically American milieu are to be avoided.[72]

These alternative suggestions led to constant changes in the names used in German performances until 1933. It was not without significance that Brecht changed the names of three of the lumberjacks for the edition of the libretto published in 1930 as part of his *Versuche* (Theatrical Experiments). This became established as the literary edition and, like the version of *Die Dreigroschenoper* published in *Versuche,* included numerous changes from the performance edition. When the directors of the Festival Neue Musik

The first scene from the premiere of *Aufstieg und Fall der Stadt Mahagonny,* with Marga Dannenberg as Leokadja Begbick, Hanns Fleischer as Willy, der "Prokurist," and Walther Zimmer as Virginia Moses. The name Dreieinigkeits-Moses (Trinity Moses) had to be changed for "religious" reasons!

Berlin (Paul Hindemith, Heinrich Burkard, and Joseph Haas) rejected the play *Die Maß-nahme* (The Measures Taken) he had written with Eisler, he changed the character's names to *Paul* Ackermann, *Heinrich* Merg, and *Joseph* Lettner.

The opera's premiere took place on 9 March 1930 in Leipzig's Neues Theater. During the final week of rehearsals Brecht, Weill, and Neher were present to assist in the staging, musical, and technical preparations. Walther Brügmann was the director, Gustav Brecher was the conductor, and Caspar Neher was responsible for the sets and the projections.

The premiere turned into one of the most protracted theater scandals of the Weimar Republic, set off this time not by disgruntled friends of traditional opera but by organized bands of disrupters planted in the audience—"Nazis, black-white-red rabble-rousers who had been paid to come as a kind of claque by instigators with plenty of capital."[73] They had already demonstrated in front of the opera house on the afternoon before the premiere; when Weill arrived with his parents and Lotte Lenya in the evening, he noticed some groups in uniform in the audience. Lenya later recalled: "The performance [was] well under way before I was startled out of my absorption by the electric tension around us, something strange and ugly . . . ; by the time the last scene was reached the riot had spread to the stage." Gustav Brecher had difficulty finishing the performance. "Panicky spectators were trying to claw their way out, and only the arrival of a large police force, finally, cleared the theater."[74]

The reactions of the right-wing press made it clear that the ruckus had to do with more than questions of contemporary opera: "General music director Brecher has deemed it appropriate to perform a piece in the opera house that is baldly Communist propaganda

Scene from the finale of the premiere of _Aufstieg und Fall der Stadt Mahagonny_, with the placards that caused the Leipzig management such consternation.

of the most evil sort."[75] Or, even more direct: "Hark, my clean Misters Brecht and Weill, your days may be just as numbered as the days of your scum city Mahagonny!"[76]

But the matter did not stop at a staged brawl and verbal attacks. On 11 March 1930, in a special session of the theater committee, the representative of the German National People's Party (the National Socialists did not yet have a seat in the city parliament) demanded that the play be immediately withdrawn. When the committee rejected his petition, the party called for a decision from Leipzig's city council. On 14 March the city council too rejected the petition, so on 16 March the second performance of the opera was free to take place.

Reports of the brawl and the political tug-of-war in the city council were given considerable coverage in the German press as a whole, leading the theaters of Essen, Oldenburg, and Dortmund to withdraw from the performance contracts they had previously signed with Universal.

The work's aesthetic qualities were almost lost sight of under the barrage of political discussion. Germany's leading music critics were principally responsible for bringing them into the spotlight. Alfred Einstein compared the opera with Wagner's _magnum opus:_

Criticism from the *Leipziger Abendpost*, 10 March 1930. The headline reads: "Sharp protest from the audience. General Music Director Brecher deals in Communist propaganda at the Neues Theater."

The first record with songs from the opera, which was released at the time of the premiere and announced in the program.

Mahagonny is meant to be a symbol, a reflection of life, but it becomes more than a symbol; by the end it has become entirely a demonstration against capitalism. *Der Ring des Nibelungen* is also directed against capitalism, but it is not a demonstration. In *Der Ring des Nibelungen* capitalism conquers the love that one can still believe exists in the world. In *Mahagonny* there is no love; there is only money, drive in all its forms, ultimate desolation, ultimate soullessness. But this itself may perhaps promote love, and the people of Leipzig who hissed and left the theater certainly felt Bert Brecht's and Kurt Weill's aggressiveness but not their seriousness.[77]

Hans Heinz Stuckenschmidt wrote: "This work is at the very peak of contemporary

**Cover design by Caspar Neher for Universal's
edition of six songs from *Aufstieg und Fall der Stadt Mahagonny*
for voice and piano, 1930.**

musico-dramatical production. Even with all its beer hall humor and its adolescent romanticism, it contributes in a highly effective manner to the legitimation of new theater and is to be passionately affirmed for this reason alone. It makes possibilities of opera for the present and the future plausible again and at the same time breaks free of its bounds."[78]

A mere three days after the premiere, on 12 March 1930, the opera was performed in Kassel (Caspar Neher's production, with Jakob Geis directing and Maurice Abravanel conducting) and Braunschweig (Caspar Neher's production, with Heinrich Voigt directing and Klaus Nettstraeter conducting). The Kassel performance ran smoothly, but a brawl had already been planned for Braunschweig. A band of National Socialist students

**Cover of arrangement of the "Alabama-Song" for salon
orchestra, published by Universal in April 1930.**

from the Technische Hochschule began the disturbance during the performance and unleashed a riot at the end. The opera had to be withdrawn after the second performance.

A good month after these performances the discussion of *Mahagonny* received fresh ammunition from Heinrich Strobel, who aired an hour-long evening program on Funk-stunde Berlin called "Für und wider Mahagonny" (For and Against Mahagonny) on 12 April 1930. After his introductory remarks, the Berlin Radio Orchestra under Theo Mackeben played instrumental versions of seven of the opera's numbers.

On 16 October the *Mahagonny* opera was performed in Frankfurt am Main as part of the festival week celebrating the fiftieth anniversary of that city's opera house. (The director was Herbert Graf, the conductor was H. W. Steinberg, and the production was by Ludwig Sievert.) The opening night ran without disturbance; not until the second

Neue Jazzmusik

Vindobona-Collection Jazz-Serie

V.C.J.Nr.		Preis Mk. Salon- / Kleines orchester orchester mit Jazz
	BENATZKY R. Aus „Die fünf Wünsche"	
106	TANGO MACABRE	2.— 3.—
107	FLIRT (Slow-Fox)	2.— 3.—
108	L'HEURE BLEUE	2.— 3.—
	DOUCET C.	
112	CHICKEN PIE, Foxtrot (H. PLATEN)	3.— 3.50
113	A SIX CYLINDER RAG-TIME (H. PLATEN)	3.— 3.50
	FOX-JUREK	
101	DEUTSCHMEISTER SLOW-FOX Jazzparaphrase über W. A. Jureks Deutsch-meister-Marsch von Frank Fox Kleines Orchester mit Jazz	3.—
	KŘENEK E. Aus „Jonny spielt auf"	
109	„LEB' WOHL, MEIN SCHATZ", Blues (J. RISSELIN)	2.— 2.50
	WEILL K.	
104	BERLIN IM LICHT-SONG (O. LINDEMANN)	3.— 4.—
114	BILBAO-SONG (H. PLATEN)	3.— 3.50
	Aus „Die Dreigroschenoper":	
102/03	TANGO-BALLADE UND KANONENSONG (J. FITELBERG)	3.50 4.—
110	BLUES-POTPOURRI (H. PLATEN) (Tanzpotpourri I) Salonorchester mit Jazzstimmen	3.50 4.50
111	FOXTROT-POTPOURRI (H. PLATEN) (Tanzpotpourri II) Salonorchester mit Jazzstimmen	3.50 4.50
	Aus „Aufstieg und Fall der Stadt Mahagonny":	
115	ALABAMA-SONG (R. ETLINGER)	3.— 3.50

KLAVIERMUSIK IM JAZZSTIL, JAZZLIEDER, U. A.

SIEHE SPEZIALPROSPEKT

Universal-Edition A. G. Wien—Leipzig

No. 140

Page from a 1931 Universal Edition catalog which includes arrangements of Weill songs for jazz band.

performance on 19 October did the organized commandos of rowdies spring into action. This performance was brought to an end only with the greatest difficulty, with the lights on, before utter chaos broke out. Nevertheless, the management kept *Mahagonny* on its program, and the opera was performed eight more times.

Still none of the three Berlin opera houses would agree to perform the work. Once again it was Weill himself who took the initiative. Since the opera houses were turning him down, he decided to try and present the work on the theater stage—even if that meant making some cuts. On 3 May 1930 he played the opera at the Deutsches Theater

Program from the performance of *Aufstieg und Fall*
***der Stadt Mahagonny* in Kassel three days after the premiere,**
on 12 March 1930.

and reported: "Yesterday I spent nearly three hours with Reinhardt and played *Mahagonny* for him and his staff. All, especially Reinhardt himself, were very favorably impressed, and I have made considerable progress. Reinhardt has a burning interest . . . [and] it seems virtually assured that it will be performed in the fall. Negotiations are already under way with Marlene Dietrich."[79] But this hope, too, was dashed: "By the way, I have heard in confidence from a well-informed source that Reinhardt received

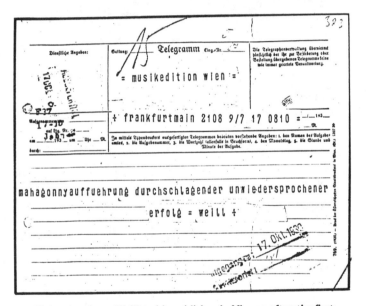

Program from the performance in Brunswick on the same day.

Telegram from Weill to his publisher in Vienna after the first
performance of the opera in Frankfurt am Main, 17 October
1930: "Mahagonny performance an incontrovertible,
smashing success. Weill."

money from heavy industry circles in the Rhine (Thyssen) . . . on the condition that he
not perform *Mahagonny*."[80]

In the end it was Ernst Josef Aufricht who made a Berlin production possible, in late
1931. He rented the Theater am Kurfürstendamm, secured in Alexander von Zemlinsky
a conductor committed to contemporary music, found money for an orchestra and a
chorus, and engaged popular actors for the leading roles—Lotte Lenya, Harald Paulsen,

Weill, Lenya, and Brecht in 1931.

First page and cast list from the program for the first
performance of *Aufstieg und Fall der Stadt Mahagonny* in Berlin.

and Trude Hesterberg. Weill cut back the orchestration as well as the score's musical
demands (for example, in the various ensembles). He also omitted the "Kranich-Duett"
and added two new numbers: "Ach bedenken Sie, Herr Jakob Schmidt" (Oh, Think It
Over, Mister Jack O'Brien) and "Laßt euch nicht verführen" (Don't Let Yourselves Be
Led Astray). On 14 December 1931 he reported: "I am rehearsing from nine in the
morning till one at night. Zemlinsky is really first class!!!"[81]

A seasoned theater manager, Aufricht launched the opening night with a large advertising campaign. He kept firing off sensational notices to the press—including one announcing that Max Schmeling would appear in the boxing scene, which turned out to be
pure hype—and he had one of the first recordings with a picture printed on the disk (a

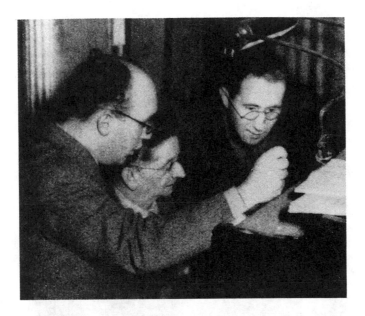

Rehearsal for the first Berlin performance of *Aufstieg und Fall der Stadt Mahagonny,* December 1931, in the Theater am Kurfürstendamm. *Left to right:* Kurt Weill; Alexander von Zemlinsky, the conductor; and Brecht.

Caricatures of the *Mahagonny* cast by Linne for the review in the *12-Uhr-Blatt,* 23 December 1931.

recent innovation from the United States) produced for the audience, with dance arrangements of the "Alabama-Song" and "Denn wie man sich bettet" (For As You Make Your Bed) performed by Emil Róosz and his artists' orchestra.

Lotte Lenya had already recorded both songs for Homocord when the opera was first performed in the spring of 1930; in 1932 she made a new recording with Telefunken. And in the spring of 1932 Electrola produced a selection from the opera with the Berlin ensemble conducted by Hans Sommer.

With the public's curiosity thus aroused, the opening night on 21 December 1931 was a great success. People came in droves to subsequent performances as well; by the spring the opera had been given more than forty times without interruption—a new record for

**Lotte Lenya as Jenny and Harald Paulsen as Alaskawolfjoe
in the first Berlin production of *Aufstieg und Fall der Stadt
Mahagonny*, December 1931.**

contemporary musical theater. The expected uproar was confined to renewed vehement
attacks from the rightist press. Clearly the social reality of Germany in the third winter of
the world economic crisis had long since caught up with the authors' vision of 1929.

 Aufstieg und Fall der Stadt Mahagonny was also the occasion of an encounter and a
short-term collaboration with Karl Kraus, whose Offenbach arrangements (*Perichole*
had been premiered in March 1931 in the Krolloper) had made a strong impression on
Weill. Kraus for his part was so taken with *Mahagonny* that he decided to present
excerpts of it in his famous series "Theater der Dichtung," evenings of readings and
lectures that included musical demonstrations. Weill had often attended his Offenbach
lectures in Berlin. Now Karl Kraus asked him to take over the piano accompaniment for
the *Mahagonny* evening, which Weill (who almost never appeared in Berlin as a per-
former or conductor of his own music) considered an honor and gladly agreed to.

**Lenya as Jenny and Heinrich Gretler as Johann Ackermann
in the first Berlin production.**

The presentation took place on 11 January 1932 in Berlin. In the first part Kraus read from works by Raimund, Wedekind, and Altenberg; the second half was devoted to Weill's opera. On 6 February Kraus repeated the program in Vienna, this time with another pianist. Shortly thereafter Weill wrote, "The Karl Kraus reading from *Mahagonny* was very interesting, but—between us—had so little to do with my own interpretation . . . that I couldn't get much out of it."[82]

The last performance in the Theater am Kurfürstendamm marked the end of this opera's performance history in Germany for a quarter of a century. *Aufstieg und Fall der*

Stadt Mahagonny was performed in three other European capitals before 1933: Prague (1930), Vienna (1932), and Copenhagen (1933).

Let us now return, though, to the time of the premiere, the spring of 1930. For a third time (after 1927 and 1929) Kurt Weill was commissioned to compose a work for Germany's most important music festival, which had moved from Baden-Baden to Berlin in 1930 and was now called "Festival Neue Musik." The focus of that year's festival was the school music movement. This subject was of burning interest to Weill, who had already ventured into this realm with his *Lindberghflug* and saw great potential in it. "Now principally two new market outlets have emerged next to the old (concert, theater, radio): the workers' choral movement and the schools. Therein, a rewarding task exists for us: to create for these new areas works of greater scope, which are nonetheless restricted in the external means to such a degree that the possibility of performance in the intended places is not hindered."[83]

The workers' choral movement was, with minor exceptions, not Weill's sphere; but he was determined to write something "decent" for the schools, so he gladly accepted the commission. Between January and May he wrote, again in collaboration with Brecht, the school opera *Der Jasager* (The Yes-Sayer). This was the last work that the two produced together in Germany.

Once again Elisabeth Hauptmann provided them with the basis for their new play. In 1929 she had translated four classical Japanese No plays into German, using Arthur Waley's English versions. One of these, by the fifteenth-century playwright Zenchiku, was entitled *Taniko* (The Hurling into the Valley). This play tells the story of a boy who joins a ritual pilgrimage by a Buddhist sect to pray for his mother. On the way he himself falls ill and loses the purity required for the pilgrimage. According to the prescribed rite, he is thrown into the valley.

Brecht and Weill were impressed by the conciseness of the plot and secularized the religious material. After their revision Weill summarized the tale as follows:

> The boy wishes to go with the teacher on a journey to the city in order to get medicine for his sick mother. The trip is dangerous; therefore, the mother does not want the boy to go. The teacher also advises against it. The boy goes, however, in order to help his mother. On the way, when they come to the most dangerous place, the boy becomes tired, thereby endangering the whole traveling party. The decision is put to him: should they turn back or should they follow the old custom, which dictates that the sick be thrown into the valley? The boy decides to be hurled into the valley. "He has said Yes," sings the chorus.

Weill continues: "We thought that students should also learn something from a didactic play. Therefore, we have introduced the concept of acquiescence [*Einverständnis*]— namely, 'It is important to learn acquiescence.' That is what students should learn. They should know that a community which one joins demands that one actually bear the consequences. . . . Through this development of 'agreement' the didactic play works in a higher sense politically, but obviously not factionally."[84]

Ernst Josef Aufricht had one of the earliest German picture
records made to help promote the first Berlin production. The
design was by the stage designer Nina Tokumbet, a friend of
Caspar Neher's. The record includes dance arrangements of two
songs from the opera, played by Emil Roòsz and his Artists'
Orchestra.

A photograph by Elli Marcus of Lotte Lenya as Jenny, with
a dedication to Weill, 29 May 1932.

This recording of selections from *Aufstieg und Fall der Stadt Mahagonny* was made by the ensemble from the first Berlin production in the spring of 1932.

Weill's music for this opera is one of the tightest scores he ever wrote. Dedicated to the Leipzig conductor Gustav Brecher, it is orchestrated for first and second violin, cello, bass (with as many string players as possible), two pianos, and a harmonium. A flute, clarinet, an alto saxophone, plucked instruments, and percussion can be added *ad libitum*. His directions further specify that "all . . . vocal parts must be sung by students. I think the boy should be sung by a 10–12 year-old, the teacher by a 16–18 year-old, the mother by a 14–16 year-old girl. Similarly, the three Students who participate in the journey should be sung by students. And finally the entire school chorus should also participate."[85]

The work opens and closes with the "Einverständnis-Chor" (Chorus of Active Consent), which attains the greatness of a Handel chorus with its extremely singable melody in canon. The clear rhythm establishes the straightforward tone of the entire work. The story actually begins in the second number, with the teacher visiting the boy at home and learning that his mother is gravely ill. A thematic figure accompanied by flowing quarter notes is introduced into this scene fifteen times, more or less as a way of articulating the exposition of the play, since the opening situation is narrated antiphonally by the teacher and the boy.

Then the mother bids farewell to her son. Her gripping "Seit dem Tag, an dem uns dein Vater verließ" (Since the day your father left us) is made much of; the ostinato accompaniment of the whole scene adds great emphasis to it. The first act ends, with commentary from the chorus, when the mother makes her decision: "Wenn es sein muß, geh mit dem Herrn Lehrer" (If you must, then go with the teacher).

The second act again opens with the chorus, which addresses the audience directly with the news that the boy is sick and too weak to continue. Here, too, Weill works with a short but all the more effective thematic figure, which is first played by the violins and winds and then at the end of the chorus is repeated three more times. It signals heightened tension and prepares musically for the decision situation. In this scene, the tenth, Weill

**Karl Kraus at one of his lecture evenings "Theater der Dichtung"
in the Mozartsaal in Berlin. On 11 January 1932 he presented
the *Mahagonny* opera, accompanied on the piano by Weill.**

begins with a two-measure phrase intoned by the piano which, with its muffled sound,
suggests death. In a long recitative interrupted only by repetitions of the opening figure
the teacher explains the ancient custom to the boy. The scene is extremely restrained, and
all the words of the teacher are articulated very carefully in a piano recitative; but when he
tells the boy the reply that is expected of him—"Ihr sollt nicht umkehren" (You shall not
turn back)—Weill suddenly changes to a fortissimo as the decisive dialogue begins.
Mighty chords introduce the question "Verlangst du, daß man umkehrt deinetwegen?"
(Do you demand that we turn back on your account?). The orchestra falls silent, and the
boy responds without any musical accompaniment, but still fortissimo, "Ihr sollt nicht
umkehren" (You shall not turn back). After this the music switches to a march rhythm
and, accompanied by relentless quarter notes (reminiscent more than anything else in
Weill's music of Eisler's war song intonation), the three students sing the confirming "Er
hat ja gesagt, er hat dem Brauch gemäß geantwortet" (He had said yes; he has answered
in accordance with the custom). Then the boy is thrown into the valley: "Da nahmen die

Freunde den Krug und beklagten die traurigen Wege der Welt und ihr bitteres Gesetz und warfen ihn hinab." (Then the friends took the jug and lamented the sad ways of the world and its bitter law and hurled him down.) The opening "Einverständnischor" is sung again as a mighty finale to the opera.

Der Jasager is a typical work of the period of *Lehrstücke* and of a time when didactic uses of art were being experimented with extensively. One may debate the plot's severity, but by now there is almost no divergence of opinion concerning the compactness of Weill's music. When the composer arrived in the United States as an exile in 1935 and was asked what he considered to be his most important European work, he answered without hesitation, "Der Jasager."[86] In terms of Brechtian theory, Weill had arrived at the point that marked his greatest insight into the functioning of society.

Der Jasager was scheduled for performance at the Festival Neue Musik alongside Hindemith's *Wir bauen eine Stadt* (Let's Build a City), Toch's *Das Wasser* (The Water), and Eisler and Brecht's *Die Maßnahme* (The Measures Taken). When the festival committee refused to perform *Die Maßnahme* on account of its political explosiveness (this play placed the decision situation of *Der Jasager* into a concrete class-warfare situation in China), Weill withdrew *Der Jasager* from the festival in solidarity with Brecht. The authors pulled strings with their radio connections to organize a "counter-performance," and on 23 June 1930 the premiere of *Der Jasager* took place in Berlin's Zentralinstitut für Unterricht und Erziehung. Neher and Brecht assumed responsibility for directing the opera, which was sung by the youth choir, youth instrumental group, and students (for the solo parts) of Berlin's Staatliche Akademie für Kirchen- und Schulmusik, with a student, Kurt Drabek, conducting. On 7 December 1930 *Der Jasager* played in a well-received matinee in Berlin's Krolloper, with the participants of the premiere under the direction of Heinrich Martens.

Brecht's severity immediately became a subject of heated debate in the press. There were attacks from the left and—worse still—acclamations from the right. Frank Warschauer, for example, a radio theoretician and close acquaintance of both authors, wrote: "No to the Yes-Sayer! Here a kind of ethical pathos that is known to be sacrosanct is proclaimed, one which contains a potent, albeit finely dispersed, dose of all the evil ingredients of a reactionary way of thinking based on senseless authority. This yes-sayer is strikingly reminiscent of the cadaverlike obedience of the yes-sayers during the war."[87] At the same time an extremely conservative Catholic paper declared: "We have not heard basic Christian truth sung more plainly and clearly than in the first bars of this gripping, even devastating play. Consent, consensus, and the offering up even of life for the suffering

Advertisement in the Berlin press for the premiere of the school opera *Der Jasager*, based on a Japanese No play, on 23 June 1930.

**Two scenes from the premiere of *Der Jasager*, with Otto Hopf
as the teacher.**

of the world . . . we know of no one who would have known how to preach this so well as
this atheist."[88] Brecht was very perturbed by these responses. He put on a test performance and then rewrote the play, renaming it *Der Jasager und der Neinsager* (The Yes-
Sayer and the No-Sayer). Weill did not participate in this revision.

Notwithstanding the heated debate over its contents, the opera became *the* event in
the school music movement before 1933 on account of its high musical standards.
Eberhard Preußner, assistant at the Zentralinstitut and an active proponent of contemporary music, made the following assessment: "What does *Der Jasager* mean for music
education in the schools? The short answer is the conquest of the schools by contempo-

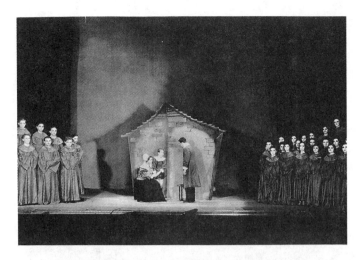

Scene from the first American performance of *Der Jasager*
by the Music School of the Henry Street Settlement (directed
by Sanford Meisner and conducted by Lehman Engel) at New
York's Grand Street Playhouse.

Advertisement for *Der Jasager* by Universal
Edition, December 1930.

rary music. . . . No other work of *Gebrauchsmusik* has been composed that is both so functional and yet also so artistic."[89]

The premiere set off an impressive run. As early as October 1930 Universal announced twenty-two planned performances; by March 1931 the number had grown to a hundred, and in October 1932 the publisher announced that the work was being performed by more than two hundred schools. Universal's Hans W. Heinsheimer himself had a hand in a Viennese performance. As a press notice explained: "A teacher has had workers'

Cast list for the film *Die Dreigroschenoper* by G. W. Pabst, 1931.

children in a suburb of Vienna learn Weill's *Jasager*. At first there were a number of concert performances, which led to a wish for a staged presentation. A play director was found in the publisher Heinsheimer, director of the stage division of Universal Edition, who was directing for the first time in his life and produced strong effects with primitive means."[90] A good example of the fact that performances of *Der Jasager* did not need to be confined to the Gymnasien [Germany's top-level secondary schools] and music schools but that the opera could actually have a very broad effect!

Brecht and Weill had just finished working on *Der Jasager* when another event boosted their popularity even further. After the tremendous success of *Die Dreigroschenoper* the company Nero-Film A. G. concluded a contract with Brecht and Weill on 21 May 1930 for a film version of the opera. This led Brecht to write a new script entitled *Die Beule—Ein Dreigroschenfilm* (The Lump on the Head—A Threepenny Film), which sharpened the play's social message considerably. The company rejected this text, Brecht refused to make changes, Weill backed him up, and between 19 October and

Lotte Lenya as Jenny in the film *Der Dreigroschenoper*.

4 November 1930 the famous "*Dreigroschen* Trial" was held, about which Brecht later wrote a sociological study. Brecht lost his trial, but a settlement was reached between Brecht and the Tobis [Ton-Bild-Syndicat] who owned Nero-Film. Weill won his trial and also reached a settlement in early February 1931. The following announcement was prepared: "The matter of *Die Dreigroschenoper* has been satisfactorily resolved. The parties have settled with each other. Kurt Weill has dropped his opposition to the showing of the film. The trials are thus finished."[91]

When the film was released, Universal published a new "sound film collection" of four songs for voice and piano. The cover included a collage of scenes from the movie.

These settlements unleashed a lively reaction in the press. Numerous voices accused Brecht and Weill of having dropped their reservations against the Nero production because of a favorable financial settlement. Weill responded to these accusations forcefully: "Allow me to make a few remarks about the various comments concerning my settlement with the Tobis. I have not settled for the sake of a monetary reward. I went to trial to keep the film production free of methods that are harmful to art and to individuals, and I settled because the Tobis agreed to consult me in the future for direction of the production. Up to now all film authors, myself included, have fought in vain for these two concessions. . . . Anyone who knows me knows that I agreed to the settlement not for material reasons but because I had attained the principal goal of the trial."[92]

The film, which in the end was based on a script by Leo Lania, Ladislav Vajda, and Béla Balázs and was filmed by the director G. W. Pabst (with Carola Neher as Polly, Rudolf Forster as Macheath, Fritz Rasp and Valeska Gert as the Peachum couple, Lotte

Lenya as Jenny, Reinhold Schünzel as Tiger Brown, and Ernst Busch as the Moritat singer), was premiered at Berlin's Atrium on 19 February 1931. The film was even more important for France than for Germany, where *Die Dreigroschenoper* was already a great success and received an additional boost in popularity from the film. Since the process of dubbing had not yet been invented, a French version of the film was made in a Berlin studio, according to practices common at the time. Featuring French actors (Albert Préjean as Macheath, Odette Florelle as Polly, Jacques Henley as Tiger Brown, and Margo Lion as Jenny), *L'Opéra de quat'sous* opened on 5 April 1931 in Paris. This film brought *Dreigroschen* fever to France, where it was attended in record numbers, and recordings further enhanced the popularity of Weill's songs. Ultraphon had already made two records in Berlin while the film was being shot (with the Lewis Ruth Band, Albert Préjean, Margo Lion, and Jacques Henley) for distribution in France. In 1931 and 1932 French record companies then produced four more recordings of *Dreigroschenoper* songs, sung by Florelle, Lys Gauty, and Marianne Oswald.

In December 1931 Weill wrote: "Friends of mine have just returned from Paris and confirm anew the spontaneous success of my music in Paris. Everyone is asking for music and records by me, and the "Mack the Knife" song is being sung on the streets."[93] A year and a half later this popularity would help him find a foothold in France as an émigré.

In spite of all the discussion about Brecht's intentions, about the trial, and about the surrounding circumstances, the film was not nearly as bad as the literature has often made it out to be. The leading Berlin film theoretician and critic Rudolf Arnheim pleaded for it as early as 1931, saying:

> The legal proceedings in the *Dreigroschenoper* case have drawn a kind of public attention that seldom comes to literary products. But with all this useful discussion G. W. Pabst's film itself has gotten the short end of the stick. The charming sweetness of Kurt Weill's music; the smoothly gliding camera, which noiselessly films the scene

The 1931 French film version, *L'Opéra de quat'sous*, made *Die Dreigroschenoper* popular in France as well. Polydor subsequently released a record of songs sung by Florelle, who played Polly in this film.

of the action; the veiled play of perspective in inner rooms covered by ghostly gratings; the ironic kitsch of the full moon and the lamenting love songs; the picturesque freshness of the beggars' market; the delicate grace with which "brutalizing and amoralizing" effects are created—we should not let all this escape us![94]

It is appropriate that this chapter about Weill's great Berlin years, which brought him both artistic recognition and broad popularity, should end with a description of the success of the filming of *Die Dreigroschenoper;* this was, after all, the work that signaled Weill's breakthrough in the Weimar Republic's artistic capital and that itself became part of the unmistakable, unique picture of that city in the second half of the 1920s.

I have already shown how Weill's and Brecht's positions started diverging more and more in their theoretical reflections on *Aufstieg und Fall der Stadt Mahagonny.* In the course of the rehearsals for the Berlin performance in the Theater am Kurfürstendamm, they got into a serious personal dispute about the production that ended in a major quarrel. For the time being, this marked the end of the Weill–Brecht partnership. The two separated—Brecht to produce *Die Mutter* (The Mother) with Hanns Eisler and Weill to complete *Die Bürgschaft* (The Pledge) with Caspar Neher.

In the end we should remember, though, that the four-year collaboration between writer and composer produced high points of German—even of European—theater that have retained their undisputed place to this day.

(1 9 3 1 – 3 2)

The Defense of Opera

The political and economic crises of the Weimar Republic intensified during the winter of 1930–31. The cabinet of Chancellor Heinrich Brüning was relying increasingly on emergency orders to govern. In January 1931, shortly after the first "Christmas of Hunger," the number of unemployed in Germany reached five million; by October 1932 the number had risen to seven and a half million. The reactionary forces of the National Socialist Workers' Party (NSDAP) and the National People's Party (DNVP) were exerting stronger pressure on democracy.

Caspar Neher at work, 1931. Neher, a childhood friend of
Brecht's and much sought after as a stage designer, played an
important part in Weill's work between 1927 and 1933.

The "Harzburg Front," which they established in October 1932, brought them into alliance with the German veterans' organization *Stahlhelm* and with heavy industry. The National Socialists were gaining influence; Adolf Hitler received thirteen million votes in the presidential elections of April 1932. The demise of the republic seemed only a matter of time.

German theater was entering a difficult period. As the economic situation worsened for a large segment of the population, theater attendance dropped off, and more and more theater managers were falling back on a "marketable" repertoire of classics and light entertainment. With state and local financial support also dwindling, opera was especially hard hit—both financially, as a particularly expensive form of theater to stage, and culturally, as the target of increasingly vehement attacks from reactionaries. Thus such a progressive man as Leipzig's opera director Gustav Brecher had to acknowledge: "It is most likely that next season things will be such that compelling financial arguments will force us above all to perform sure-fire operettas in addition to a few musical masterpieces, primarily of German origin—Pfitzner, Strauss."[1] In July 1931, in spite of a large protest campaign throughout the country, the Prussian Landtag decided to close Berlin's Krolloper, whose work since 1927 had become synonymous with repertoire renewal and a commitment to contemporary opera. Whereas the three Berlin opera houses staged a total of sixty operas during the 1927–28 season, the number had shrunk in 1931–32 to a mere sixteen. In the face of such circumstances most composers had stopped writing operas altogether.

Not Kurt Weill. He was convinced that opera could be further developed, even in these times. He not only fought passionately for this idea but above all worked for it in practical ways. As early as 1930, in the wake of the political uproar over the *Mahagonny* premiere in Leipzig, he had expressed his conviction "that the path I've chosen is correct and that it is out of the question to give up this path just because its beginnings happen to run into a strand of the fiercest cultural reaction and, like all great innovations, encounter violent opposition."[2]

Weill formulated his credo of an opera of "large form"—which, contrary to the half-hearted stances of many theater managers, should at this very time be greeted with particular interest on the part of audiences—in numerous articles in the Berlin press in 1931–32, articles whose titles themselves sum up his agenda. In August 1931 he wrote in "Zur großen Form!": "I do not see why, in as troubled a time as now, when the interest of the individual in questions of the whole is heightened to an extreme, the public should avoid theater that addresses the great questions of the day. Naturally, the form these addresses take plays a decisive role. Today we are on the way to a form of theater which projects the great, leading ideas of the time onto simple, typical processes. The recognition that the large form of theater is more necessary than ever today gives us justification to believe in a future for opera."[3]

Weill expanded on the question of what this kind of opera of "large form" might look like in an article entitled "Wirklich eine Opernkrise?" (Actually an Operatic Crisis?) in the summer of 1932: "Our era conceals within itself an abundance of great ideas and human or generally valid subjects. If one resolves to free opera from the sphere of naturalistic theater and to see in it that heightened form of theater best suited to translate great ideas of the time into a timeless humanistic form, then a new belief in the future of opera is produced quite by itself."[4] When Weill penned these lines, his opera *Die Bürgschaft* (The Pledge) had already been premiered in Berlin.

After *Aufstieg und Fall der Stadt Mahagonny* he had searched for a long time for new opera material and had considered a number of projects in the process. In December 1929, apparently under the influence of Piscator's 1928 dramatization of Jaroslav Hašek's novel *The Good Soldier Schweik,* he considered writing an opera based on the same story. In early August 1930 he was looking at Jack London and wrote that "a plan for a Franz Kafka opera is taking shape."[5] But by the end of August he wrote: "I have been working with Caspar Neher on an opera libretto for about two weeks."[6]

Ever since they had first met while staging the *Mahagonny* songspiel's premiere at Baden-Baden in July 1927, joint theater work had brought Weill and Neher together time and again. As Weill's relationship with Brecht continued to cool from the spring of 1930 on, his contact with Neher grew, and soon a cordial friendship had developed between them, all the more so as Weill was strongly drawn to Neher's wife, Erika. In the course of numerous conversations about the concept of a "timeless" opera of "large form," Neher directed Weill in mid-August 1930 to a parable written by Johann Gottfried Herder in 1774 entitled *Der afrikanische Rechtsspruch* (The African Verdict), which he recommended to the composer as suitable opera material.

Alexander the Great comes to a distant African province one day and witnesses a trial there. Two men are arguing before the king. One has sold the other a sack of grain in which gold was hidden. The buyer notices the gold and wants to return it, but the seller insists that everything that was in the sack now belongs to the buyer. The king learns that the two contenders have a son and a daughter. He rules that the two children shall be married so that the gold will then belong to them. Alexander is utterly astonished and declares that in his country both men would have been decapitated and the gold would have gone to the state. The African king then asks Alexander if it rains in his country and if the sun shines. To Alexander's astonished "Yes" the African replies, "Then it must be because of the innocent animals that live in your country, because the sun should not shine nor should the heavens rain down on such people."[7]

Kurt Weill was taken by this project, which seemed to contain every possibility for the kind of opera libretto he had in mind. When Caspar Neher suggested that he himself could write the libretto, Weill agreed. However this decision may have been reached, it posed a great risk, since this was Neher's first literary effort. But he brought a wealth of theater experience to the project of crafting a tale suitable for opera. It speaks for the close affinity between the two that at such a crucial phase in the composer's development, when he was striving to create a completely new kind of opera, Weill—who had worked with such experienced theater authors as Kaiser and Brecht—would have entrusted the libretto to the "neophyte" Neher. Later, in the years after 1935, Neher was to work with Rudolf Wagner-Régeny as the librettist for three more successful operas.

In May and June of 1931 Weill took an automobile trip through France and Spain. Neher joined him in Zazaux near San Sebastián, having just completed a first draft of the text, which he now wanted to revise jointly with Weill. Afterward Weill composed the opera, finishing it by October 1931. *Die Bürgschaft,* an attempt to pour epic opera into a large, timeless form, became his most extensive score. Two commenting choruses—one beside the stage and one on the stage—accompany the action; characters frequently break out of the plot and address the audience directly; and a large choral cantata further interrupts the action. The music includes grand orchestral sections (such as a "barbaric march" at the outbreak of the war) as well as vocal numbers that are highly differentiated in their musical design. Frequent use is made of Weill's old stylistic principle of integrating elements of popular music into opera. A rogues' trio, for example, which appears in every act (in a changing configuration), contains a rather shabby waltz as its "recognizable melody." But this is all there is in the way of cheerful sounds; as Ernst Bloch noted, "The amused humor is gone. Weill does not want to paper over the difficult time."[8]

Die Bürgschaft is set in the imaginary land of Urb. The main characters are the cattle dealer Johann Matthes, his wife Anna and daughter Luise, and the grain dealer David Orth and his son Jakob. The sentence is pronounced by the judge of Urb.

In the prologue the cattle dealer, who has gambled away all his money, is visited by his creditors. He runs to his friend the grain dealer for help. Without hesitation Orth offers to make a pledge for his friend. The commenting chorus sings, "Es ändert sich nicht der Mensch, es sind die Verhältnisse, die seine Haltung verändern" (It is not people themselves that change, it is only circumstances that change their conduct).

The first act takes place six years later. Herder's parable now goes as follows: Matthes buys a sack of grain from Orth and finds that a great deal of money is hidden in it. Orth knew that when he handed it over to him; he also knew that Matthes needed some money until his ship came in and that he would pay him back. Matthes first is silent and then, pressed by blackmailers, rushes to Orth and tries to give him the money back. Orth refuses, and the two agree to bring the case before a judge. At the end of the act the two principal characters sing, "Die Verhältnisse sind es, die seine Haltung verändern. Der Mensch ändert sich nicht" (It is only circumstances that change their conduct. People themselves do not change).

Act 2 opens with the verdict. The judge of Urb decides to marry the two children to each other and give them the money. But then Ellis, the commissar of the Great Forces that will soon take over Urb by violence, appears on the scene. He revises the sentence, has Matthes and Orth imprisoned, and confiscates the money. The cattle dealer's wife discovers that her daughter, Luise, has disappeared.

By the beginning of the third act, six more years have passed. Want and deprivation reign in Urb. Matthes and Orth have finished serving their prison terms and have now regained a degree of prosperity. The chorus reviews the events of the intervening years. A war broke out in Urb, and when it was over, want and deprivation spread throughout the land; brutality and violence grew rampant. Anna Matthes dies and the mob discovers that Matthes has been guilty of betrayal. He flees to Orth's house to seek help from his old friend. But the world has changed: Orth refuses to help him. The two fight. Orth wrestles Matthes to the ground and hands him over to the mob. Matthes is killed. The chorus concludes the opera with the observation, "Alles vollzieht sich nach einem Gesetz, dem

Program from the premiere of *Die Bürgschaft*, Weill's most
extensive score, at the Städtische Oper Berlin-Charlottenburg,
10 March 1932.

Gesetz des Geldes, dem Gesetz der Macht" (Everything follows one law, the law of money, the law of power).

In spite of its "timeless" and generally "human" aspects, there could be little question as to the targets of the opera. Words put into the mouth of the commissar of the Great Forces would soon become terrifying reality in Germany. "The system I represent needs new ground in order to anchor its existence"—who would not draw parallels to the catch phrase *Volk ohne Raum* (a people without room)? "If the land does not deliver us what we expect, we will have to resort to other means to force the land to meet our expectations"—did Hitler's emissaries not deal with the governments of Europe in this tone just a few years later? "In the sixth year after the arrival of the commissar war broke out. The army marches day and night, through fields and meadows, with tanks and cannons. Thus they march into the pit that will devour them"—was this not a visionary premonition of Hitler's war?

The National Socialists took the attack seriously. The 9 March 1932 issue of *Der völkische Beobachter* printed the following reaction: "The Städtische Oper Charlottenburg intends to give Germanness a slap in the face in the first half of March with the premiere of a new Kurt Weill opera, *Die Bürgschaft*. . . . This Jew has seen how his last opera [*Mahagonny*] led to trouble in Leipzig. . . . It is utterly incomprehensible, then, that an author who presents thoroughly un-German works is to be heard again at a theater supported by German taxpayers! May Israel be edified by this new opus of Weill's."

This piece of invective appeared the day before the premiere. Carl Ebert, the director of the Städtische Oper, did not let himself be swayed by it, though—something the Nazis did not forget. A few days after Hitler came to power on 30 January 1933 Ebert was "relieved" of his position, in no small measure because of his commitment to *Die Bürgschaft*.

Weill and Neher were constantly present during the last two weeks of rehearsal. Carl Ebert was directing the play, and the conductor was Fritz Stiedry. Ebert later described the atmosphere, especially Neher's strong personality: "During the rehearsal discussions— the best ones were with Fritz Stiedry (*Macbeth*, *Bürgschaft*) . . . —it was exciting to watch Caspar, to see how 'it' worked inside him, how his face was drawn in inner tension almost into a grimace, how he waited for the key word that would unleash his creativity."[9]

The premiere on 10 March 1932 at Berlin's Städtische Oper was a great success both for Weill and for the work. Although they did not overlook certain weaknesses in Neher's text and in the length of the work, the leading critics unanimously declared that Weill had blazed a new trail. Alfred Einstein wrote:

> This opera wears the face of the time, without, as in *Mahagonny*, holding a fist under the nose of the time. This opera is no longer a play or a dream, it no longer belongs to the "sphere of the beautiful"; it speaks directly to everyone. . . . Weill draws on the stylistic expression of his most mature work, *Der Jasager*, on that peculiar and convincing synthesis of the most modern hit rhythm and the most traditional Baroque arioso. . . . Strange that we are happiest when Weill breaks through the rigidity of formulas, when we hit upon a golden vein of musical inventiveness. . . . If there is a serious "opera of the times," it is *Die Bürgschaft* of Kurt Weill and Caspar Neher.[10]

Hans Heinz Stuckenschmidt discussed Weill's departure from Brechtian theater in a piece entitled "Weill am Scheidewege" (Weill at the Crossroads):

> If one were to strip Weill's music of all that gives it melodic and tonal contour, it would still have its magical impulse for plot. It is typical music of interjection, which, rooted in recitative, carries the action whenever words are damned to impotence. Brecht's epic theater uses such musical interjection with great artistic clairvoyance. Didactic theater needed it to give shape to its abstractions. Weill, separated from Brecht, is

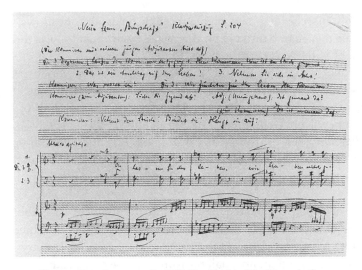

**Manuscript of a scene that Weill added to *Die Bürgschaft*
during rehearsals.**

seeking to make himself independent. His ambition drives him to pure opera; the strongest representative of functional music is using theater as a function of musical form.[11]

The political opponents of the progressive and avant-garde artistic developments of the Weimar Republic had grown much stronger than they were in 1930 when *Mahagonny* opened, however. They had already attained decisive power in many local and regional governments. *Die Bürgschaft* did not conform to their agenda. On top of indictments by the Nazi press, the *Kampfbund für deutsche Kultur* (Strike Force for German Culture), an organization of the NSDAP led by Alfred Rosenberg, began exerting pressure on theaters that had already signed options or contracts to perform Weill's new opera. Hamburg, Coburg, Königsberg, Duisburg, Stettin, and Leipzig all gave in and withdrew *Die Bürgschaft* from their programs—one sign of the political situation in Germany in mid-1932. Universal conveyed the following excerpts from two theater directors' letters to Weill: "Coburg: Considering the special constellation of the audience in Coburg I will scarcely be able to do the *Bürgschaft*. As you know, the entire right-wing press has made a particularly solid front against the work. . . . Hamburg: Unfortunately I cannot do the *Bürgschaft* at the moment. I have not been permitted. Since, as you know, we have to reckon with certain influences at present, I simply have to bow to these pressures."[12]

Two directors did not conform. A few weeks after the premiere the opera was performed in Düsseldorf (with W. Iltz directing and Jascha Horenstein conducting) and Wiesbaden (with Paul Bekker directing and Karl Rankl conducting). Paul Bekker had more to say about *Die Bürgschaft* in a book of "letters to contemporary musicians" (*Briefe an zeitgenössische Musiker*) that appeared not long thereafter. In his "Letter to Kurt Weill" he took up the question of the extent to which Weill's concept of a "timeless

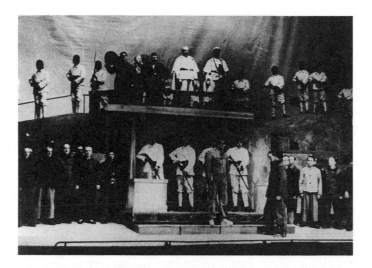

Scene from the premiere of *Die Bürgschaft*.

opera" meshed with the political allusions in Neher's text. Bekker professes to be an adherent of "political opera," which, as in Mozart's *Don Giovanni,* he sees as "great and lasting precisely because it has soaked up contemporary reality completely and has only left its costume." Speaking directly to Weill, the letter closes: "So I think that you will write a folk opera [*Volksoper*] for us again, with or without chorus. All the undercurrents of political thinking and feeling could flow into this, returning to their origins, and here the joy of being could have free play, the joy that overcomes all the tragedy of circumstances and that finds its life goal in a constantly renewed affirmation."[13]

Weill must have read Bekker's book, for soon the term *Volksoper* turns up for the first time in his discussions of new projects. The increasing difficulties with theaters—which the performance history of *Die Bürgschaft* had shown clearly—forced Weill to reconsider things. The months of May to July 1932 became a time of search and reflection before he settled into a concrete piece of work. In May he wrote to his publisher: "Having established the genre of school opera with the *Jasager* I now want to develop a new type of work which I would like to call the 'layman's opera'—that is, operas which can be performed by laymen, this time not by children, but by adults. I believe . . . that with such pieces, which aren't necessarily dependent upon opera houses, I will best be able to demonstrate how I plan to help myself when the theaters are too dumb and cowardly to perform my works."[14] There are direct links between these reflections about easily comprehensible works, as well as the projects he considered as possible "folk operas," and Weill's later work in the United States, especially the phase of *Down in the Valley.*

Soon thereafter Weill mentioned as possible projects *Romeo und Julia,* "a folk opera that takes place in a market hall, a love story of simple young people"; *Onkel Toms Hütte* (Uncle Tom's Cabin), "a simple folk opera based on the famous novel"; and "a play with music based on an actual event from the Genoa peace conference of 1910." In addition he was considering an opera on Georg Kaiser's play *Die jüdische Witwe* (The Jewish Widow) and a school opera *Naboths Weinberg* (Naboth's Vineyard). Also, a "musical folk play with a clear political line" would be appropriate now, a play "for proletarian circles."[15] None of these projects came to fruition, however.

Toward the end of June 1932, in search of performance possibilities outside opera houses, Kurt Weill contacted Berlin's revue king Erik Charell, director of the Großes Schauspielhaus (formerly the Zirkus Schumann) and creator of the new genre of the revue operetta, who had launched his house with *Im weißen Rössl* (In The Little White Horse). Charell did not show much enthusiasm for any of Weill's proposed projects but suggested instead that Weill compose a musical play on the old German silent picture *Das Kabinett des Dr. Caligari* (The Cabinet of Dr. Caligari). On 28 June 1932 Charell, Weill, and Neher saw the film together, and two days later Georg Kaiser was invited to join in the collaboration—an invitation he immediately accepted. Three days of intensive work followed, and on 7 July Weill, Kaiser, and Neher presented Charell with a first prospectus, which was rejected. Unsuccessful though this episode was, it did bring one important result. Through the coincidence of Charell's suggestion of an expressionist silent film, the expressionism "expert" Kaiser had been brought in. Thus the long-interrupted working relationship between Weill and Kaiser (who had never lost touch with each other personally) was resumed. Weill wrote: "The Kaiser–Neher–Weill collaboration has gone so well that I am firmly convinced that it will bear fruit beyond the Charell project. I would like this team to write folk plays which would be somewhere between opera and spoken drama."[16]

Soon Georg Kaiser made Weill such an offer. In the town of Grünheide Weill began the last work that he would complete in Germany, *Der Silbersee* (The Silver Lake). On 29 July Weill wrote:

> Kaiser wants to write a musical folk play with me. He has come up with a very nice, truly Kaiserian idea on which we have been working for several days. I believe that we will already have an outline for this play by the beginning of next week. It isn't to be an opera, but a work between genres. It remains up to me whether it is a "play with music," that is, with simple songs sung by plain actors, or whether I want to make greater musical demands and write music of the length and difficulty of, say, an Offenbach musiquette.

After only a short period of intensive joint work, a first draft of the text was completed, which Kaiser simultaneously prepared for book publication by Kiepenheuer Verlag. The story of the *Wintermärchen* (Winter Fairy Tale), as it is called in the subtitle, shows clear ties to the situation in Germany in mid-1932. Five unemployed young men are living in a cottage on the edge of town. Driven by hunger, they rob a grocery store in town. The robbery is discovered, and Severin, their leader, is shot by the policeman Olim as they try to escape. Olim soon regrets his action; when he wins the jackpot in the lottery, he buys a mansion, gets Severin out of the police hospital, and takes him in, hoping to restore him to health and to make up for what he has done to him. Two impoverished members of the nobility, Frau von Luber and Baron Laur, work as servants in the mansion. A niece of Frau von Luber named Fennimore is brought to the mansion to entertain Severin. She tells him the legend of the nearby silver lake, which can freeze over even in summer to save those in need. A grand conspiracy on the part of the two housekeepers does Olim out of his mansion. While the two conspirators revel in their triumph, Severin and Olim, now both without means, run to the silver lake to drown themselves. When they get there, they find that the lake has frozen over, although the winter is long past and the sun is shining. Led, as it were, by Fennimore's voice, Severin and Olim step out onto the lake and disappear into the distance: "Wer weiter muß, den trägt der Silbersee" (Those who must go on will be carried by the silver lake).

Weill wrote sixteen self-contained musical numbers for the play. He realized his wish to write a "work between genres" both in terms of its musical demands (the parts of Fennimore and Severin require trained voices, and a chorus is used) and in terms of its orchestration (the score calls for twenty-four instrumentalists).

In *Der Silbersee* Weill's characteristic European theater style is very impressively developed. The music begins with an overture, whose polyphonic richness, runs of fifths, and contrapuntal complexity immediately make one sit up and listen. In the first scene the unemployed young men bury a figure symbolizing hunger. Weill set the lines "Wir tragen den Toten zu Grabe" (We are carrying the dead to the grave) to a gripping funeral march (*alla marcia funebre*). Then Severin sings "Der Bäcker bäckt ums Morgenrot das allerbeste Weizenbrot" (When at dawn the sky turns red, the baker bakes the best wheat bread), an aggressive song that approaches the style of Eisler's war songs and articulates the young men's right to a dignified existence. This is followed, in the grocery store scene, by a slow waltz by the sales clerks, "Wir sind zwei Mädchen, die an jedermann verkaufen" (We are two girls who sell to everyone). This song—which the girls sing while they destroy groceries to keep the prices high—is set to a spare waltz rhythm. In places Weill distorts the harmonies to the point where a laugh sticks in the throat of the listener. Then comes the robbery and Olim's shot. The chorus comments on the action in a style that is severe, at times almost exhortatory. When Olim wins the lottery money, an agent gives him advice on how to invest it. Weill wrote one of his most biting, and also most beautiful, tango adaptations for this scene. Again, as in *Die Bürgschaft,* money is at the center of the plot and drives the characters. Bourgeois icons are shattered when the violins accompany such lines as "Das produziert die Krone des Gewinns: Zins und Zinseszins!" (This is what brings the greatest profit: interest and interest on interest!) with a shabby tango beat. At the end of the first act Olim and Severin arrive at the mansion. The first thing they hear is "Fennimores Lied," with its refrain "Ich bin eine arme Verwandte" (I am a poor relative).

When Fennimore is asked to entertain Severin at supper, she first performs a comical dance on the tabletop using two bananas—inspired by Charlie Chaplin's famous fork and roll dance from the movie *Gold Rush*—accompanied in the orchestra by a sharply syncopated fox-trot rhythm. Then she immediately launches into the "Ballade von Cäsars Tod" (Ballad of the Death of Caesar). The apocalyptic march that Weill composed for this number gives musical force to its explosive power. An analogy is clearly being drawn between Caesar and Hitler: "Er verfolgte seine frechen Ziele und sah schon als Herrn der Römer sich" (He pursued his brazen goals and already saw himself as lord of the Romans). The song's conclusion, supported by weighty octave runs in the orchestra, again holds plenty of political explosive power with its line "Cäsar wollte mit dem Schwert regieren und ein Messer hat ihn selbst gefällt" (Caesar wanted to reign with the sword, and a knife cut him down).

This is followed by a duet between Severin and Fennimore that is musically closely related to the "Kranich-Duett" in *Mahagonny*. The accompanying arabesques in the woodwinds paint a picture of the silver lake as a poetic, heightened metaphor of great force. The purity of the silver lake is meant as an alternative both for the lovers on the stage and for the listener.

The third act again opens with an orchestral prelude in which motifs from the overture are taken up and expanded. Severin, who does not know that it was Olim who fired the shot, is still looking for the perpetrator. He sings a grand aria of revenge, "Es wird nicht vergessen, es wird nicht vergeben" (It will not be forgotten, it will not be forgiven), which is vocally extremely challenging. This is followed by the conspiracy and triumph of the two plotters. They sing as a duet the "Lied vom Schlaraffenland" (Song of Never-Never Land), a bitterly malicious, aggressive piece that is frequently interrupted by the orchestra. Severin and Olim, who have found each other and are reconciled, are chased away and decide to die together.

The grand finale at the silver lake is introduced by a long, quasi-pantomime scene in which Severin and Olim discover the miracle of the frozen lake. The chorus leads them and at the same time comments on their thoughts and actions. Then the rhythm suddenly changes, and a light orchestral allegretto provides a transition to Fennimore's visionary song, which guides them both over the lake. Once again Weill returns to the rhythm of "Fennimores Lied," not unlike a barcarole, before Fennimore's voice and the chorus merge in the final sequence: "Wer weiter muß, den trägt der Silbersee" (Those who must go on will be carried by the silver lake). Nine orchestral measures, now pianissimo, close the work and leave the listeners to their own thoughts and reflections.

Weill had completed the composition by the end of October 1932, and again he himself took the initiative in finding performance possibilities. On 13 November he drove to Dresden to present the work to the manager Reucker. "He was extremely pleased with it and we have already talked about casting (Ponto as Olim, Reiner as Severin), stage director: Gielen, set designer: Neher, conductor: Busch. That would be a performance the likes of which we could scarcely get in Berlin."[17] Eight days later came the rejection: "Reucker has rejected a performance of the work because he finds it too crass and biting for what he called his 'Court Theater subscription audience.'"[18] Immediately Weill began negotiating again, this time with the Deutsches Theater in Berlin (it is "offering us a truly imposing premiere with a major cast and the fullest accommodation of all our desires") and with Leipzig (theater director "Sierck is enthusiastic. Brecher has called me to say that he himself will conduct").[19]

The Deutsches Theater also clearly had misgivings, however, and did not pursue the matter further, so the possibility of a Berlin premiere once again evaporated for Weill. At

**In March 1932 Weill and Lenya moved into this house at
Wißmannstraße 9 (now Käthe-Kollwitz-Straße) in the artists'
suburb of Kleinmachnow.**

that point Universal concluded a contract with Leipzig and drew Magdeburg and Erfurt into a joint premiere. On 2 January 1933 the publisher informed the composer of its decision.

Thus the year 1932 ended, and with it came a major rupture in Weill's personal life. At the beginning of March Weill and Lenya had moved into their own house in the artists' suburb of Kleinmachnow, a good half-hour's drive from Berlin. Their growing professional obligations—Weill's frequent trips away from Berlin for performances and negotiations, and Lenya's burgeoning career in theater, cabaret, film, and recording studio— had left them with less and less time for each other in the years since the premiere of *Die Dreigroschenoper.* In the fall of 1931 Lenya had spent three months in the Soviet Union with Erwin Piscator's crew filming Anna Seghers's short story *Der Aufstand der Fischer*

(The Fishermen's Uprising). This trip did not result immediately in a film, however; not until 1934 did Piscator complete a film, and it did not have Lenya in it. Weill had also taken a number of lengthy vacations in France, Switzerland, and Spain by himself. In short, the two had been growing apart.

Lotte Lenya accepted an offer to participate in a Viennese production of *Aufstieg und Fall der Stadt Mahagonny* in April 1932 (the production opened on 26 April in the Raimund-Theater and had eleven performances), and there she met the singer Otto Pasetti, a member of the local ensemble. They took a liking to each other and decided to live and travel together for a while. Lenya suggested a divorce to Weill in the summer of 1932; presumably she was also aware of his attraction to Erika Neher. Weill agreed, and a Berlin lawyer was hired to take care of the necessary formalities. In spite of this decision, the two maintained a friendly relationship and told each other in an extended correspondence about their various plans and doings. By the time the divorce was made final on 18 September 1933, Weill had been out of Germany for six months.

The Nazis and Weill

Like so many other German artists and intellectuals, Kurt Weill was not fully aware of just how deadly serious a turn had been taken in political developments in Germany. Although he had been a constant target of vehement attacks from the NSDAP and the DNVP press ever since *Die Dreigroschenoper,* and especially since the *Mahagonny* opera, he did not believe that the National Socialists stood a real chance of coming to power. Meanwhile, though, the pace of events picked up. On 17 November 1932 the cabinet of Chancellor Franz von

Weill in 1933, the year he left Germany for France.

Papen resigned, and on 19 November Reich President Hindenburg offered Hitler the position of chancellor of a parliamentary majority. By this time Hitler was confident enough of his own strength to reject the offer and demand total state power for the NSDAP instead. Hindenburg still hesitated.

Two days after Weill had completed the score of *Der Silbersee* in Kleinmachnow (it is dated 1 December) the transitional cabinet that Hindenburg had put together under the former Minister of Defense Kurt von Schleicher took office. Schleicher openly admitted that his objective was "to give German politics a breathing space of twelve weeks while negotiations are held between those in power and Hitler."[1] In the bitterly cold winter months of 1932–33 the fate of the Weimar Republic was sealed.

Weill and Neher were intensively occupied with a film project in January 1933. The "Europa-Film" company in Berlin was working on a film adaptation of Hans Fallada's successful novel *Kleiner Mann, was nun?* (Little Man, What Now?), which Rowohlt had published in early 1932. Berthold Viertel was lined up to direct the film, and Fallada himself was to write the script. Neher and Weill were asked to provide the sets and the music, and they had long conversations about it. Weill wrote: "In this way I hope . . . to realize at least something of the new form of musical film I have in mind. . . . In accordance with the subject matter I will write as popular a music as possible and in particular am going to center it on a song with the refrain, 'Kleiner Mann, was nun?'"[2]

Lenya in front of the Reichstag building in Berlin in 1932.

GEORG KAISER
DER SILBERSEE
EIN WINTERMÄRCHEN
IN DREI AKTEN

GUSTAV KIEPENHEUER VERLAG · BERLIN

Cover designed by Caspar Neher for the libretto of *Der Silbersee,* the last work to be published by Gustav Kiepenheuer Verlag before Hitler's accession to power in January 1933.

This project never materialized, however; political events prevented both Weill and Viertel from continuing their work on the film, which was eventually made in the summer of 1933 under the direction of Fritz Wendhausen, with music by Harald Böhmelt and sets by Caspar Neher.

We do not know if Kurt Weill heard the radio broadcast of the torchlight procession with which the SA celebrated Hitler's accession to power on 30 January 1933. But again, his reaction was similar to that of many German intellectuals: dismay mixed with the conviction that Hitler and his henchmen stood little chance of governing for long, that it was all just a "Hitler chimera," as Brecht called it. Six days after the seizure of power Weill wrote, "I consider what is going on here so sickening that I cannot imagine it lasting more than a couple of months." At the same time he admitted, "But one could be very wrong."[3] Hans W. Heinsheimer replied by return mail from Vienna: "I cannot agree that the course in Germany might only be a nightmare lasting a few months. I am filled with the deepest pessimism because I believe that only now will we pay the price for underestimating the opponent, that only now will we see that they will maintain a better, firmer, and more ruthless hold on everything than the Republicans ever dared to do over fifteen years. So how will this situation concretely affect *Silbersee?*"[4]

Rehearsals had already begun for the work's premiere in Leipzig, Magdeburg, and Erfurt when Hitler came to power. Naturally it took weeks, even months, for the NSDAP's

**Ernst Busch (*standing*) as Severin in the highly successful
Magdeburg production of *Der Silbersee* in 1933.**

"reorganization of German cultural activity" to be implemented throughout the country. Whereas the new regime turned almost immediately to "cleansing" the radio, as the most important of the mass media, provincial theater remained relatively undisturbed, at least in the first weeks. The case of *Der Silbersee* reflects the course of developments.

Of course the Nazis intervened massively, but the theaters stood by the work, and the premiere was able to take place. The Leipzig director Detlef Sierck remembered:

> The Nazis came into power, and one of their town councilors, a man called Hauptmann . . . asked me to drop the play. Otherwise, he told me, something would happen. So I got together with Kaiser, Weill, and Neher, since it concerned them personally as well, but we decided to go ahead, feeling the play to be artistically as well as politically very important. On the morning of the opening Dr. Goerdeler called me and advised that it would be best for me to fall ill and postpone the opening for a couple of weeks, and then everything could be let quietly drop. I told him that I thought it was a time

ALTES THEATER

Sonnabend, den 18. Februar 1933

Außer Anrecht

Uraufführung

„Der Silbersee"

Ein Wintermärchen von Georg Kaiser — Musik von Kurt Weill

In Szene gesetzt von Detlef Sierck

Musikalische Leitung: Gustav Brecher

Leipziger Sinfonie-Orchester

Olim	Erhard Siedel
Severin	Alexander Golling
Frau von Luber	Lina Carstens
Fennimore	Gretl Berndt
Laur	Ernst Sattler
Der dicke Landjäger	Wilhelm Engst
Alter Arzt	Karl Huth
Junger Arzt	Walter Kiesler
Krankenschwester	Gert Riederer
Erster	Max Noack
Zweiter	Martin Flörchinger
Dritter Bursche	Joachim Gottschalk
Vierter	Hans Tenhoff
Ein Diener	Artur Nicklas
Lotterieagent	Albert Garbe
Eine Zofe	Irmgard Fischer
Ein Sänger	Hans Lißmann

Chöre gesungen von Mitgliedern des Opernchores, Leitung Konrad Neuger

Bühnenbilder: Caspar Neher

Änderungen vorbehalten

Kleinere Pause nach dem vierten Bild

Größere Pause nach dem zweiten Akt (zehnten Bild)

Rückgabe von Eintrittskarten wegen Umbesetzungen ausgeschlossen

Einlaß 19½ Uhr   Anfang 20 Uhr   Ende 23 Uhr

Preis des Programms 30 Pfg.

Program from Leipzig's Altes Theater, one of
the theaters participating in the joint premiere
of *Der Silbersee* on 18 February 1933, the
others being in Magdeburg and Erfurt.

221549

SECHS STÜCKE AUS DER MUSIK ZUM SCHAUSPIEL

VON

GEORG KAISER

DER SILBERSEE

VON

KURT WEILL

UNIVERSAL-EDITION, WIEN / LEIPZIG

No. 10.471

The last publication of Weill's music by
Universal was a selection of six songs from *Der
Silbersee* for voice and piano, in February 1933.
The drawing for the cover is by Max
Oppenheimer (Mopp).

when it would be disastrous not to stand by one's opinion and give in. He then told me
that he had information that the SA and the Nazi Party would block the opening, and
he would seriously advise me to call the whole thing off. I said I wouldn't. Only two
people can call off the play, I told him—he, as the mayor of Leipzig, or I, as the sole
person responsible for the Altes Theater. He answered that if things went badly he
might not be able to cover me.[5]

The premiere on 18 February 1933 turned out to be a memorable occasion. Kaiser
and Weill had traveled from Berlin to Leipzig, along with many of their acquaintances—
theater people and journalists. Hans Rothe writes: "Everyone who counted in the German Theater met together for the last time. And everyone knew this. The atmosphere
there can hardly be described. It was the last day of the greatest decade of German culture
in the twentieth century. The Nazis' barracking and yelling were somewhat disturbing.
But in spite of that, it was a great evening, certainly the most impressive theatrical evening
I have ever been present at."[6] The performances in Magdeburg (where Ernst Busch played
the part of Severin as a guest from Berlin) and Erfurt were similarly emphatic successes.

The last Weill recording to be released in Germany before the war, of two songs from Der Silbersee, came out in February 1933. Lenya also recorded two songs from this work under the direction of Gustav Brecher, but the record was not released.

Right after the premieres the Berlin label Gloria released a recording of the "Lied vom Schlaraffenland" and "Der Bäcker bäckt ums Morgenrot" sung by Ernst Busch and conducted by Maurice Abravanel. This record could still be put on the market for a little while; but a second one that Electrola recorded at the end of February with Lotte Lenya and Gustav Brecher could not be released. Universal published a piano reduction in February 1933, as well as an edition of selections entitled *Sechs Stücke aus der Musik zum Schauspiel "Der Silbersee"* (Six Pieces from the Music to the Play "Der Silbersee").

Only a few real reviews could appear in the Berlin press, which had already been subjected to a heavy dose of *Gleichschaltung*. Hans Heinz Stuckenschmidt, for example, had to publish his article in the New York journal *Modern Music*. Rolf Nürnberg, in a review entitled "Großer Kaiser-Weill-Erfolg in Leipzig" (Huge Kaiser–Weill Success in Leipzig), gave a detailed assessment of the piece and then went on to write: "In order to attend a theater performance today that engages its audience and does not let the culture of theater wither away; in order to find theater atmosphere and theater work, one must leave the precincts of Berlin and go to Leipzig."[7]

The attacks in the Nazi press were all the more vehement. The *Leipziger Tageszeitung* wrote: "Kaiser, though not himself a Jew, belongs to the circle of Berlin literary Hebrews. His latest clumsy piece of staged junk is called *Der Silbersee* and has "music" by Weill. As is well known, this is the gentleman who gave us the whores' songs from the Three Penny and Mahagonny world. A person who gives himself over to such vile things, who goes

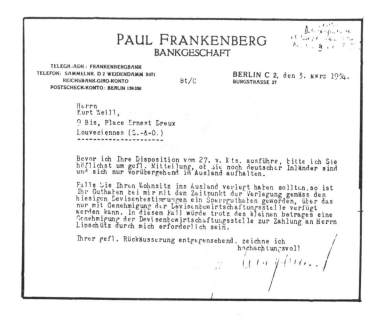

Letter of March 1934 from Weill's Berlin bank to his Louveciennes address, telling him that his assets are frozen.

along with Brechtian and Kaiserian dirt and is thus of its nature and its sort, should not be treated as a serious composer."[8]

The *Völkischer Beobachter* openly threatened those who participated in the premiere:

Detlef Sierck has rendered the Jewish literati . . . a service that he may pay for dearly. . . . One must treat a composer like Weill with distrust, especially when he, as a Jew, allows himself to use a German opera stage for his un-German purposes. . . . The most shameful thing is that the general music director of the city of Leipzig, Gustav Brecher, has lent himself to such a performance! A man with any sensitivity— and of all times five days after the fiftieth anniversary of the death of Richard Wagner, in the middle of the commemorations by the opera house that is unfortunately still entrusted to him!—would have rejected this kind of presentation! Recently, at the commemorative celebrations, Mister Brecher scrutinized our Führer rather closely in the Gewandhaus. I had the opportunity to observe this. Now he will come to know the Führer and the . . . power that emanates from him much better![9]

The threat would be tragically fulfilled seven years later, in 1940, when Brecher, fleeing before the advancing Hitler army, committed suicide in the Belgian town of Ostend.

The campaign to withdraw *Der Silbersee* was first mounted in Magdeburg, a center of German militarism and headquarters of the *Stahlhelm* and its head, Franz Seldte. On 21 February, three days after the premiere, the following "community declaration" was issued:

With indignation and the sharpest of protests the German public in Magdeburg objects to the degradation of art to the one-sided, un-German propaganda of Bolshevist theories that has taken hold in the Magdeburger Stadttheater. The performance of the play by Georg Kaiser and Kurt Weill is a slap in the face of the national population. With shameless importunity this play preaches the idea of class hate and contains innumerable open and veiled invitations to violence.

The Magdeburger Stadttheater, kept afloat through difficult times by the tax pennies of the entire population, should be supporting the cultural and national ascent of the German people, but through the hand of its director Götze it has become an instrument of utterly inartistic attempts at Bolshevization.

The public, represented by the undersigned associations and organizations, therefore demands in the name of countless citizens, including those not included in them, the immediate withdrawal of the play.

NSDAP, Kreisleitung Magdeburg/Women's League of the NSDAP, Kreis Magdeburg/Strike Force for German Culture, Landesleitung Sachsen-Anhalt/Stahlhelm, Association of Soldiers from the Front, Gründergau Magdeburg/German National People's Party, Kreisverein Magdeburg/Strike Force of the Professional Middle Class/Association of Queen Luise.[10]

The theaters could no longer withstand the pressure. On 27 February the Reichstag went up in flames in Berlin; by the beginning of March *Der Silbersee* had been withdrawn from all three theaters. With the close of the last performance in Leipzig, on 4 March 1933, Weill's music fell silent in Germany for the next twelve years of the brown night.

When news reached Weill, the day after the Reichstag fire, of the wave of arrests which had taken place that same night and which had included numerous intellectuals—especially writers and journalists—he no longer doubted that he, too, was personally in danger. He fled the house in Kleinmachnow, leaving it in the care of the maid, and moved first to a hotel in Westend and soon thereafter, at the beginning of March, to the home of Caspar and Erika Neher.[11] On 15 March Weill—who already had his eye on France—met the French film director Jean Renoir in Berlin to discuss possible projects. Again, urgent warnings reached him to leave Berlin and Germany. On 21 March, the "Day of Potsdam," on which a ceremony was held in front of the Garnisonskirche at which Hindenburg officially, and with great pomp, handed over power to Hitler (power that Hitler had already been exercising for nearly two months), Weill hesitated no longer. He packed his personal belongings, climbed into the Nehers' car with a small suitcase, and drove with them via Luxembourg to France. On 23 March 1933 Weill arrived in Paris. The Neher couple returned to Berlin, but Weill rented a room in the Hotel Splendide. Germany lay behind him; his life as an émigré had begun.

In order to understand the further development of the composer, it is essential at this juncture to take a brief look at the treatment that both the person and the music of Kurt Weill received at the hands of the Nazi regime from 1933 on. Weill became a preferred, if not indeed the prime, symbol in the crusade against "Jewish cultural bolshevism" and the "degenerate art of the mechanical age," as the progressive concepts and artistic directions of the Weimar Republic were now called.

The indescribably low level of the attacks and vituperations and the filthy language of the invectives hurt the sensitive Weill (who naturally got word of it all in exile) as much as the ban on his music, the destruction of his published music and recordings, and the desecration of his Jewish beliefs. His decision to break radically with Germany and to take leave altogether of German and European traditions in his music—as he did from about 1938 on in the United States—has its basis here. This is important to bear in mind whenever we think about the "two Weills."

As early as the end of 1931 the "theoretical mouthpiece" of the NSDAP, the *National-sozialistische Monatshefte* (published by Adolf Hitler with Alfred Rosenberg as editor), had contained a key article by Walter Trienes about the work of Weill and Brecht. Entitled "Neudeutsche Opern'kultur'" (New German Opera "Culture") it said for example:

> Detailed observations and investigations regarding the Weill–Brecht type itself are surely unnecessary, since much too much has already been made of these "bearers of culture." But critical illumination is needed of what we can expect from these people regarding their "attempts at education." . . . The most conspicuous aspect of Weill's music is jazz rhythm. If Weill is intentionally bringing Negro rhythms into German art music, he is only making practical application of what the Jew Bernhard Sekles as a director of the Hochsches Konservatorium in Frankfurt am Main pronounced in his introduction to a class on jazz music: that a transfusion of Negro blood could not hurt us. So the people that brought forth a Bach, Mozart, Beethoven, and Wagner needs to be rejuvenated with Negro blood. . . . In summary one can only say over and over again that Brechtian texts and Weillian music are never to be regarded as German art.[12]

In 1933 a whole series of "Bekenntnisse zur neuen deutschen Musik" (Affirmations of New German Music) appeared, soon after the establishment of the Nazi dictatorship; here again, everything that Weill had stood for in the years since 1925 was dragged through the dirt. People who had little voice before 1933 because of their poor quality now styled themselves as "expert" writers. Here are three examples from the year 1933. Helmut Kötzsch:

> Of course the likes of Weill, Brecht, Křenek, Wagner-Régeny saw only the negative side of people and worked only destructively, taking pleasure in relativizing whatever existed, in breaking apart and destroying, and without any belief in elemental humanity, without a connection to the nation, without an authentic ethos, without a future, and ultimately without meaning.[13]

Friedrich Walter:

> What all has washed over us! Here contemporary opera—there school opera, youth and school music, *Gebrauchsmusik*, amateur and community music. Only a complete lack of critical faculties (toward their own output), hubris, and a lack of instinct are to blame that a development could take hold in our music which can only be understood as a *sin against the spirit*. For how else are we to explain the abstruse concoctions of

**This book by the "anti-Semitic specialist" Christa Maria Rock
appeared in Munich in late 1935. Weill was, of course,
listed in this *Musical ABC of Jews*.**

those bygone years? Certain sorts of composers cropped up among us who came from all over the world and found their sought-after Eldorado here where they could dispose of their wares. Clever little heads, but strangely enough they did not know how to distinguish between such elementary things as a chorale and a fox-trot; they might write a Salvation Army song one day and a choral fantasy the next (Weill).[14]

One of the displays at the exhibition "Entartete Musik," part
of the Reich Music Days in Düsseldorf in 1938.

Karl Grunsky:

As a natural basic form of human existence the Jew in his lasciviousness seems to be
drawn to the world of whores and pimps. *Die Dreigroschenoper* and *Mahagonny*
swarm with vulgarities. . . . One would think that such coarseness would be rejected
everywhere. But that is not so: W. E. Schäfer payed homage to the "talented piece."
Nor was there any opposition along Berlin's Kurfürstendamm. Why the Jew Max
Reinhardt withdrew the announced Berlin performance of *Mahagonny* is not
clear. . . . To complete this betrayal, modern jacks-of-all-trades even write didactic
and school plays especially for our schools—Weill his *Jasager,* which was received as a

Cover of the brochure for the exhibit "Entartete Musik." The Star of David, the caricature of a black jazz musician, and the saxophone were used by the Nazis as symbols of the "degenerate" progressive music of the Weimar Republic.

message of glad tidings. Young squawkers who are seeking their way without any sense of what is *völkisch* are supposed to work with these musical greats! Jazz, *Jonny, Dreigroschenoper*—these are their lifeblood. Since Adolf Hitler has become Reich chancellor, such pranks are now a thing of the past. The tide has begun to turn. German music is gradually liberating itself from the deadly embrace.[15]

In 1935 the so-called Institute for the Study of the Jewish Question published its "standard work" entitled *Die Juden in Deutschland* (The Jews in Germany). The Nazis counted this book alongside *Mein Kampf* as one of their "books for the home," and it was issued in large print runs year after year. In the chapter on "Jews as 'Stewards' of German Culture" Kurt Weill was the focus of the discussion of music:

> This list [from Mendelssohn to Offenbach and Korngold] would be incomplete, however, were it not to include the name of the Jewish composer in whom the line descending from Offenbach's can-can operetta has reached its preliminary high point: Kurt Weill. . . . The indescribably banal melodies he added to the libretto that Bert Brecht pieced together from stolen texts is still fresh in our memories. In addition to the anarchistic didactic play *Der Jasager,* the so-called opera *Mahagonny* also arose in conjunction with this evil literary bolshevism. . . . It hardly seems possible today that this kind of nonsense, this monstrous spawn of snooty nihilism, was at one time actually performed on German stages with the participation of German musicians, singers, and actors.[16]

At the notorious exhibition "Entartete Musik" (Degenerate Music), part of the so-called Reichsmusiktage (Reich Music Days) mounted in Düsseldorf in 1938, several "display placards" were devoted to Weill, and the old *Dreigroschen* records were played as typical examples of "degeneration." An accompanying brochure was written by Hans Severus, a government official who had organized the exhibition and had taken over the direction of the Deutsches Nationaltheater in Weimar. The brochure's cover—a caricature of a black man wearing the Star of David and playing the saxophone—left no question as to the Nazis' cynical agenda. The text that Severus wrote is similarly pernicious: "What has been brought together in the exhibition is the reflection of a veritable witches' sabbath and of the most frivolous intellectual and artistic cultural bolshevism and a reflection of the triumph of the subhuman, of arrogant Jewish impudence and complete intellectual imbecility."[17]

The publisher of the leading German musical lexicon, the "Riemann," planned a new edition in 1938–39, because the eleventh edition edited by Alfred Einstein in 1929 could clearly no longer be reprinted without revisions. A relatively unassuming Nazi partisan, Josef Müller-Blattau of the University of Königsberg, was commissioned to prepare the new edition. In February 1939 Schott released the first two issues, a total of 128 pages comprising the letters A to D. This is as far as the new twelfth edition ever got, though, for the interventions were still too minimal for the Nazis.

> One would have expected, now that the Reich of Adolf Hitler has carried out the ultimate separation between what is non-Jewish and what is Jewish in the area of cultural, intellectual, and scholarly life, that the new Riemann would show a suitably radical departure from the editorial practice of an Einstein. But what has happened? All the Jewry that had embedded itself in our culture in the last decades is honored with extensive tributes. . . . Some day the whole brood will march back in through the door where the Abes and Abrahams hide their grinning faces—by "legal means," of course. The Kestenbergs, Kerrs, and company all have reason to be thankful to the German professor of the University of Königsberg, Müller-Blattau.[18]

LEXIKON DER JUDEN
IN DER MUSIK

Mit einem Titelverzeichnis
jüdischer Werke

Zusammengestellt im Auftrag der Reichsleitung
der NSDAP. auf Grund behördlicher, parteiamtlich
geprüfter Unterlagen

bearbeitet von

Dr. Theo Stengel
Referent in der Reichsmusikkammer

in Verbindung mit

Dr. habil. Herbert Gerigk
Leiter des Amtes Musik beim Beauftragten des Führers
für die Überwachung der gesamten geistigen und weltanschaulichen
Schulung und Erziehung der NSDAP.

Title page of the official Nazi "lexicon" of Jewish musical
personalities, first published in 1941. Its most extensive
slanderous article was devoted to Weill.

A further "reckoning" with the music of "the time of decay" appeared in 1940, in a book by Walter Trienes entitled *Musik in Gefahr* (Music in Danger). Here he wrote, for example: "The ethical nadir was reached in *Die Dreigroschenoper* and the *Stadt Mahagonny* by the nihilists Brecht and Weill. . . . The Jews' blasphemy against God found pictorial expression in the impious pictures of a Grosz (Jew), and it returned in Weill's (Jew) *Mahagonny*; Toller's (Jew) *Feuer aus den Kesseln* [Draw the Fires] and Wolf's (Jew) *Matrosen von Cattaro* [The Sailors from Cattaro] found their musical counterpart in Landé's (Jew) Communist oratorio *Potemkin* and Weill's (Jew) piece of class warfare, *Die Bürgschaft*."[19]

Weill's name did not make it into the new "Riemann," which was prevented from going beyond the letter D, but he was given "suitable" attention in the official Nazi *Lexikon der Juden in der Musik* (Lexicon of Jews in Music), which was first published in 1941 by the Berlin publisher Hahnefeld and went through numerous reprintings. Let us

close our selection of Nazi voices on Kurt Weill here, a selection whose hate and igno-
rance are indicative of the overall official cultural policy of the NSDAP from 1933 to 1945.
According to this lexicon, Weill was "inseparable from the worst subversion of our art.
His stage works show baldly and unscrupulously the Jewish-anarchistic tendency. . . .
His *Dreigroschenoper* written jointly with Bert Brecht . . . was touted by Jews and their
panderers as a revolutionary upheaval of all musico-dramatic art."[20]

Thus sullied by those who now ruled Germany, Kurt Weill received due appreciation
and honor from those who represented true German culture from 1933 on: the exiles.
Several important books on the music of the Weimar Republic were published by émigré
presses, books that made clear how significant a role Kurt Weill had played in the years
since the premiere of *Der Protagonist* in 1926 in Dresden. It is good to know that these
books, too, made their way to Weill. In 1934 Zurich's Atlantis Verlag published Paul
Bekker's book *Wandlungen der Oper* (Changes in Opera). In the chapter on
"Nachkriegsoper" (Postwar Opera) Bekker described the innovations of *Die Dreigroschenoper* and the *Mahagonny* opera in detail and then went on to say: "The most
powerful and, for the time being, last attempt of this sort [an opera that strives to enliven
the voices] is Weill's *Die Bürgschaft*. Here another kind of connection is shown between
speech and song. . . . It rests not on their blending and mutually intensifying each other
but on their running alongside each other on different, closely related levels. Word and
melodic speech appear no longer as an organic but as a combined unity."[21]

In spite of all the official attempts at eradication, the old recordings of Weill's music
were secretly kept and listened to by many German families. The London cultural histo-
rian John Willett recounts a wonderful example of this:

> In the summer of the Munich crisis my friend Tim Bennett went to look at the
> Weißenhofsiedlung at Stuttgart, that showpiece collection of thirty-three houses by
> outstanding modern architects from Behrens to Le Corbusier. . . . In one of the three
> most uncompromisingly functional houses on the whole estate—those built by the
> Dutch Communist architect Mart Stam—Tim had been asked in to have tea and listen
> to the banned records of *The Threepenny Opera*. And I have before me the dingy grey
> book which his unknown host gave him: an English translation of *The Great Hunger*
> by the Norwegian novelist Johan Bojer. On the flyleaf is written "Memento of an
> afternoon spent in Stuttgart in Mart Stam's house, to music by Kurt Weill. 13 Aug.
> 1938."[22]

When this dedication was written, Kurt Weill was already living in the United States.
He was one of many thousands of representatives of German intellectual life (if one
counts the less prominent or even not at all prominent) who had been forced to leave their
homeland and were now participating in an unprecedented "exodus of the intellect" to
every corner of the earth.

(1 9 3 3 – 3 5)

9

Interlude: Exile in France

When Kurt Weill arrived in Paris on 23 March 1933, he did not enter the city as an unknown figure. Not only had the songs of the *Opéra de quat'sous* become widely popular in France, but since 11 December 1932 Weill's name had come to the attention of the Parisian musical world and the critics. On that evening a Weill concert had taken place in the Salle Gaveau that was quite enthusiastically received by both the public and the press. The idea for the concert had come from the Parisian music patron Vicomte de Noailles, who had written to Weill in Berlin in August 1932 inviting him, "on the basis of the great success of the *Drei-groschenoper* music in Paris, to give a concert of my works in Paris during the course of the winter."[1] Weill decided on the *Mahagonny* songspiel and his school opera *Der Jasager*, thus deliberately selecting two of his newer works for musical theater for his Parisian concert debut. He handed over the preparations for the concert tó his friends Hans Curjel and Maurice Abravanel. Both works were performed in German in concert form. Curjel added four numbers from *Aufstieg und Fall der Stadt Mahagonny* to the songspiel–this "Parisian version" became the basis for later performances as well–and he enlisted Lotte Lenya and Otto Pasetti as soloists, along with other singers. For *Der Jasager* the ensemble from the Berlin premiere (including the Youth Chorus and Youth Instrumental Group of Berlin's Staatliche Akademie für Kirchen- und Schulmusik) made the trip to Paris. Maurice Abravanel conducted both works.

The concert took place as part of a series offered by the chamber music society "La Sérénade," whose members included France's leading composers. Many prominent people came to the concert; the audience that night included Igor Stravinsky, Darius Milhaud, Arthur Honegger, André Gide, Jean Cocteau, Pablo Picasso, and Fernand Léger.

André George, a leading Parisian music critic, wrote: "We have heard two unique works that not only captivate the listener with their richness of imagination and expressivity but also, once heard, will not easily be forgotten."[2] Emile Vuillermoz summarized the evening's impact thus: "It has been quite a few years since Paris has felt so intense and so noble a tremor."[3]

A mere three months had passed since this concert when Weill arrived in Paris. His very first days there were filled with meetings with Jean Renoir and René Clair; Weill was eager to realize the film plans in France that they had discussed in Berlin. Nothing came of this, however, and by the beginning of April Weill was already at work on a new theater project.

A troupe called "Les Ballets 1933" had formed in Paris under the direction of the choreographer George Balanchine and was now looking for works to perform in a multi-part ballet evening. The artistic director, Boris Kochno, had already secured financing from a wealthy Englishman, Edward James, who was married to Tilly Losch, a German dancer living in Paris. James made only two stipulations: that his wife be given a role and that one of the works be composed by Kurt Weill, whose music he had held in especially high esteem ever since the December concert, which he had attended. James and Weill met on 9 April, and James told the composer that he had already arranged for a guest performance in London after the Paris performance scheduled for 27 May. Weill accepted the commission with two stipulations of his own. First, since he did not want to write an "ordinary" ballet but already had in mind a plan that would require a librettist, he wanted James to ask Jean Cocteau to participate. And second, since none of Weill's works had ever been performed in England, he wanted the Parisian concert featuring *Mahagonny* and *Der Jasager* to be repeated in London, running simultaneously with the ballet performance there. James agreed and spoke to Cocteau the following day.[4] Cocteau declined on account of the shortness of time. Doubtless thinking of the advertising appeal

Ein sensationeller Erfolg von

KURT WEILL IN PARIS

MAHAGONNY
DER „JASAGER"

Kurt Weill wurde am 11. Dezember bei einer Aufführung seiner Opern „Mahagonny„ und „Jasager" in Paris stürmisch gefeiert.

Emile Vuillermoz schreibt darüber:

„Voilà bien des années que 'Paris n'a pas eu l'occasion d'éprouver une émotion aussi intense et aussi noble. Il faut que ces spectacles soint offerts de nouveau à notre foule. La Sérénade doit aller jusqu'au bout de sa mission en faisant l'effort nécessaire pour tirer parti de sa victoire".

Les Nouvelles Littéraires (André George):

„. . . une oeuvre singulière, que l'on n'attendait plus, qui vous charme ou vous bouleverse, et qui, une fois entendue, ne s'oubliera jamais".

DIE BÜRGSCHAFT

Oper in 3 Akten. Text von Kurt Weill und Caspar Neher

Aufführungen in Basel — Düsseldorf · Wiesbaden Hamburg - - Königsberg — Duisburg - Stettin

Ein Erfolg von Stetigkeit und Dauer!

DER SILBERSEE

Schauspiel von Georg Kaiser. Musik von Kurt Weill

Uraufführung am 18. Februar 1933 in Leipzig — Magdeburg ·· Erfurt

(Gemeinsamer Vertrieb mit der Firma Felix Bloch Erben, Berlin)

UNIVERSAL - EDITION A. G.,   WIEN — LEIPZIG

Advertisement for Weill operas by Universal Edition, January 1933, referring to the triumphant success of the first Parisian Weill evening on 11 December 1932 in the Salle Gaveau.

**One of the popular French *Dreigroschenoper*
records, with Lys Gauty singing the part
of Jenny, 1932.**

the "trademark" Weill–Brecht would have in Paris after the success of the *Opéra de quat'sous*, James suggested Brecht as the author. Weill consented.

Bertolt Brecht was now also in the first stage of his exile and was staying along with his family in Carona, Switzerland, as a guest of the writer Lisa Tetzner. He left for Paris as soon as Weill's news reached him, arriving by the end of the second week of April. By this time James, Kochno, Balanchine, and Weill had already decided to produce a *ballet chanté*. Again it was the financier who suggested the idea. Tilly Losch knew Lotte Lenya from Berlin, and James had been fascinated by Lenya's performance in *Mahagonny*. He had already notified her in Vienna and had contracted both her and Otto Pasetti.

The ballet with song *Die sieben Todsünden* (The Seven Deadly Sins) was written between 15 April and the beginning of May (Weill completed the piano reduction on 4 May). By the end of April Brecht was on his way back to Switzerland.

The ballet is essentially a bitter work. It tells the tale of a family in Louisiana that decides to send their daughter Anna to the big cities to make a career as a dancer and earn enough money to build a nice new house back home. Anna consists of two persons—Anna I (the singer, the "rational" one, who manages her sister and constantly warns her not to give into her natural feelings) and Anna II (the dancer, the girl degraded into a commodity). A prologue and an epilogue frame the seven stations of the ballet that Anna must travel through, representing at the same time the "deadly sins." Brecht turns the sins into virtues, declaring that they are sins only for the petits bourgeois, who cannot afford them under the constraints of a capitalist society because they are not allowed to lead a natural, human life.

Brecht had already developed the underlying idea of splitting a person into two fundamentally different personalities in his play sketch *Die Ware Liebe* (The Ware Love—

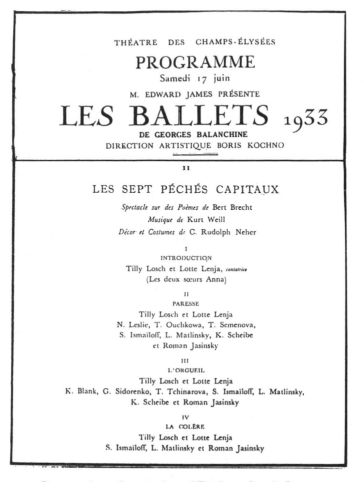

THÉATRE DES CHAMPS-ÉLYSÉES

PROGRAMME

Samedi 17 juin

M. EDWARD JAMES PRÉSENTE

LES BALLETS 1933

DE GEORGES BALANCHINE
DIRECTION ARTISTIQUE BORIS KOCHNO

II

LES SEPT PÉCHÉS CAPITAUX

Spectacle sur des Poèmes de Bert Brecht

Musique de Kurt Weill

Décor et Costumes de C. Rudolph Neher

I
INTRODUCTION
Tilly Losch et Lotte Lenja, *cantatrice*
(Les deux sœurs Anna)

II
PARESSE
Tilly Losch et Lotte Lenja
N. Leslie, T. Ouchkowa, T. Semenova,
S. Ismailoff, L. Matlinsky, K. Scheibe
et Roman Jasinsky

III
L'ORGUEIL
Tilly Losch et Lotte Lenja
K. Blank, G. Sidorenko, T. Tchinarova, S. Ismailoff, L. Matlinsky,
K. Scheibe et Roman Jasinsky

IV
LA COLÈRE
Tilly Losch et Lotte Lenja
S. Ismailoff, L. Matlinsky et Roman Jasinsky

**Program from the premiere of *The Seven Deadly Sins* at
the Théâtre des Champs-Elysées in Paris, 17 June 1933.
The performance was given by "Les Ballets 1933," a troupe
formed under the direction of George Balanchine, who also
choreographed the work.**

[*Ware*, meaning commodity, is a play on the word *wahre*, meaning true—trans.]), a study for his later play *Der gute Mensch von Sezuan* (The Good Person of Szechwan). Kim H. Kowalke's assumption that both Brecht and Weill knew Theodore Dreiser's novel *An American Tragedy*, which had been filmed in 1931 by Josef von Sternberg, is also reasonable. There "the protagonist, Clyde, and his alter-ego, Gilbert, confront deadly sins with religion and family playing destructive roles."[5]

Weill's music for *Die sieben Todsünden* again shows him at the peak of his European theater style. Whereas his last work in Germany had sought to create more of a chamber orchestral sound, characterized mainly by winds, in *Die sieben Todsünden* he uses a large orchestra and achieves his effects above all by a virtuosic treatment of the strings. For the first time Weill succeeds in incorporating jazz elements not only in the winds but in the direct interplay between winds and strings. And the melodic invention is as strong as ever. The prologue and epilogue enclose the action as if they were one great Weill song.

The most brilliant idea of all was to have a male quartet sing, often a cappella, the parts of Anna's family (her parents and grandparents), who keep up a narrow-minded running commentary on the girl's journey. Reminiscent of the excesses of German male glee club singing, this scoring attains an extreme measure of comedy and caricature.

Aside from these family choruses, however, the music almost completely avoids earlier parodistic effects. The solo songs make their strongest impact when they are directly juxtaposed with the quartet.

The ballet proceeds by sin, as follows:

Number 1. Sloth. In a park in the first city they reach, the sisters carry out little blackmail tricks on a number of couples to extract money from them. Bone weary, Anna II falls asleep. Anna I has to rouse her and get her back to work. Weill's music for this scene, into which the family later interjects itself from its place of commentary next to the stage, is strongly dancelike, a harried tarantella with typical chromatic transitions.

Number 2. Pride. Anna has gotten a job in Memphis as a dancer in a small, dirty cabaret, where no one is interested in the dancers' art but only in exhibitions of nudity. When Anna II refuses, Anna I has to break her of her pride and force her to dance. This scene is continuously accompanied by Anna I, with the waltz "Als wir aber ausgestattet waren" (But when we were outfitted). Weill's harmonic treatment and his orchestration show musically what kind of work Anna has taken on here.

Number 3. Anger. Anna is a statistician in a film studio. When she notices a star ruthlessly torturing a horse, she indignantly steps in and is immediately fired. But Anna I forces her sister to apologize so that she can get her job back. Sung by Anna I and the family, the entire scene in the studio is composed by Weill as a shimmy fox-trot. Here the winds in the orchestra take precedence, and the scene is very dancelike.

Number 4. Gluttony. Anna herself has become a star now, and her contract requires her to maintain a certain weight. Anna I keeps an eye on her and insists that she eat as little as possible. The entire scene is commented on only by the family. More than three-quarters of the time the four soloists sing a cappella, with pizzicato strings added only twice. Weill executes a master stroke of musical caricature here, debunking popular barbershop style precisely by his artful reconstruction of it.

Number 5. Lust. Anna II now has a boyfriend, Edward, who is very rich and heaps presents on her. She also has a lover, Fernando, who is poor and takes the presents away. Anna I has to get Anna II to renounce the lover and return to the rich boyfriend. Anna I and the family accompany the scene vocally.

Number 6. Avarice. Edward, ruined by Anna II, has shot himself. A second boyfriend has also thrown himself out of a window for the same reason. When Anna II wants to use a

**Lotte Lenya (*right*) and Tilly Losch (*left*) as the sisters Anna I and
Anna II in the premiere of *The Seven Deadly Sins*.**

third man in the same way, Anna I forces her to give him back his money so that she will not get a bad reputation. This scene includes a grand tenor aria sung by the father, "Wer seine Habsucht zeigt, um den wird ein Bogen gemacht" (He who shows his avarice will be avoided by others). With a wide vocal range—reaching to a high A—the father sings at times almost liturgically about what is most sacred to him: money.

Number 7. Envy. Anna II is often exhausted now. She sees other girls giving in to all the natural things that are denied her. In a grand ballet, "Die Letzten werden die Ersten sein" (The last shall be first), however, she becomes the triumphant heroine, while the other girls wilt and clear the alleyway for her. Weill composed this conquering last part of the scene as a popular march, but a painful metamorphosis takes place beneath its jubilant sounds.

The epilogue closes the ballet with Anna I and Anna II returning to Louisiana. "Jetzt haben wirs geschafft, Anna" (We've done it, Anna), sings Anna I, to which Anna II responds, speaking, with a broken "Ja, Anna," followed by six final orchestral measures.

The premiere took place on 7 June 1933 at the Théâtre des Champs-Elysées in Paris. George Balanchine did the choreography and Caspar Neher the sets; Maurice Abravanel was the conductor. Tilly Losch and Lotte Lenya played the parts of the two Annas, and the troupe "Les Ballets 1933" danced.

In addition to *Die sieben Todsünden* (which ran under the title *Les Sept Péchés Capitaux)* five other short ballets were on the program: *Les Songes* (The Dreams) by Darius Milhaud, *Errante* (The Wanderer) based on music of Schubert with instrumentation by Charles Koechlin, *Fastes* (Pomp) by Henri Sauguet, *Mozartiana* with music of Mozart orchestrated by Tchaikovsky, and *Les Valses de Beethoven* (The Waltzes of Beethoven) orchestrated by Nicolas Nabokoff.

Brecht had come from Carona again for the premiere, so the Weill–Neher–Brecht–Lenya team was reunited as in the old Berlin days. The reception of the evening by the audience was very mixed. *The New Yorker*'s Paris correspondent, Janet Flanner, described it well:

> "Les Ballets 1933" was presented by Edward James, new optimistic British art patron, at a cost of a million francs. The program consisted of six Balanchine ballets, only half of which, or around 500,000 francs' worth, the public appeared to enjoy. The three granted admiration were "Fastes" . . . "Les Songes" . . . and "Les Valses de Beethoven." . . . The other trio—like dishes on a table d'hôte of which you could select one though you weren't expected to like all three—consisted of "Mozartiana" . . . "Errante" . . . and lastly, "Les Sept Péchés Capitaux" . . . a concoction for which no one seemed to have an appetite but yours truly.[6]

Since the ballet, despite its French title, was sung in German, apparently no one in the hall apart from the numerous German émigrés understood what it was actually about. The émigré press greeted Brecht's and Weill's new work all the more joyously. Walter Mehring, for example, wrote: "It was a grand evening. Artists and interpreters were celebrated by an elite in the fashion to which one was accustomed in the great age of German theater art."[7]

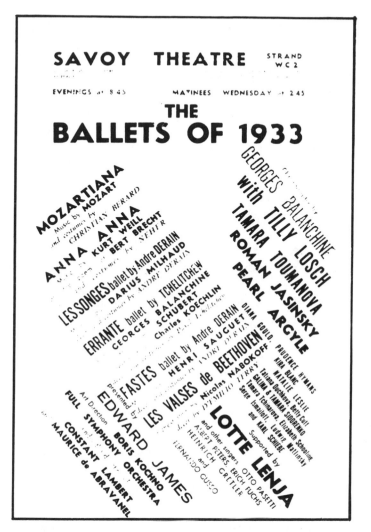

Advertisement for a guest performance by "Les Ballets 1933"
in London, 1–15 July 1933. Here *The Seven Deadly Sins* played
under the title *Anna Anna*.

The ballet program was performed a total of seven times in Paris, ending on 19 June, and then the production traveled to London, where it opened on 28 June at the Savoy Theatre. Even before the departure, "La Sérénade" had put on a second—again very successful—concert performance of *Mahagonny* on 20 June 1933 in Paris (with Lotte Lenya, Otto Pasetti, Albert Peters, and others, conducted by Maurice Abravanel), this time paired in the first half with works by Alfredo Casella and Jean Français. Having learned from their experience in Paris, James and Weill translated Brecht's libretto in great haste into English, Lotte Lenya learned the new text in a few days, and it ran in London under the title *Anna Anna*. The work's reception in London was also marked by a lack of comprehension and rejection. A total of fourteen performances of the ballet program were held through 15 July.

This was followed on 18 July, again at the Savoy Theatre, by the agreed-upon performance of the *Mahagonny* songspiel—paired, however, not with a second work by Weill but with Milhaud's *Les Hymnes*. Edward James, who apparently had seen the photographs of the 1927 premiere of the Weill work in Baden-Baden, came up with a performance that combined a staged with a concert approach. He had the singers appear inside a boxing ring, as they had in the German premiere. Again the critics reacted negatively, this time with a certain amount of ridicule. Under the title "Songs Sung in a Boxing Ring on Stage," one London newspaper wrote: "Into the ropes stepped singers, among them Fraulein Lotte Lenja, who declaimed odd little scraps of music with an American jazz flavour and seemed rather depressed about it. This music . . . soon gets on the nerves, for it is all of the same colour."[8] Weill's first foray into England had failed dismally; he himself did not experience the disaster personally, as he was enjoying a vacation in Italy at the time.

Die sieben Todsünden was performed only one more time during Weill's and Brecht's lifetimes, in Copenhagen in 1936. Not until after Brecht's death was the text published under the title—not authorized by Weill—*Die sieben Todsünden der Kleinbürger* (The Seven Deadly Sins of the Petits Bourgeois).

In July 1933 Weill wrote to his sister while on vacation in Positano, Italy: "I am still not sure about the further course of my life, but I am not thinking about that too much. All sorts of work plans are gradually forming—also a good sign."[9] The Neher couple also spent some time with Weill, who did not return to Paris until early August. Naturally, developments in Germany were the main topic of conversation. At this time Weill also

In November 1933 Weill moved into this house on the Place Dreux in the Parisian suburb of Louveciennes.

carried on an extensive correspondence with Georg Kaiser, who, following his "removal" from the poetry division of the Preußische Akademie der Künste, had withdrawn to Grünheide and was going into Berlin only occasionally. How must Weill have felt when he read the following lines written to him by Kaiser's daughter? "Recently my father and I were in the Eden Bar, where a tireless piano player was performing—and suddenly he broke into your unforgettable song of the shark with its teeth. At that point, solemnly thinking of the creator of this melody, we dropped our knives and forks and took in the sounds as if they were a delicacy we had not tasted for a long time. Yes, dear Mister Weill, we do not forget, we have a long and unshakable memory."[10]

In spite of all the recognition that Weill received in Paris, his financial situation was not rosy. In his haste to leave Berlin he had not taken along any large reserves of money; and, according to Nazi legislation, he was not allowed to transfer any money from his Berlin account out of the country. The bank informed him, after asking him if his stay abroad was temporary: "If you have moved your residence abroad, then your assets here were frozen at the time of the move in accordance with currency regulations and may be accessed only by permission of the currency control office."[11] Such permission was of course not forthcoming for the émigré Weill. The problem was compounded by the ban on Weill's music in Germany, which dried up his main source of royalties. On top of all this, Universal also stopped its monthly payments to Weill and terminated its contract with him in October 1933. So he was exceedingly pleased when the Vicomte and Vicomtesse de Noailles invited him to live with them for a while in their spacious Parisian apartment, allowing him to move out of his rather expensive hotel room. He also received a commission from Radio Paris in the fall of 1933. And finally in November—again thanks to arrangements made by the Noailles—Weill moved into a cottage that had once been the servants' quarters for the château of Madame Dubarry in the Parisian suburb of Louveciennes, near Saint-Germain. For nearly two years this cottage would provide him with the necessary quiet to compose.

Almost at the same time that Weill was moving to Louveciennes, another important performance of one of his works was given—one that ended, however, on a shrill note of discord and made him suddenly aware that the shadow of the Nazis was pursuing him even here.

In November 1933 Maurice Abravanel conducted two concerts by the Orchestre de Paris. The program included three songs from *Der Silbersee,* sung by the famous soprano Madeleine Grey. Abravanel describes what happened:

> I will never forget that performance at the Salle Pleyel. Great applause after each song and, at the end, a real triumph, with shouts of *"bis."* But to my ears, louder than all that was a voice yelling, "Vive Hitler!" Grey, bless her soul, focused on the cheers, and she prompted me to go back onstage. Again there were bravos, but this time they were clearly overshadowed by Florent Schmitt's and his friends' [French Nazi sympathizers] insults. Kurt came backstage with an infinitely sad look. "Did I need that?" he said. . . . In the morning Kurt was on the phone, and I went back to town to have coffee with him. He was very sad.[12]

CONCERTGEBOUW
AMSTERDAM

PROGRAMMA

VAN HET

ABONNEMENTS-CONCERT

(SERIE B)

DONDERDAG 11 OCTOBER 1934, 's avonds 8¼ uur

DIRIGENT

BRUNO WALTER

SYMPHONISCHE FANTASIE (SYMPHONIE No. I).......... KURT WEILL
    Sonate   (GEB. 1900)
    Largo
    Rondo
                Allereerste uitvoering

DERDE CONCERT (C GR. T., OP. 26) voor piano en
    orkest .... SERGE PROKOFIEFF
    Andante — Allegro   (GEB. 1891)
    Andantino — Variaties
    Allegro, ma non troppo

        Solist: de componist

    — PAUZE —

VIERDE SYMPHONIE (E KL. T., OP. 98) .... JOHANNES BRAHMS
    Allegro non troppo   (1833—1897)
    Andante moderato
    Allegro giocoso
    Allegro energico e passionato

Steinway & Sons' Concertvleugel

Begin tweede deel = 9.45, einde ± 10.30 uur

Program of the world premiere of Symphony No. 2, conducted by Bruno Walter, Amsterdam, 11 October 1934. The announcement says "Symphony No. 1," since Weill's original First Symphony, composed in 1919, had been withdrawn by the composer.

These events of the years 1932 and 1933 undoubtedly flowed into the score Weill was now working on, that of his Second Symphony. The symphony was a commission from the music patron Princesse de Polignac, to whom it is dedicated. Weill had started work on it in January and February 1933 while he was still in Germany, and he completed it in February 1934. Since his First Symphony, composed in 1921, had never been released for performance, Weill now referred to the new symphony as his first; at times he also used the name *Symphonische Phantasie* or *Drei Nacht-Szenen: Eine symphonische Phantasie* (Three Night Scenes: A Symphonic Fantasy).

Although Weill always refused to ascribe programmatic content to this symphony, it is surely an expression of this sensitive artist's reflections on the events of his time. At least certain dark, painful notes point in that direction, as does an occasional feverishness and breathlessness. The symphony is written in tripartite form (sonata – largo – rondo) and is a veritable model of proportion. It clearly shows Weill's theater experience, especially that of his last great stage works (at times one can imagine that one is listening to the score of *Die Bürgschaft, Der Silbersee,* or *Die sieben Todsünden*), but he expressly conceived the

Program from a performance of stage works by Kurt Weill in Rome, 29 December 1933.

work as a "pure musical form." The thematic material is introduced in the opening funeral march. This is followed by an allegro in sonata form, which gives the symphony's first movement its name. The second movement takes up the funeral march again and develops it with many elaborations. The third movement, an exuberant rondo, weaves the thematic threads of the preceding movements into a grand finale. The movement's sparkle pays homage to Mozart and Haydn, while its romantic traits bring Schubert and Mahler to mind. Although a number of the musical predecessors whom Weill greatly revered thus exert an influence, Weill's own contribution is what makes this symphony what it is, expressing its unbroken musical power even in a foreign land.

Bruno Walter conducted the premiere in Amsterdam with the Concertgebouw Orchestra on 11 October 1934. Weill attended the rehearsals and wrote enthusiastically to Lotte Lenya: "The rehearsal was wonderful. Walter makes it great, and they are all very enthusiastic, especially the whole orchestra. It is a good piece and sounds outstanding." [13] Walter continued to promote the work: he played it with the Concertgebouw Orchestra in Rotterdam and The Hague that same fall, with the New York Philharmonic in New York in December 1934, and in Vienna in the spring of 1938.

Later, after he came to the United States, Weill told a reporter: "I write absolute music in order to—how can I say it?—control my own style. You must turn away from your own habitual way occasionally." [14] The Second Symphony was to be Weill's last symphonic work for the concert hall, however.

Weill traveled to Rome at the end of 1933 and attended a performance there on 29 December of *Der Jasager* and *Mahagonny* as part of the longstanding series of concerts of the "Accademia di Santa Cecilia," thanks to Hans Curjel, who had taken the initative for the concert. *Der Jasager* was sung by the Zurich Youth Choir under the direction of Robert Blum, and *Mahagonny* was sung once again by Lenya, Pasetti, Peters, and others, with Maurice Abravanel conducting. The audience's reception was not quite as enthusiastic as it had been in Paris, but unlike his London experience, this first performance in Italy was a satisfactory success.

In the meantime Weill had established closer ties with Darius Milhaud and Jean Cocteau in Paris. Milhaud, whose ballet music for *La Création du Monde* (1923) was the first European symphonic work based on jazz rhythms and blues, had known Weill since the days they had spent together in Baden-Baden in 1927. He admired Weill's music and often welcomed him as a guest in his and his wife Madeleine's home. Weill saw Jean Cocteau for the first time soon after the latter had declined the ballet commission, and the two discussed the possibiity of collaborating on a Faust opera—a project that never came to fruition, however. Weill was an even more frequent guest in Cocteau's home, often along with Lotte Lenya. A song came out of one of these evenings in a funny way. Lenya tells the story: "Kurt and I were invited to dinner at Cocteau's one evening. Cocteau tried to speak a few sentences in German. Kurt expressed his surprise at this attempt and asked Cocteau if he really spoke German. Cocteau replied, 'Yes—all nouns!' He then excused himself, went into another room, and returned a few minutes later with a sheet of paper. On it were the first lines of 'Es regnet.' Kurt encouraged him to finish the poem, which Cocteau eventually did. Kurt corrected some of Cocteau's grammar-school German and set it to music." [15]

If this was decidedly an occasional composition, a second song was written expressly for a famous actress and singer around the same time. In the summer of 1933 Marlene Dietrich was in Paris to make some records and open her newly completed Hollywood film *Song of Songs,* directed by Rouben Mamoulian. She also had to get her passport extended, as she was not yet a U.S. citizen. When she went to the German embassy to take care of this, the German ambassador handed her a message from Goebbels asking her to return to the Ufa Studios in Berlin, an offer that Dietrich declined as categorically as Fritz Lang had when he had received a similar proposal slightly earlier. Later Marlene Dietrich wrote: "The reply I gave the Hitler regime when I was asked in Paris to return and become the 'reigning queen of the German film industry' is, I think, generally known." [16]

Cover of a single sheet of a song written for Lys Gauty and published by Weill's new publisher, Heugel, in Paris in 1934.

During her stay in Paris she also met with Kurt Weill and asked him to write something for her. Out of this request came Weill's setting of a poem by Erich Kästner, "Der Abschiedsbrief " (The Farewell Letter). Marlene never sang Weill's song, however. About six months later he suddenly received a telegram from Hollywood: "Would it interest you to come here and work with Sternberg and me on a musical film length about six months stop please let me know if you want and can stop Paramount will take care of the rest fondly yours Marlene."[17] Of course Weill was interested, and a number of telegrams were

**Cover of another single sheet of a song written for Lys Gauty,
from 1935. These two songs, sung in the cabarets of Paris,
were a huge success.**

exchanged, with, among others, the director Josef von Sternberg; but this project, too, fell apart.

As mentioned earlier, at the beginning of October 1933 Universal informed the composer that the ten-year contract signed in 1924 would have to be terminated because of the "completely absent German market" and that Weill could consider himself free of the contract for the last year. So, doubtless with the help of friends like Milhaud and Honegger, on 31 October 1933 he signed a new contract with the renowned Parisian music publisher Heugel, which had a division for "light" music, the Editions Coda. In June 1934 two songs that Weill had composed for the popular singer Lys Gauty (who had already made a recording of two *Dreigroschen* songs in 1932) were published under this imprint: "Complainte de la Seine" (The Seine's Lament) and "Je ne t'aime pas" (I don't

Cover of a single sheet of "Youkali," the tango melody from
Marie Galante, now with words by Roger Fernay.

love you), both on texts by the French writer Maurice Magre. Gauty sang these songs with resounding success in the cabarets of Paris.

Weill was busy with two other theater projects from September 1934 into 1935. The first, arranged by Heugel, was a joint project with Jacques Deval for a stage version of that writer's successful novel *Marie Galante*. Together they made it into a play with music; seven of the scenes contain instrumental and vocal compositions by Weill.

This is the exotic tale of a girl named Marie living in Panama City. Marie had been abducted a few years earlier from her home in Bordeaux by a sailing captain and brought to Latin America, where he had abandoned her when she refused to submit to him. Here she is supported by an elderly Japanese man who turns out to be a spy. He promises Marie money for the return trip if she will carry out some assignments for him. Marie agrees and dies on a spying mission. She finally returns to Bordeaux in a coffin.

Four songs from *Marie Galante* for voice and piano published by Heugel in 1934, with a picture of Florelle, the lead in the Paris production, on the cover.

The music includes daringly orchestrated instrumental pieces (such as a "Panama Military March" and a saccharine cabaret number in the form of a fox-trot), as well as a number of songs. What is most astonishing about *Marie Galante* is that Weill's four main "French" songs, especially Marie's homesick lament, were so good and so authentically French that they went beyond the performance to become widely popular in France. Heugel published seven of the songs separately in 1934, and in 1935 a tango melody from the play that had originally been purely instrumental was issued, now with words by Roger Fernay. This tango, called "Youkali," likewise achieved considerable popularity. A further indication of the resonance these songs found in many French people came ten years later, when a hopeful France was looking with the rest of Europe toward the Allied invasion and the opening of the Second Front. Along with all the other songs of the Resistance, people were singing a song from Weill's *Marie Galante:* "J'attends un navire" (I'm waiting for a ship).

Weill's remarkable ability to absorb with his musical sensitivity the very essence of a foreign musical sphere and let it flow into his own compositions had been strikingly demonstrated. Soon similar things would happen in America.

The premiere of *Marie Galante* took place on 22 December 1934 at the Théâtre de Paris, with Florelle, who had played the part of Polly in the French version of the *Dreigroschen* film, in the title role. The production was not a success, however, and ran only a short time.

At this time Weill was already hard at work on another project, the operetta *Der Kuhhandel* (literally, *The Cow Deal;* the English version went under the title *A Kingdom for a Cow*) on a libretto by Robert Vambery. Weill knew Vambery, the former chief dramaturg of the Theater am Schiffbauerdamm, from their work together on the performances of *Die Dreigroschenoper* and *Happy End*. Having likewise emigrated to Paris, Vambery showed his libretto to Weill in the fall, and the composer was immediately interested.

The play takes place on an imaginary island shared by the republics of Ucqua and Santa Maria. The head of sales for an American arms manufacturer, Waterkeyn Armaments Corporation, comes from Cleveland to Santa Maria. First he buys the country's major newspaper and uses it to publish reports of large weapons purchases by the neighboring republic of Ucqua. Then he calls on the president of Santa Maria and persuades him to place a similarly large order with his firm. Because this greatly exceeds the poor country's financial resources, a new biannual tax is levied. The president makes one further attempt to rescue the situation before war breaks out. He has his army stage a maneuver on the border with Ucqua and simultaneously calls for a peace conference, which closes with a gala banquet for the visiting delegation. The arms dealer sees that he is about to lose his booty and incites the defense minister, Conchas, to a coup d'état that is carried out during the banquet. Conchas storms into the room as the new president, provokes the delegation from Ucqua, and calls on the people to defend their national honor against the "sworn enemy."

The effects of these affairs of state on simple people are shown in the love story of two villagers, Juan and Juanita. Juan's livelihood depends on a dairy cow that is taken away from him when he refuses to pay the new tax. He is drafted into the army of General Conchas. When Conchas stages a "referendum" after his coup to make the foreign banks believe that his government enjoys popular support, Juan is selected to express his approval as a "representative of the simple people." But instead of answering Conchas's questions with the rehearsed "Yes," he boxes the general's ears. Juan is immediately sent away to the front and—like all the inhabitants of Santa Maria—survives the war only because the weapons delivered by Waterkeyn turn out not to work. Conchas promptly does an about-face in light of the new situation, expounds on the benefits of peaceful

Flier from the premiere of *A Kingdom for a*
Cow **at London's Savoy Theatre, 28 June 1935.**

coexistence to his people, and retracts the declaration of war against Ucqua. Surrounded
by the jubilant throng, he forgives Juan and gives the happy couple his blessing.

Here was a play that held out every possibility for Weill to create something along the
lines of Offenbach's operettas, to which he had long felt a strong affinity. It contained
numerous references to the political events of the past two decades in Europe, to debates
over armament and disarmament within the League of Nations, and to various peace
conferences, and it also had a viable plot and a romantic love story.

The composer began to work intensively, writing pieces of varying musical structure:
songs and choruses, ariettas and jazz-inspired numbers. A major turning point came after
large portions had been completed: Vambery, who had been searching in vain for performance possibilities in Paris, secured a contract for the premiere in London. The contract
stipulated, however, that the work be reshaped to fit the standard model of West End
theater. Two Englishmen, Desmond Carter and Reginald Arkell, were brought in. They
completely changed the piece, defusing it and smoothing it over, so that nothing remained
of Weill's and Vambery's original intention of writing an operetta in the style of Offenbach.[18]

Der Kuhhandel is clearly a transitional work. There is much in it that is still reminiscent of Weill's most recent works—from *Mahagonny* through *Der Jasager* and *Die*

Bürgschaft to *Die sieben Todsünden*—but at the same time it represents a new attempt to capture the "simple forms of musical theater." As this was his only attempt at operetta, it is doubly a shame that the work was interrupted.

The English version that now came into being, *A Kingdom for a Cow,* with its clear turn to anglicisms and new stylistic elements, points toward Weill's later work in the area of musical plays. The premiere of *A Kingdom for a Cow* took place on 28 June 1935 at London's Savoy Theatre. Weill had already traveled to England several times since January to participate in the English revision, and he was also present at the premiere. Although it received generally friendly press, it was not a great hit with the audience and was discontinued after a run of only three weeks. "The end of *A Kingdom for a Cow* was also the end of *Der Kuhhandel,* for Weill never returned to the German-language version."[19]

An important decision in Weill's private life came during those weeks in London in the spring of 1935. On one of his visits there he spent some time with Lotte Lenya, who had separated from Otto Pasetti after more than two and a half years. For the first time in years she and Kurt Weill were alone in each other's company once more. His relationship with Erika Neher had also ended; they had not seen each other since March 1934, when the Nehers had stayed with him for two weeks in Louveciennes.

The relationship between Weill and Lenya had never ceased to be friendly. They had seen each other at various performances and had told each other about their plans and projects in an extensive correspondence. Apparently they both realized that they needed each other as much as ever—in any case, they decided to end their separation and live together again. In the summer of 1935 Lotte Lenya moved back in with Weill in his cottage at Louveciennes.

Weill had been occupied for some time with a piece of work that would be decisive for the further course of his life. The early history of this project goes back to 1933, to Chicago, where a large pageant entitled *The Romance of a People,* based on episodes from the Hebrew Scripture, was commissioned by a number of Jewish organizations for presentation at the World's Fair. Isaac van Grove, at that time director of Chicago's Civic Opera, composed and conducted the music. The idea for the project, as well as the fundraising and production, had come from Meyer Weisgal, an officer of the Zionist Organization of America and a theater enthusiast. A Jew born in Poland in 1895, Weisgal had gone to America with his parents as a child. When he read, after Hitler's accession to power, that Max Reinhardt, whom he greatly admired, would have to emigrate, he spontaneously sent him a telegram: "To Max Reinhardt, Europe: If Hitler doesn't want you I'll take you."[20]

Of course this telegram never reached Reinhardt. But in November 1933 Weisgal went to Paris and met him there for the first time in order to present him with a plan for a new religious pageant that would be of top artistic quality this time. After thinking it over, Reinhardt agreed and recommended that he entrust the text to Franz Werfel and the music to Kurt Weill. Weisgal consented, so Reinhardt contacted Werfel and Weill, arranging with Weisgal for the four of them to meet in the early summer of 1934 at his residence near Salzburg.

**A discussion of the planned New York performance of *Der Weg
der Verheißung* at Schloß Leopoldskron, Max Reinhardt's
luxurious residence near Salzburg, in May 1934. *Left to right:*
Franz Werfel, Reinhardt, and Kurt Weill.**

Max Reinhardt's offer reached Weill in mid-December 1933, and he immediately agreed to participate in the project. The material prospects aside—so far he had composed some artistically interesting but hardly very successful things during his exile—the offer to work with material from the history of the Jewish people came at a time when Weill was trying to reach a fundamental decision. Events in Germany had affected him deeply. He had been forced to leave the country where his family had lived since the fourteenth century, the country in whose intellectual and musical traditions he had grown up and to whose musical development in the Weimar Republic he had made more than a negligible contribution. Now he had been reduced to silence and was being insulted in unworthy language; even in Paris, as events had shown, he was not left in peace. Kurt Weill gave up on Germany.

He neither wanted (as did many bourgeois émigrés) to write works that would shield and protect Germany—German culture and music—from the attacks of the Nazis nor was able or willing (as were many politically conscious émigrés later on) to write works for a future liberated Germany. It was not his style in any case to participate in an active political way in the anti-Nazi struggle. For Weill a painful process had begun of constructing a new persona, of removing Germany from his thinking and his music. How hard this was for him can be glimpsed from an interview of June 1934, when he was asked if he missed Germany: "In my innermost heart I have never left it!"[21]

**Weill in Salzburg in 1934, during consultations about *Der Weg
der Verheißung*.**

Weill in Salzburg in 1934.

The new project was suited to reinforce his decision, and of course it tapped into Weill's deep roots in the Jewish religion. Besides, it held out the prospect of a trip to the United States if Reinhardt's and Weisgal's plans came to fruition.

In May 1934 the meeting between Weisgal, Reinhardt, Werfel, Weill,and Rudolf Kommer (an associate of Reinhardt's) took place at the Schloß Leopoldskron, Reinhardt's luxurious residence near Salzburg. Franz Werfel had brought a first draft of the text, which he read aloud. Then they discussed it. As Weisgal describes it, "three of the best-known un-Jewish Jewish artists, gathered in the former residence of the Archbishop of Salzburg, in actual physical view of Berchtesgaden, Hitler's mountain chalet across the border in Bavaria, pledged themselves to give high dramatic expression to the significance of the people they had forgotten about till Hitler came to power."[22] And then: "I cried. Weill cried. Werfel cried. Finally, Reinhardt cried. Then I knew we had something."[23] By the end of this memorable meeting, a contract for the play had been signed, with an agreement that it would be completed by mid-1935 and premiered in New York by the end of 1935.

A month later, in June 1934, Reinhardt invited Werfel and Weill for further discussions to Venice, where he was staging *The Merchant of Venice*. There the next concrete steps in the collaboration were mapped out.

As soon as Weill returned to Louveciennes, he began working, "putting to paper all the Hebraic melodies I had learned from childhood. . . . In several days' memory seeking, I had written about two hundred songs, and then I began work at the Bibliothèque Nationale to trace their sources as far as possible. Many, I discovered, had been composed in the eighteenth and nineteenth centuries. . . . Those I dismissed, retaining only the old music, and with that as my guide, I attempted to create music of the same mood that would communicate naturally and inevitably the stories of the Old Testament."[24]

Originally he had conceived of the composition as taking the form of a large oratorio—David Drew points to Arthur Honegger's *Le Roi David*—and came around only after some resistance to Reinhardt's notion of something more along the lines of opera. But then he worked on it with great intensity. On 6 October 1934 he wrote to Reinhardt: "I have now composed more than half. . . . Of course, for now I am only doing the explicitly musical numbers and am skipping over the parts that I will be able to figure out only jointly with you. . . . In fact I am now more than ever convinced that it will be necessary to fill some of the roles with singers—that is, high-caliber singers such as you are envisaging."[25] What Weill is referring to here is his argument with Werfel's conception of a largely spoken drama. We will come back to this work at the time of its premiere.

By August 1935 Weill was working with great concentration on this composition with only minor interruptions. In the middle of that month a further consultation took place at the Schloß Leopoldskron, to which Reinhardt (who had just finished filming his *Midsummer Night's Dream* in the United States) came directly from New York with Meyer Weisgal. Weill was informed of the project's latest status: everything was set for a premiere in December 1935 at the Manhattan Opera House, which had already been rented and was being prepared. Rehearsals would start in the fall, and the composer, of course, would need to be on hand. This came as no surprise to Weill, since the trip to New York to prepare the performance had always been part of their discussions.

Back from Salzburg, Weill applied for travelers' visas at the American Consulate in Paris. Naturally Lotte Lenya was to go, too. Weisgal took care of booking ship passage, since he also had to return to New York.

At the beginning of September 1935 the three of them boarded the SS *Majestic* in Cherbourg. On 10 September Weill and Lenya first stepped onto American soil in New York harbor. A new phase of their lives had begun.

III

The United States

Robert Chrisholm as Macheath and Steffi Duna as Polly in the first American production of *The Threepenny Opera*, directed by Francesco von Mendelssohn and premiered at Broadway's Empire Theatre on 13 April 1933. The production was an utter flop, thanks to a poor translation and inadequate staging, and it had to be withdrawn after only twelve performances.

Facing page 237: Weill and Lenya in New York in September 1935.

10

Group Theatre and the Playwrights' Company

Whereas Kurt Weill had been greeted as something of a celebrity when he arrived in Paris, he arrived in New York a virtual unknown. Neither the single performances of the Violin Concerto (Cincinnati, 1930) and *Der Lindbergh-flug* (Philadelphia, 1931) nor the two amateur performances of *Der Jasager* (New York and Salem, Massachusetts, 1933) had attracted much public attention. His greatest European theatrical success, *Die Dreigroschenoper,* had completely flopped when it opened in New York in 1933 on account of a poor translation and an ill-conceived production. Weill had set great hopes on that opening. When Universal had informed him of the contract—Hitler had already come to power by then—he had replied, "If the music is done well there and my name is given the proper exposure, in half a year I could have the same position in New York that I have in Paris."[1]

The Threepenny Opera, translated by Gifford Cochran and Jerold Krimsky, opened at the Empire Theatre on 13 April and was withdrawn after only twelve performances—a colossal failure in Broadway terms. The critic from the *New Yorker,* while allowing that Weill's music had "a very new and fascinating rhythm," dismissed the production as a whole, writing sarcastically that "the general effect is that of a show being put on by amateurs in Fortnum & Mason's window, where tweed coats and sport sweaters lie draped about jars of greengages and Yorkshire pudding just as if it were the most natural juxtaposition in the world."[2]

The apparently total misunderstanding of the play on the part of the director and actors—a sign of their lack of knowledge about the Brecht–Weill concept of epic theater—makes one think almost involuntarily of the nearly identical failure of Brecht's and Eisler's *Die Mutter* on 19 November 1935 in New York and of the sarcasm with which Eisler later looked back on it: "It was terrible. What was happening onstage looked like something from the Tegernsee [a Bavarian village] farmer's festival. It was just horrible."[3] Brecht, Eisler, and Weill were meeting frequently at that time, and Weill held Eisler's music for *Die Mutter* in very high esteem.

Of course, Weill's name was known to a small circle of specialists in contemporary European music; some avant-garde composers who had studied in Europe, such as George Antheil and Marc Blitzstein, knew him well. To help Weill get off to a successful start in the United States—which was all the more urgent as various complications had caused the opening of *The Eternal Road* to be postponed indefinitely—the League of American Composers presented a Weill evening on 10 December 1935, to which they invited New York's leading music critics, producers, and publishers.

Lotte Lenya appeared with a chorus of ten singers and two pianists and sang excerpts from Weill's European stage works, from *Mahagonny* to *Marie Galante.* By intermission half the audience of about a hundred and fifty had left; the evening turned out to be an utter failure and brought Weill no important contacts. Weill shared this kind of bitter experience with many other émigrés, who learned that the American art market, determined by the law of commerce and not at all comparable to what they had been used to in Europe, had little interest in contemporary European art. It soon became clear that Weill would not be able to make a living in this country on the basis of his European oeuvre. He would have to give American theater a try.

The United States was just reaching the pinnacle of a decade of exceptionally diverse cultural development which played against the backdrop of one of the most serious economic crises it had ever experienced. After the "Black Friday" stock market crash on 25 October 1929, the wave of the Great Depression had washed over the land; in 1930–31 millions of Americans lost their jobs and their savings. President Hoover's government proved incapable of mastering the situation, and in November 1932 Franklin D. Roosevelt was swept into office with a large majority of votes. Upon taking office in March

1933, he presented his program for combating the crisis, the package of laws and measures called the "New Deal" that would set the course of American politics for the next several years. Along with programs to create jobs and provide social services, the New Deal also included a number of federally funded cultural projects.

Since thousands of theater people were among the unemployed, the Federal Theatre Project was established in the summer of 1935 under the auspices of the Works Progress Administration (WPA). This project financed hundreds of productions by progressive theater troupes in more than twenty states over the next four years and put more than ten thousand people back to work. The Federal Theatre Project was directed by Hallie Flanagan, who had formulated the goal of a "free, adult, uncensored theater" at the start of the project.[4] Here was an outlet for dissatisfaction with a private theater business that functioned on the basis of purely commercial criteria and was ruled by virtually omnipotent wealthy producers, offering next to no opportunities for artistic experimentation.

Well before the inception of the Federal Theatre Project two counter-movements had been founded in New York. Shortly after a large actors' strike on Broadway in August 1919 (in which the actors and their union protested against repressive measures taken by the producers) the playwright Lawrence Langner, the director Phillip Moeller, the designer Lee Simonson, and the actress Helen Wesley, as well as Maurice Wertheim and Theresa Helburn, had founded the Theatre Guild, which was to work over the next decade to carve out a space within Broadway for theater guided by artistic criteria. Brooks Atkinson, theater critic for the *New York Times* and authentic chronicler of New York theater, assessed its significance thus: "The Guild annihilated provinciality in the American theater. Once it was established, Broadway became an active part of the theater of the world."[5] Thanks to the Guild, not only did twentieth-century European drama come to New York in the 1920s and early 1930s, but above all, through numerous premieres of new works that would never have been ventured by mainline producers, the way was paved for a whole generation of American playwrights, from Elmer Rice and Maxwell Anderson to Eugene O'Neill and William Saroyan. The Theatre Guild began to lose some of its influence and significance in the early 1930s, as it became increasingly conservative and no longer in tune with the aspirations of a younger theater generation that had acquired a social and political conscience through their experience of the crisis of the Depression. Nonetheless, the Guild has continued to this day, though it is now "no more than an organizational shell."[6]

In early 1931 a group of young directors, playwrights, and actors left the Guild to found their own organization, the Group Theatre, under the direction of Harold Clurman, Cheryl Crawford, and Lee Strasberg. "Through these young people, all of whom had extraordinary talent, the original spirit and principles of the Guild have permeated the theater."[7] The Group Theatre launched its first performance, a production of Paul Green's play *The House of Connelly,* in the spring of 1931. In January 1935 it had its biggest success up to that point with Clifford Odets's *Waiting for Lefty.*

Such, in broad outline, was the situation of American theater and especially of those enterprises that emerged in opposition to the commercial business of Broadway. This was where Kurt Weill would find a foothold in a new country.

The founders of the Group Theatre, *left to right:* Harold Clurman, Cheryl Crawford, and Lee Strasberg, in 1933.

He met the director Harold Clurman at a party in the spring of 1936. Clurman, who had visited Europe as a student and was a friend of Aaron Copland and hence also well versed in music, was familiar with *Die Dreigroschenoper* and was pleased to meet its composer. Weill for his part knew the Group Theatre and respected its progressive goals and its repertoire. He asked Clurman the all-important question, whether the Group Theatre saw any possibility of doing a play with music. In the next few days Clurman brought together the composer and the other leading people of the theater—Lee Strasberg and his wife, the actress Paula Miller, and the director Cheryl Crawford. They discussed various plans and projects. It was Weill who suggested an American *Schweik.* The suggestion was well received, and they agreed to set to work on it.

The playwright Paul Green, who was closely associated with the Group Theatre, was asked to write the book. Born on a farm in Lillington, North Carolina, in 1895, Green had won the Pulitzer Prize in 1927 for his first play, *In Abraham's Bosom,* "the first play on Broadway that told the harsh story of Negro life without any of the usual clichés, sentimentalities, or melodramatica."[8] In 1931 the Group Theatre had performed his *House of Connelly* with great success. When he met Weill, Green had a teaching post at the University of North Carolina at Chapel Hill.

Together with Cheryl Crawford, Weill went to Chapel Hill in May 1936, and a first draft of *Johnny Johnson,* as the American *Schweik* from World War I would be called, came out of an intensive period of joint work with Green. Cheryl Crawford wrote: "We spent days at the local library reading newspaper articles about the period. . . . At night we talked, and soon a rough scenario began to evolve."[9]

Back in New York, Weill set to work on the composition, and the play was completed at the Group Theatre's annual three-month "summer camp" at Pine Brook, in Trumbull,

Kurt Weill and Cheryl Crawford at Paul Green's house in Chapel Hill, North Carolina, working on *Johnny Johnson*, in May 1936.

Connecticut. "Kurt worked at the piano below my bedroom, so the songs were drilled into my head day and night. We called the script *Johnny Johnson* after our hero, an ordinary simple soldier who hated war and tried to stop it."[10]

Kurt Weill gave his first lecture in the United States at the summer camp, on the question "What Is Musical Theater?" His notes from that lecture have survived. For the first time he was writing in English, but all his corrections and notes for further remarks were in German. Weill grasped the situation in the United States very accurately in his notes: "Metropolitan—worst example of old-fashioned opera (museum) on the one side, musical comedy, which tries to be sophisticated and low brow at the same time, on the other side. Nothing between. Enormous field for a musical theater. Collaboration of playwright and composer."[11]

The collective working style of the Group Theatre may have reminded Weill of his years of collaboration with Brecht. The Group had rented a ten-room apartment on West Fifty-seventh Street, where they worked, rehearsed, and talked, and where they also cooked and ate together. Any of the actors who might be in need of an apartment slept there too. During the three summer months they worked together in a roomy house with a large garden in Pine Brook. Kurt Weill was very quickly assimilated into this collective —out of which would later come such famous actors as Stella Adler, Lee J. Cobb, and Elia Kazan, who made his career as a Hollywood film director.

Rehearsals for *Johnny Johnson* began in New York in October 1936. A small rehearsal stage was rented for the purpose. Although Weill had written music that could be sung by actors, there were still great difficulties, as the American actors—unlike the actors Weill had worked with in Berlin—were completely unused to singing. Nervousness mounted when rehearsals were moved to the large Forty-fourth Street Theatre. Not until the tryouts did the ensemble gain enough confidence to look forward to the premiere with some equanimity.

The story of *Johnny Johnson* begins on 6 April 1917 in a small Southern town. The mayor unveils a peace monument made by the town's tombstone mason, Johnny Johnson. The people sing hymns of peace until news arrives of the United States' entry into the World War, at which point the mood changes completely. Only Johnny sticks by his opinion that "war is about the low-darndest thing the human race could indulge in." From his sweetheart Minny Belle he learns of President Wilson's proclamation that this will be the war to end all wars forever. Upon hearing this, Johnny signs up for the army voluntarily.

The next scene shows him at the recruiting office. Rejected at first because of his naive answers to the intelligence test, he is immediately drafted when he simply strikes down a Hun-like sergeant. "Crazy or not, he's our man!" Sailing out of New York harbor on a troopship, Johnny engages the Statue of Liberty in a dialogue.

The next scene shows him in a foxhole in the battlefields of France. Wounded Frenchmen pass by as Johnny and his comrades dream of home; Johnny, of course, is dreaming especially of Minny Belle. Explosions from three giant cannons wrench the soldiers out of their dreams. Johnny volunteers to go and deal with a German sniper in a graveyard. When he fails and the two meet, it turns out that the German is only sixteen years old. Johnny puts Wilson's proclamation into the boy's pocket and sends him back to the German line. After this, Johnny is wounded and sent to a hospital in Paris, where he is tended by a French nurse. When he hears of a great offensive being planned by the Allies, he smuggles vials of laughing gas out of the hospital, makes his way into military headquarters, and anesthetizes the officers. He stops the offensive and celebrates peace with the soldiers in the trench in a general's uniform. When the officers awaken from the anesthesia, they resume the war. Johnny is arrested and sent back to the United States, where he spends a number of years in a mental hosptial. There he organizes a "League of Nations" with his fellow inmates, many of whom look like U.S. senators from the war years. Released after ten years, Johnny now sells toys as a peddler. When a boy asks him for a tin soldier, Johnny explains to him why he does not sell them and then wanders on, repeating his motto, "We'll never lose our faith and hope and trust in all mankind."[12]

Weill's music for *Johnny Johnson* is just as heterogeneous as the play itself. The score already includes many elements of a typically American "musical play"—smooth melodic and harmonic contours in the style of popular hits; but in the realistic and gripping war scenes the European Weill is still very much in evidence. This is true both of the orchestral parts, especially the march passages, and of a number of choruses and songs. "Johnny's Song," the most important vocal number, comes at the very end of the play. The melody has been introduced orchestrally in the first scene, when Johnny expresses his thoughts on peace during the unveiling of the peace monument; now, at the close, he sings the song as a kind of credo of the path he has traveled, which the listener has been following for two hours. Here Weill is already adhering to a large extent to American conventions. A hillbilly banjo is added to the orchestra in a number of places, and even

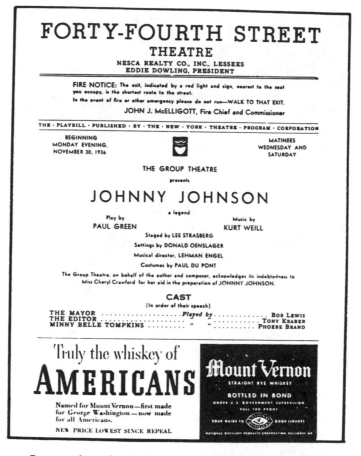

Program from the premiere of *Johnny Johnson* at New York's
Forty-fourth Street Theatre, November 1936.

the end (for the first time a major Weill song follows the popular American practice of raising the final refrain a step) shows that the composer is well on his way to adapting to his new environment. The main love song between Johnny and Minny Belle in the first act ("O Heart of Love") also furnishes proof of this. The music starts unexpectedly, however. The overture is, except for a few tacked-on measures, simply an orchestral version of the "Lied vom Branntweinhändler" (Song of the Brandy-Seller) from *Happy End* (1929). The melody is first played by the trumpet and then taken up by the strings and the clarinet. The somewhat cloying melody—which in *Happy End* serves to parody Lilian Holiday's "purification" efforts—has a completely different effect in this new, full orchestration. Weill surely wanted the overture to suggest something of the *Schweik* that is being presented here.

Echoes of *Happy End* are also heard (though only in the first few measures) in another song, "Mon Ami, My Friend," which the French nurse sings at Johnny's bedside in the

The trench scene from the premiere of *Johnny Johnson*.

hospital. This starts out like the old "Bilbao-Song" before settling into the new, smoother American sound. A tango is also featured in Weill's score. In the recruiting scene the officer sings "Captain Valentine's Tango," which clearly contains elements of parody.

The strongest musical number is the "Song of the Guns" in the second act. While Johnny and his comrades lie in the foxhole dreaming of home ("Johnny's Dream" is a very kitschy piece in which Minny Belle's voice soothes the soldiers), three giant cannons appear, raising their threatening heads over the soldiers and out toward the audience. An unseen chorus sounds from their huge openings: "We are the cannons you have made. You soldiers lying here under the sky, how many of you will still be alive tomorrow?" Weill has the male chorus begin singing a cappella, in a warning, penetrating tone; he then adds a harmonica and finally the strings, which also end the entire play with a moving closing figure.

Johnny Johnson is thus a work of transition from Europe to America. Weill's European conception of the theater still resonates here—this was still in demand with the progressive Group Theatre and in an anti-war piece—but he is also already working with the musical forms that give the American "musical play" its specific character.

The premiere of *Johnny Johnson*, on 19 November 1936, in the Forty-fourth Street Theatre, was directed by Lee Strasberg. The conductor was the then unknown Lehman Engel, who would later become one of the most sought-after musical directors on Broadway. The actors included Lee J. Cobb and Elia Kazan; the title role was played by Russell Collins.

The premiere was a resounding success and led to sixty-eight performances of that production—in Broadway terms a fairly short run, however, which meant that the play was not successful financially. Apparently audiences were accustomed to seeing either straight drama or musical comedy; they were taken by surprise by this new form and were

Telegram from Harold Clurman wishing Weill success on the
night of the premiere of *Johnny Johnson*.

also "not ready for an ardent plea against war, let alone a musical without production
numbers, with speeches delivered against a musical background, and a leading man who
doesn't sing a note until the final moments of the play."[13] In May 1937 *Johnny Johnson*
was quite successfully performed by theater groups of the Federal Theatre Project in
Boston (with a run of four weeks) and Los Angeles (with a run of six weeks).

The reception among critics was very mixed. Whereas Burns Mantle ranked the play
among the year's top ten[14] and the *Morning Telegraph* certified that "Johnny's Song" was
already being "hummed, sung and whistled on streets, in subways, in bathtubs and on
terraces,"[15] other reviewers were more reticent. The most important review for Weill was
undoubtedly a lengthy piece by Marc Blitzstein that appeared in *Modern Music,* the
journal of the League of American Composers. After confessing that he has "written
some harsh things in the past about Kurt Weill and his music," Blitzstein allows that "I
wish now to write a few good things." He then launches into an extensive discussion of
the music of *Johnny Johnson*. Addressing himself to his fellow music critics, he writes: "I
wonder if the music-critics, who will doubtless spend a lot of time worrying that Weill's
score is not sufficiently American or folksy—I wonder if they will have noticed that Weill
has practically added a new form to the musical theatre."[16]

In the meantime the New York music publisher Chappell had signed a contract with
Weill. A letter Weill wrote to Max Dreyfus at Chappell when *Johnny Johnson* was in its
fifth week makes it clear how little the newcomer understood about the market forces in
American popular music. Weill starts out by describing audience reactions, how people
are humming his melodies as they leave the theater, but then goes on to say directly: "And
yet it seems not possible to have these songs sung over the radio, played in dance orches-
ters [sic], in nightclubs, on records etc. . . . . Frankly, things of this kind never happened to
me before."[17] *Johnny Johnson* was not performed again during Weill's lifetime after the
1936–37 performances in New York, Boston, and Los Angeles.

"The first imaginative and exciting entry in a season of old, dead-tired waxworks. My God, if we don't grab onto something really big when it comes along, even if it does have its flaws, the theatre may go right on as it started this year. Makes you laugh, cry and and boil. The first anti-war play to use laughing gas in its attack on the stupidity of mankind, and to my mind the most effective of all satires in its class."

—ROBERT BENCHLEY
New Yorker

JOHNNY JOHNSON

A GROUP THEATRE PRODUCTION
PLAY BY PAUL GREEN • MUSIC BY KURT WEILL

"Paul Green's poetic concentration and his aloofness have combined to give him singular power and he uses it in *Johnny Johnson* on big game. Ferociously funny scenes. The best of it commands, with the theme itself, both respect and admiration. It has released the inventive gusto of the Group. Lee Strasberg has directed it with extraordinary sensitiveness and power, with resourceful humor and vivid imagination. The best of it is living and stinging stuff."

—JOHN ANDERSON
N. Y. Evening Journal

"Credit for the Group's finest and freshest show can be squarely split four ways: To Russell Collins for his good humor and dignity as *Johnny Johnson*; to Donald Oenslager for a series of arresting and imaginative sets; to Poet-Playwright Green for a profound and witty evangelical address; to Composer Weill for the haunting ballads which immensely help to articulate the play."

Time Magazine

44TH ST. THEATRE
West of Broadway
Telephone: LAckawanna 4-4337
Eves. 8:40. Prices 55c to $2.75. Mats. 55c to $2.20

266

Advertisement for *Johnny Johnson*. The picture in the top right corner is of Russell Collins, the first actor to play the title role.

Only seven weeks after the premiere, while *Johnny Johnson* was still on Broadway, the repeatedly postponed premiere of the big Reinhardt project finally took place at the Manhattan Opera House. After three years of preparation, a financial collapse of the production, and countless technical difficulties, a project was now under way that in its sheer scope was without parallel in the American theater of the 1930s.

The postponement of the premiere originally planned for December 1935 resulted from a decision by Reinhardt that assured the project monumental greatness but also guaranteed its financial ruin. In the summer of 1935 the Vienna stage designer Oskar

**Brian Morgan as Johnny Johnson in the 1937 Los Angeles
production sponsored by the Federal Theatre Project.**

Strnad, whom Reinhardt had secured for the overall design, became so ill that he had to withdraw his participation. Reinhardt then turned to the American designer Norman Bel Geddes, with whom he had already worked when he was a guest director for a New York play. Guy Stern writes: "Bel Geddes, as gifted a stage designer as he was grandiose (if not megalomanic), designed sets that necessitated the complete rebuilding of a theater."[18] Since the producer, Meyer Weisgal, had had such a production in mind from the start, Bel Geddes's conception did not faze him at all; instead, he set himself all the more energetically to raising the necessary funds. The remodeling of the theater soon began. Nearly everything except for the outer walls was changed: rows of seats were removed, new walls were erected—and of course the work was not completed on schedule.

In the meantime the text had been translated into English by Ludwig Lewisohn, with additional song lyrics by Charles Alan, and the original title *The Road of Promise* (a literal translation of *Der Weg der Verheißung*) had been changed to *The Eternal Road*.

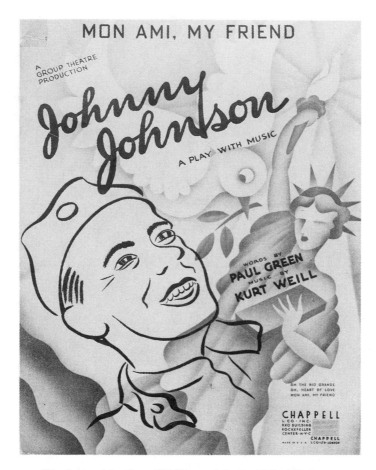

The first publication of Weill's music in the United States: a single sheet of the song "Mon Ami, My Friend" from _Johnny Johnson_, spring 1937.

Alluding to the delay, Reinhardt sent Weill a card with a picture of the grand hall at Schloß Leopoldskron for Christmas 1935, with the lines "Here it was still a 'road of promise.' Now it has become—at least until the premiere next year—an 'eternal road.' But you continue to be an oasis of joy, peace, and harmony along this road."[19]

Weill almost became a sacrifice to Bel Geddes's gigantomania, however. At the beginning of September 1935 Bel Geddes decided on a design that would leave no room for an orchestra and would necessitate using playback—that is, music on records—for the performance. This was too much even for Reinhardt, who immediately sent Weill a telegram, which reached him while he was still aboard the _Majestic_. As soon as he arrived in New York, Weill turned to the conductor Leopold Stokowski so as to have a well-known partner to help out in the debate. He explained the problem to him and asked him

Sketch by Benedikt Dolbin of a rehearsal of *The Eternal Road*.
***Left to right:* Werfel, Reinhardt, and Weill. Lenya can be**
seen in the background.

to express an opinion. He also explained the nature of his composition to the conductor:

> I have attempted something here—with Max Reinhardt's enthusiastic support—that has often been tried but never so completely followed through on. I have composed about three-quarters of Werfel's text, and in such a way that my music, which for the most part will be interpreted by singing actors rather than singers, covers the whole range from the spoken word through intermediary half-spoken and half-sung stages to pure song. It is these intermediary stages, which should always arise out of music and flow back into music, that to a large extent will come out of the rehearsals, since it cannot be notated. For this kind of musical theater, in which the word is always embedded in music, it is naturally even more necessary than for opera to have a flexible, responsive, adaptable orchestra. Do you believe that this is possible if the music is recorded and played back?[20]

Stokowski's answer has not survived. But a compromise was finally reached for the performance. Large portions of the music were recorded by RCA Victor on sound film, and only a small ensemble of musicians remained in the stage area. The conductor was faced with the difficult task of coordinating live and recorded music.

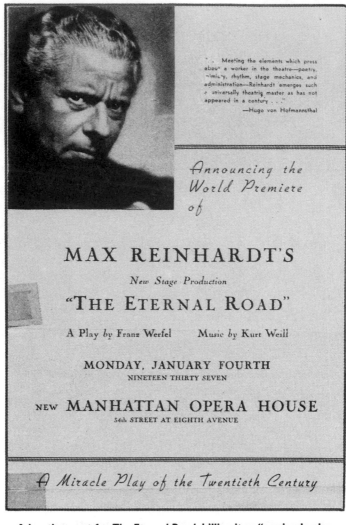

Advertisement for *The Eternal Road*, billing it as "a miracle play of the twentieth century."

Finally the day of the premiere at the Manhattan Opera House arrived, 4 January 1937. Weisgal tells the story:

I got to the theatre about ten minutes before the opening. The air was vibrant with expectation, the more so as the packed audience had no idea what to expect. We had no curtain; all the effects were based on lighting—$60,000 worth of it. When the first lights went on dimly they revealed only the small synagogue, and the Jews, men, women and children, huddled together in fear—nothing more. Then the *chazan* . . . began to chant "And God said to Abraham . . ." Slowly the stage began to light up, revealing the depth and height of five broad ascending tiers, and finally, at the top, the choir—one hundred singers in the robes of angels, a heavenly host. The audience caught its breath and one could hear a collective "A-ah." I knew the play was made.[21]

The Eternal Road opens with a Jewish congregation gathered in a synagogue. The rabbi tells them that the Jews are about to be expelled from the country they have long been living in. There is no direct reference to Germany, but the parallels are all too painfully clear.

Now the congregation begins to read excerpts from Hebrew Scripture. Beginning with Abraham and ending with the prophets, the biblical scenes show in condensed form the long wanderings of the Jewish people. As the little congregation disappears into darkness, the biblical scenes dissolve into a large pageant that takes up the entire gigantic stage. At the end of the performance the congregation itself takes up the "eternal road" to a different land, perhaps the Promised Land. In Franz Werfel's text the two levels of the play stand out clearly from each other. The scenes in the synagogue use prose, while the acted-out scenes taken from the Bible are written in verse. Weill's music likewise separates the two levels from each other. In the synagogue scenes he uses a number of original Jewish songs and melodies; the rabbi's psalmody (with echoes of the evangelists' parts from Bach's Passions) is particularly impressive. Here the music has a chamber quality, making the contrast all the stronger to the large oratorio forms that Weill uses for the pageant. The composer had already developed a special affinity for choral singing, which he combines in *The Eternal Road* with recitative and orchestra to create a compelling dramatic form.

Composed in 1935, while he was still in France—and at a time when his sister, Ruth, and her husband had just emigrated to Palestine and when Weill's parents, now both over sixty, were also planning to emigrate there—*The Eternal Road* shows Kurt Weill's Jewish side, a side of his personality that he had repressed during his many years in Berlin. But

The premiere of *The Eternal Road* at the
Manhattan Opera House, 4 January 1937.

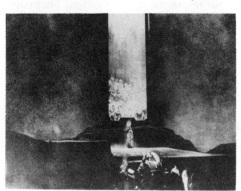

**Sketch by Harry Horner of the stage for the New York
production of *The Eternal Road*, giving a sense of the enormous
dimensions involved.**

now, in writing a composition about the odyssey of his people, he once more became strongly aware of this source of his art.

The premiere was an enormous success. Max Reinhardt, an experienced choreographer of large mass scenes onstage, had created a monumental production, and the conductor, Isaac van Grove, brought out the full effect of Weill's music. Norman Bel Geddes's stage designs were of dimensions never seen before.

In the center stood a huge mountain reaching from the orchestra pit up to the rigging loft. The people on the "road" climbed up the many levels of this mountain in the pageant. The little synagogue was at the base of the mountain, where the first rows of the theater had been removed. About two hundred and thirty actors (including Sidney Lumet, who was later to become a successful Hollywood director), forty dancers, and a chorus of a hundred singers were involved in the production.

When the production opened on January 7, 1937, the four acts ran until three o'clock the next morning, and exhausted the audience. But the critics left at midnight after

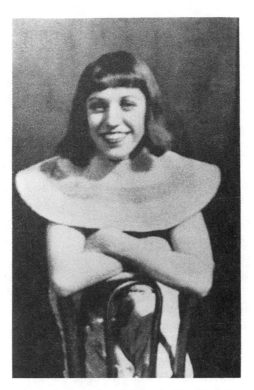

Lenya in the role of Miriam in *The Eternal Road*. This constituted her debut in the United States.

seeing the first two acts, and most of the notices were rhapsodic. Beginning on the second night, the last two acts were furtively discarded, and *The Eternal Road* was a hit. There was not an empty seat during the 153 performances. But after the play opened the producers discovered that the operating expenses were greater than the revenue from capacity audiences and the production lost $5000 a week.[22]

Naturally, the critics from the daily press focused on the play as a visual spectacle. Brooks Atkinson described the performance as "one of the few notable productions of the season" and commented: "Kurt Weill has composed a triumphant score that gives 'The Eternal Road' enormous emotional vitality."[23] Paul Bekker, who himself had emigrated to the United States in the meantime, discussed Weill's music in some detail in the German-language *New Yorker Staatszeitung und Herold*. He reminds the reader of the genre of nineteenth-century melodrama and of Robert Schumann's *Manfred*, "in which the problem of the connection between the spoken and the sung word was taken up again." Weill, he wrote, had now incorporated this genre in a completetly modern work, because "he is a born theater musician, not in the sense of theatrics but in the sense of a form of theater we are seeking today that goes beyond pathos and illusions."[24] One of America's best-known music critics, David Ewen, devoted an extensive article entitled "A

Musical Modernist" to Weill. Discussing both *Johnny Johnson* and *The Eternal Road,* he concluded: "That two such diametrically opposite musical expressions should have been produced by the same composer proves an almost phenomenal versatility of style. Weill is quite as much at home in symphonic music as in the opera; he roams as freely and gracefully in strict classicism as in jazz. He can produce a complex orchestral work, a titillating song-hit or a lyrically beautiful aria with equal ease."[25]

The Eternal Road not only made Kurt Weill's name more widely known in America as a composer of unusual musical theater; it also brought Lotte Lenya her first artistic assignment in the United States. She played and sang the role of Miriam.

The eccentric production history was surely the reason that this large work was not performed again during Weill's lifetime. As successful as *The Eternal Road* had been with both the critics and the public, Weill had still not earned much money from it. The question of his material well-being was all the more pressing as he now had to support his parents, who had emigrated to Palestine in the meantime. Nor was life in New York City inexpensive. So there were no elaborate festivities when Kurt Weill and Lotte Lenya took the official step of remarrying each other on 19 January 1937—wedded this time by a justice of the peace in North Castle, not far from New York City.

In his financially straitened situation Weill, like many European émigrés, cast an eye toward Hollywood. Cheryl Crawford from the Group Theatre was just planning a trip to Hollywood to discuss a number of projects, providing an opportune moment for Weill to establish contacts in the film industry with her help. So Weill and Crawford left for California right after the wedding, while Lotte Lenya moved into Crawford's apartment on Beekman Place, with a view of the East River.

From the end of January through June 1937 Weill met a number of scriptwriters, producers, and directors, as well as quite a few old acquaintances from his Berlin days now living in California's large colony of émigrés. The film director Fritz Lang, who had been working in Hollywood since 1935 and had had his first major American success with the film *Fury* in 1936, showed considerable interest in working with Weill, but they were not able to get started on a joint project immediately. One contact made during this time was to have great significance three years later: this is when Weill got to know Ira Gershwin, brother of the composer George Gershwin. Weill had already met the two brothers shortly after his arrival in New York, and he had attended a dress rehearsal of *Porgy and Bess.* Now he met Ira again, and the two took a liking to each other, although they did not specifically think of working together at this point.

In March a concrete commission came out of the various vague discussions that Weill had been having. The director William Dieterle, whom Weill had known in Berlin as Wilhelm Dieterle, was planning one of Hollywood's first "anti-Nazi films," as film history now terms the two hundred or so films (of varying artistic quality) made in the United States between 1938 and 1945 with anti-Fascist subject matter. Dieterle was planning a film on the Spanish Civil War, and he was immediately taken with the idea that his fellow émigré Weill should write the music for it. At first the film was to be called *The River Is Blue,* but then the title was changed to *Castles in Spain.* Weill wrote the music for it in March and April and was then confronted for the first time with the reality of

Weill and Lenya with the songwriter Ann Ronell (*left*) in New York in 1937.

Hollywood: the producer rejected his score as not being sufficiently accessible. Weill did receive a check for his efforts, but his music was sent to the archives. Ultimately the film was released in 1938 under yet another title, *Blockade,* with music by Werner Janssen. Somewhat disillusioned, Weill returned to New York. One of his first impressions of Hollywood had been confirmed: "They hate any kind of enthusiasm here. . . . It is a strange mixture of organization and confusion. . . . It is the craziest place in the world and I have never seen so many worried and unhappy people together."[26]

Upon his return to New York, Weill was greeted by a letter from Ernst Josef Aufricht from Paris. Aufricht was preparing a production of *Die Dreigroschenoper* to be held during the Paris World's Fair. For the role of Mrs. Peachum he had secured the famous

Weill on his first visit to Hollywood in the spring of 1937.

singer Yvette Guilbert, who naturally wanted more solo numbers. (The only solo for her part in the original opera was the "Ballade von der sexuellen Hörigkeit.") Aufricht sent Weill two sets of lyrics she had written, asking him to set them to music. Weill composed these as *Deux Chansons d'Yvette Guilbert* and sent them to Paris with strict instructions that they be used only for that production. The lyrics were probably sung to Guilbert's own melodies, however.

In the summer of 1937 Weill and Lenya drew the formal consequences of their break with Germany and started the process of applying for American citizenship. According to American immigration law, they first had to be registered as immigrants and obtain immigrant visas. Up to this point they had been using the visitor's visas they had obtained

At Paramount's sound studio in Hollywood in April 1938. *Left to right*: Weill, the director Fritz Lang, the conductor Boris Morros, and two unidentified technicians, listening to recordings for the film *You and Me*.

in Paris, which were valid for two years. One had to enter the United States from abroad in order to be eligible for an immigrant visa, so Weill and Lenya went to Canada in August 1937 so that on their return trip they could apply for immigrant visas at the Canadian–American border. Only then did they receive the necessary visas. Weill and Lenya put in their applications for U.S. citizenship on 27 August; it took until 1943 for their application to make its way through the bureaucracy.

Two projects that remained unfinished occupied Weill in the fall of 1937 and the spring of 1938. In mid-August 1937 President Roosevelt gave a speech on Roanoke Island that attracted a good deal of attention. Roosevelt spoke of the hopes of the many opponents of Hitler who had come to the United States and of their experiences of present-day America. He called on people to look to the early history of their country, where the foundations of current democratic ideals lay. It was time to consider this more carefully.

Soon after reading this speech in the newspaper, Weill wrote to Paul Green and suggested a plan for a joint play: "It is this 'comprehensive view' which we have to give—a picture of early America."[27] Green agreed, and together they developed an idea for a play to be called *The Common Glory,* but it never got beyond the preliminary sketches.

Weill's next project also had to do with the country's early history, with the "American dream." The young playwright Hoffman R. Hays had written a play entitled *The Ballad of Davy Crockett* for the Federal Theatre Project, which told the story of this legendary folk hero who went to Washington as a congressional delegate from Tennessee and fell at the Alamo in 1836. Between January and March 1938 the two worked energetically on a "musical play" to be called *Davy Crockett.* Work on this progressed well: a libretto with seven scenes and a first draft of the piano reduction, which Weill expressly called "incomplete, for rehearsal purposes only," have survived. The material, which is treated like a ballad (two singers comment on the action in a folk style), contains two original waltzes and several numbers in the style of early Western music, including a "Peasant Dance."[28]

Apparently both projects were slated for performance as part of the Federal Theatre Project, and their abandonment had to do with the Project's increasingly precarious financial situation. Long before the Project was officially terminated on 30 June 1939, a number of theater troupes had to stop work. Paul Green describes how work on *The Common Glory* was broken off: "We got on near the middle of this thing, [with] great plans, and we were set. Then Mrs. Flanagan called up on the phone, and she said, 'I've got terrible news,' and I said, 'What?' And she said, 'They're going to kill the Federal Theatre.'"[29]

Once again Weill had invested time and energy in projects that did not come to fruition. In March 1938, however, he received a concrete invitation to work with Fritz Lang on a film for Paramount called *You and Me,* based on a short story by Norman Krasna. Lang later described it as "a fairy tale inspired by Brecht and his *Lehrstück* style."[30] With such intentions, it was only logical that Lang should commission Weill to write the music.

Weill spent April and May in Hollywood writing the score, which also contained songs. The film—starring George Raft and Sylvia Sidney—tells the story of a New York department store owner whose social conscience leads him to employ former convicts and integrate them back into society. One of the former convicts, a young woman, falls in love with a nonconvict department head. When some of the others—in spite of all attempts to improve them—plan a grand robbery in the store, the young woman, their former accomplice, leads them back onto the path of virtue. Moved by her actions, the department head marries her.

The film's traces of the Brecht–Weill didactic play that Lang later referred to are, to be sure, small enough. Weill, who developed an extensive score, was again confronted with the practices of the dream factory. The producers cut out large sections of his music, and a popular film music composer, Boris Morros, was commissioned to rewrite some sections. The completed film contained only two Weill songs, "You Can't Get Something for Nothing" and "The Right Guy for Me" (with lyrics by Sam Coslow). For a second time Weill returned to New York feeling decidedly disillusioned. He did not go back to the studios of Hollywood for another five years.

Sheet music of a song from the film *You and Me*, 1938, with the
leads, Sylvia Sidney and George Raft, pictured on the cover.

Nonetheless, the film brought in so much money that Weill and Lenya were able to leave the hectic big city and rent a little house in Suffern, about an hour's drive from Manhattan. They moved there during the summer of 1938.

In November another group of authors split off from the Theatre Guild to found their own production company, where they would be in a better position to realize their artistic intentions in performances of their plays. Five of the most successful playwrights of the day—Elmer Rice, Maxwell Anderson, Robert E. Sherwood, Sidney Howard, and S. N. Behrman—founded the Playwrights' Company. Brooks Atkinson, speaking of the "Big Five," describes the reactions of the private producers: "When the news got around that five influential playwrights were renouncing commercial management, Broadway was not altogether pleased. . . . Some managers believed that the Playwrights' Company foreshadowed the end of the commercial manager. . . . In 1938 and 1939 the Playwrights' Company and the Theater Guild dominated the cultural aspects of Broadway."[31]

**Weill in Hollywood during the time when the film _You and Me_
was being completed, May 1938.**

Starting on 15 October 1938, with the premiere of Sherwood's _Abe Lincoln in Illinois_,
the Playwrights' Company produced four Broadway plays in the 1938–39 season alone.
The second of these was _Knickerbocker Holiday_, by Maxwell Anderson and Kurt Weill.
The program from the premiere told the story of how this came to be:

> It was at a theatrical party in New York some three years ago that Anderson and Weill
> first met. . . . "I'd like to write a play with you," were the composer's first words to
> the playwright. There is no record of the precise reply made by Anderson, but it was a
> gentle answer to the effect that the idea in all probability was a good one and that he'd
> give it some thought. A couple of years passed. . . . The scene now shifts to April

Maxwell Anderson (*right*) and Kurt Weill (*at the piano*) with the two leads, Walter Huston and Jeanne Madden, during a rehearsal for *Knickerbocker Holiday* in early October 1938. This was the second of four plays produced on Broadway by the Playwrights' Company in the 1938–39 season.

1938, to Anderson's home in the country at New City, N.Y. Weekend guests at that place were Weill and his wife. "Kurt," said the dramatist suddenly, "do you think we can make a musical comedy out of Washington Irving's *Father Knickerbocker's History of New York?*" Unfortunately, the chronicler has no record of the exact reply that Weill made to Anderson on this historic occasion. It was, however, in the affirmative. A day or so later Hollywood beckoned to Weill and he was off for the West on a four-week contract. "If the idea works out," Anderson said to him in parting, "I'll have the book ready upon your return."[32]

Next to Eugene O'Neill, Maxwell Anderson was the most important American playwright of the time. Born in Pennsylvania in 1888, he had started out after World War I as a journalist. After a first unsuccessful tragedy in verse, in 1924 he wrote the brilliant anti-war play *What Price Glory?* — "one of the most exciting and provocative plays ever produced on Broadway,"[33] with Laurence Stalling, his colleague from *The World*. The play was enormously successful in Germany as well, where Carl Zuckmayer translated it under the title *Rivalen*. The Berlin performance (at the Theater in der Königgrätzer Straße under the direction of Erwin Piscator, with Fritz Kortner and Hans Albers in the lead roles) became a hit in March 1929.

After the unexpected success of *What Price Glory?* Anderson devoted himself fully to drama. Starting in 1925, he wrote at least one play every year, and in 1933 he was awarded the Pulitzer Prize for *Both Your Houses*. In 1936–37 three of his plays had successful runs on Broadway. In Maxwell Anderson Kurt Weill now had an American partner who was both experienced and famous.

By the time Weill returned from Hollywood toward the end of May 1938, Anderson had written a first draft. The play was discussed a number of times by the members of the Playwrights' Company, and by September it was completed.

Knickerbocker Holiday is based on the classic book by Washington Irving (1783–1859) about New York City, from its founding by Dutch seafarers through its heyday and the end of Dutch rule under Peter Stuyvesant in 1664. It is the first important comic-satiric work of American literature, a portrayal of the "illustrious" pioneer days, with a strong emphasis on the "follies in steering the young colony's little ship of state."[34]

The play is told as a story within a story. It opens with the writer Washington Irving sitting in his study, working on his book about New York. He leads the audience into the scene of New Amsterdam in 1647 and introduces the main characters, including the young man Brom Broeck and his sweetheart, Tina Tienhoven, the daughter of the mayor. Without informing her, her father has already promised her hand to the new Dutch governor due to arrive shortly, Peter Stuyvesant.

First page of the manuscript of the first version of the music for *Knickerbocker Holiday*, which Weill gave to his friends Maxwell and Mabel Anderson, inscribing it "To Mab and Max as a token of my undying affection."

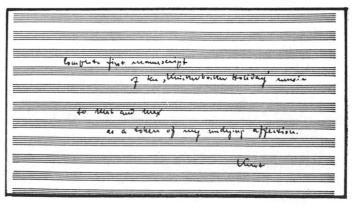

VOCAL GEMS
WORDS AND MUSIC (COMPLETE)

☆

PLAYWRIGHTS PRODUCING COMPANY, INC.

presents

WALTER HUSTON

in

THE NEW MUSICAL COMEDY

"KNICKERBOCKER HOLIDAY"

Book & Lyrics by MAXWELL ANDERSON

Music by KURT WEILL

☆

Staged by JOSHUA LOGAN

Settings by JO MIELZINER

☆

VOLUME 1 – CONTENTS
WASHINGTON IRVING'S SONG
OUR ANCIENT LIBERTIES
HOW CAN YOU TELL AN AMERICAN
WILL YOU REMEMBER ME?
YOUNG PEOPLE THINK ABOUT LOVE
SEPTEMBER SONG

PRICE 1.00

CRAWFORD MUSIC CORPORATION
RKO Building — Rockefeller Center — New York
Printed in U.S.A.

Cover of a selection of six songs, including "September Song,"
written expressly for Walter Huston, for *Knickerbocker Holiday,*
published in New York in 1938.

In the first act the city councilmen are preparing a gala reception for the governor. The "high point" of the celebration is to be the execution of Brom, who has hit the mayor and, as a friend of the Indians, is a source of discomfort anyway with his ideas about freedom. He is arrested and sentenced. Cleverly, he asks to be hanged in the traditional fashion by the neck and not, according to the horrible new method, by the waist, which causes the delinquent to die an agonizing death. The council lets itself be duped and, naturally, has him strung up by his waist just as the governor enters. The governor pardons Brom and then asks to be left alone with his promised one, whom he presses to marry him immediately. But Brom intervenes, and Stuyvesant has him put in jail again. This is where the second act begins. While the army leaves for a maneuver, preparations are made for the governor's wedding. Meanwhile the Indians attack the city. Brom escapes from jail and throws himself into the fray to restore peace. In the course of this he frees Stuyvesant, who now, however, realizes that Brom is a rival for Tina and insists that Brom's sentence of execution, which he had originally lifted, be carried out. At this point the writer intervenes and tells Stuyvesant that he should let mercy rule for a number of reasons, not the least of which is his reputation. And so it happens; the governor even gives up Tina, so nothing more stands in the way of the happy ending.

Anderson's text is full of ironic allusions to the era of the New Deal and the politics of President Roosevelt. His Peter Stuyvesant exhibits many of Roosevelt's traits, while Brom Broeck is an embodiment of the opponents of Roosevelt's politics. At first Anderson's attacks were even sharper, but his colleagues in the Playwrights' Company persuaded him to tone them down somewhat. As Elmer Rice relates: "The rest of us were strongly pro-Roosevelt, and though, of course, we had no control over Anderson's script, we did succeed, mainly by cajolery, in getting him to delete some of the more pointed references to the New Deal."[35] Anderson expressed his views about this in an essay entitled "A Preface to the Politics of *Knickerbocker Holiday.*"

The final version of the play still contained plenty of satiric bite. In the priceless execution scene the city council is made utterly ludicrous. Even the suggestive names of the venerable dignitaries—two of them are named Vanderbilt and Roosevelt—delighted the audience: "Toward the end of the play, when Stuyvesant orders the Council to pull on the rope that will hang Brom Broeck—by the neck this time—it is Councillor Roosevelt who first throws down the rope and announces: 'No! Ve vouldn't pull. My name iss Roosevelt, und ven I get a idea, it shticks. Ve vouldn't pull.' When President Roosevelt saw the production in Washington, Time Magazine reported that he 'tossed his head and roared with laughter,' for surely it was he and his policies that the author wrote of."[36]

If the announcement that Maxwell Anderson had written his first musical play added weight to the publicity, the casting of Walter Huston as Peter Stuyvesant further heightened public interest. Huston was then one of the most popular stage and film actors in America. He had first become known in 1924 in the premiere of O'Neill's *Desire under the Elms* and had been made famous above all by two roles that he played in long successful runs on Broadway. In 1931–32 he played the baseball player in Ring Lardner's *Elmer the Great,* and in 1934–37 he played Samuel Dodsworth in Sidney Howard's dramatization of *Dodsworth,* the novel by Sinclair Lewis. Since 1929 he had also been sought after as a Hollywood actor.

When rehearsals for *Knickerbocker Holiday* began, Huston was still tied up with film work in California. The director, Joshua Logan, explained the role and the play to him in long telephone conversations. Huston wished he could have a nice song with which the aging Stuyvesant could perhaps impress the young Tina a bit. When the director passed on this request to the composer, Weill sent Huston a telegram: "What is the range of your voice?" The actor promptly cabled back, "I have no range. Appearing tonight on Bing Crosby program. Will sing a song for you." Weill listened to the program and came to Maxwell Anderson the next morning saying, "Let's write a sentimental, romantic song for him."[37]

**Walter Huston as Peter Stuyvesant in the premiere of
Knickerbocker Holiday at the Ethel Barrymore Theatre,
19 October 1938.**

Thus, within a few days "September Song" came into being, a song whose melody came from *Der Kuhhandel*. Just as the "Moritat von Mackie Messer," added on Harald Paulsen's request, had become Weill's most popular European melody, so this song, written especially for Walter Huston, has remained to this day Weill's most popular song in America.

The music for *Knickerbocker Holiday* consists of twenty-eight numbers, including a multitude of songs, of which four became particularly well known. Principal among these, of course, was the lyrical "September Song" with its refrain:

> Oh, it's a long, long while
> From May to December.
> But the days grow short,
> When you reach September.

The melody ascends first by a major third and then immediately by a fifth; after a lift the voice falls by a second, giving the song its characteristic, striking line. The other especially successful songs were "It Never Was You," a duet between Tina and Brom; "There's Nowhere to Go but Up!" sung by Brom; and "How Can You Tell an American?" in which Brom sings of his ideals from the time of the founding of America.

A young musician assured Weill that his score had captured the American style better than ever: "I've never seen such a superb work of prosody. It is downright amazing for a

Cover of the single sheet of "September Song" that was issued
after the film version of *Knickerbocker Holiday* was released
by United Artists in the summer of 1944. The leads, Nelson
Eddy and Constance Dowling, are pictured.

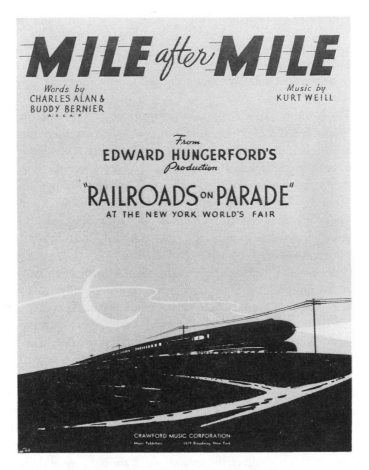

Cover of the single sheet of the song "Mile after Mile" from the
pageant play *Railroads on Parade,* written for the railroad
industry's exhibit at the New York World's Fair of 1939.

foreigner. . . . 'How Can You Tell an American?': a very good song, a daring song. . . . I
would like to give these pages to students so that they can see the quality of the workman-
ship. One would really have to describe the whole song. It is American."[38] Maxwell
Anderson also wrote to his colleague Elmer Rice about Weill's music, saying, "Weill's
music is the best I have ever heard for any musical show, better even than Sullivan's. If the
words are only half as good and we have the right actors, we should come off very well."[39]

The New York premiere on 19 October 1938 at the Ethel Barrymore Theatre was
Weill's first big hit on Broadway. Joshua Logan was the director, and Weill's old friend
Maurice Abravanel (who had likewise been in the United States since 1936) conducted.
Contrary to common practice in the United States, Kurt Weill orchestrated his own music
and carefully watched over the quality of the interpretation during the musical rehearsals.

The critics, who had already been positive during the tryouts in Boston and Washington, continued to write glowing reviews. The *New Yorker* critic, for example, in a review entitled "Maxwell Anderson, with Music, " first highlighted the text's wit and intelligence and then went on to say, "In 'September Song' and 'To Our Ancient Liberties' Kurt Weill has written a couple of the best songs of the year, and I like everything else he wrote for Mr. Anderson's show, too."[40]

Knickerbocker Holiday had a run of 168 performances; although this did not spell huge financial gains for the Playwrights' Company, it meant that they did not lose anything on their first musical work. Right after *Knickerbocker Holiday* Weill and Anderson began working on a new joint venture, *Ulysses Africanus.* The basis for this project was the historical short story *Eneas Africanus* by Harry Stillwell Edwards, about a Negro slave from the South. This was to be a broadly conceived musical folk play incorporating traditional black music. Anderson offered the lead role to Paul Robeson, who declined. But various other commitments of Anderson's led to interruptions in their work, and the play remained unfinished.

Weill and Anderson had developed a cordial friendship through working together. The two families saw quite a lot of each other; when Weill and Lenya gave up their rented house in Suffern in May 1941 and bought their own house in New City, Anderson and Weill became next-door neighbors, which further enhanced their association. In 1940 the two jointly wrote a commissioned work, the radio cantata *The Ballad of Magna Carta,* which was broadcast throughout the country by CBS on 4 February 1940.

The subject of *Magna Carta,* the fundamental English charter of 1215 whereby King John, under pressure from his barons, was forced to confirm and extend their privileges, was a celebration of America's freedom more than five months after the outbreak of the Fascist war in Europe. Weill had this to say about the music: "It's a ballad like the old Scottish ones, set to music, but between the stanzas there are prose passages, sometimes spoken, sometimes in recitative. Even the spoken parts, though, are in rhythm, so that the whole thing has a definite pattern."[41]

Weill had also been busy working on another commission in 1939. At the end of April the doors opened on the New York World's Fair. Expositions by large industry dominated the United States' section, emphasizing America's leading role in the world economy. This meant that there was plenty of money and room for artistic experimentation, as well as spectacular presentations. Thus the director Joseph Losey and the composer Hanns Eisler wrote a new kind of color puppet trick film called *Pete Roleum and His Cousins* for the oil industry's pavilion. Kurt Weill was commissioned to write a musical work that would demonstrate locomotive production and the achievements of the overland railroads. The result was *Railroads on Parade,* with words by Edward Hungerford, a sixty-minute open-air spectacle with a "cast" of chorus, orchestra, and fifteen historical locomotives. Weill spoke of it as a "circus opera" and brought in the director's assistant Charles Alan and the conductor Isaac van Grove from Reinhardt's monumental production *The Eternal Road.* For his composition Weill made frequent use of quotations from colonial American songs. The high point was the representation of the meeting between the tracklayers in the building of the first transcontinental railroad. "Mr. Weill has continued to give the visual

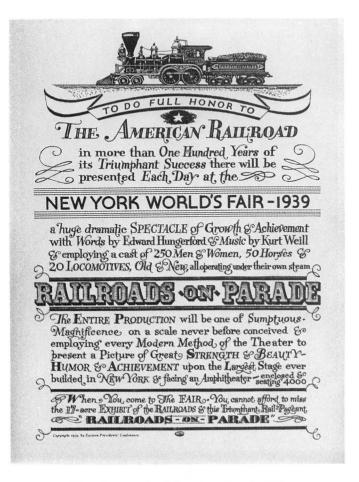

Advertisement for *Railroads on Parade*, 1939.

action precisely the right musical background. The use of the whistles of the fifteen old locomotives for a colloquy between them when the first trains from the East and the West meet in Nevada is amusingly worked out."[42]

When asked in an interview about the "functional character" of this *Railroad* music, Weill formulated a response that was often quoted later, one that can stand as a kind of guiding principle for all his music: "I have never acknowledged the difference between 'serious' music and 'light' music. There is only good music and bad music."[43]

By the end of 1939 he had written stage music for two productions of the Playwrights' Company. Likewise falling into the category of functional music, these purely instrumental works were also gestures of friendship toward his colleagues Sidney Howard (*Madam, Will You Walk?*) and Elmer Rice (*Two on an Island*).

II

Composer of Musicals

If Kurt Weill had transferred the European model of a "play with music" to the American theater with *Johnny Johnson* in 1936, with *Knickerbocker Holiday* in 1938 he had made his first contribution to the shaping of an independent form of American musical theater that would soon gain international standing: the musical. Although the early history of the musical reaches back to the nineteenth century, its real development came in the 1930s. Weill was of no small significance in this development: "In driving Weill out of Germany, Hitler inadvertently did Broadway a favor."[1]

For a better understanding of the context in which Weill's works were written, let us consider for a moment the general outlines of this development. As Joachim Sonderhoff has written, "American musical theater has no tradition, but it has a wildly turbulent and exciting early history."[2] In 1844 Palmo's Opera House was opened in New York (with a French guest ballet performance), and in 1883 the Metropolitan Opera House was opened (with Gounod's *Faust).* But until the 1930s opera in the United States was restricted to pure, as Weill wrote, "museum-piece" reproductions of European works and performance syles. Opera had exerted no influence up to that point on the development of an American form of musical theater, whose roots lay much more in the entertainment industry of the nineteenth century—above all, in burlesque, vaudeville (sometimes also called variety), and extravaganzas.

These three entertainment forms were mixtures of dance, ribald humor, circus elements, and song. *The Black Crook* of 1866 was the first long-running show, "an incredibly rediculous melodrama loosely based on the *Faust* legend."[3] Minstrel shows emerged in the late 1850s and enjoyed great popularity over the next fifty years. The idea was to have white actors portray African-Americans (who were still barred from the stage at this time). Decked out with blackened faces, thickly made-up lips, and wigs, they would present their jokes and sketches, as well as song and dance numbers. Done in what was often a crude parody of Southern speech patterns, the minstrel show became a vehicle of discrimination against African-Americans.

The first decade of the twentieth century brought new forms. Composers who had emigrated from Europe (such as the Irishman Victor Herbert and the Czech Rudolf Friml) developed light opera, an American form of operetta. George M. Cohan created the form of musical comedy in 1904 with *Little Johnny Jones,* and Florenz Ziegfeld established his annually produced follies in 1907, a form of American revue that reached its high point in the 1920s.

Although the stars—from the comedian W. C. Fields to the singer and dancer Fred Astaire—drew large crowds, all these forms of musical entertainment were characterized by two important deficiencies. First, they consisted of individual numbers that were loosely strung together but lacked a fully developed plot or book. Likewise, the shows always contained one or two musical hits but lacked any through-composed music. Writing about the years between 1910 and 1930, Brooks Atkinson remarked: "The standard musical show lingered for more than a decade. . . . The written material for *Lady Be Good* in 1924 was worthless, but George Gershwin's title song, with its descending refrain, delighted everybody, and his 'Fascinating Rhythm' has outlived the show and him. . . . Nobody can remember the theme of *Gay Divorce* in 1932, but no one can forget Cole Porter's rueful melody he called 'Night and Day.' "[4]

The year 1927 marked the real birth of the new genre of the musical—or "musical play," as it was often called—in the United States. The composer Jerome Kern and his librettist, Oscar Hammerstein II, adapted a novel by Edna Ferber for a work by the same title, *Show Boat.* For the first time there was a real unity between text and music, book and score. The story of life on board a Mississippi steamboat was also realistic and

The creators of the musical *Lady in the Dark*. *Left to right:* Moss Hart, Kurt Weill, and Ira Gershwin. This work was such a success that it ensured Weill's complete financial independence.

captured the spirit of the day. But *Show Boat* was followed by an incomprehensible silence. Sound movies had just become popular and were tempting the public as a new attraction and Hollywood was taking over the country's most successful songwriters. By the mid-1930s only two more works had appeared that gave real evidence of a new development of the genre: *Of Thee I Sing* (late 1931) and *Let 'Em Eat Cake* (1933). Both came from the same team: George S. Kaufman (book), Ira Gershwin (song lyrics), and George Gershwin (music). At the high point of the Depression these musicals, with their social critique, burst in on the public like a bombshell, thanks in no small part to the fabulous songs by the Gershwin brothers. Richard Rodgers's *On Your Toes* (1936) must also be mentioned, a sentimental story from the world of ballet with a dance insert choreographed by George Balanchine that lasted nearly eleven minutes and became such an important constitutive element that later musicals could not do without it.

Kurt Weill's first works for American musical theater thus came right in the middle of the phase when the musical had just gotten off the ground. The old forms were still held high in public esteem (Billy Minsky's burlesques at the Oriental Theatre on Broadway, the moving picture variations of the Ziegfeld Follies, carried on into the 1930s with a number of films called *Broadway Melody of 19—,* and so on). Weill was one of the agents of renewal, a fact that has so far received scant attention in Europe. As Stanley Green writes: "In spite of its brief run of about four months, *Knickerbocker Holiday* is generally accepted as a significant milestone in the development of the American musical theatre."[5]

From 1938 on we must speak of the American Weill and measure the significance of his work against the standard of its genre within the development of American theater. His decision to work within the musical theater of Broadway, which was so fundamentally different from European musical theater, to write for a public that had different expectations of a "musical play" than Europeans had of contemporary musical theater, makes it seem beside the point to measure his American works against his European ones, or vice versa. Once the decision had been made to break radically with Germany, Kurt Weill became an American composer. To cite Stanley Green again: "Indeed, it was characteristic of the man, both in his work and in his personal life, that he never looked

Manuscript page of Weill's score for the "Glamour Dream" from
Lady in the Dark.

backward. The challenge of the present was what concerned him, whether it was a new country or a new musical project. His impatience with self-pity, combined with his complete disinterest in anything that was not of immediate concern, enabled him to adjust to every new situation within the shortest possible time and with the most efficient results."[6] His very next project would bring him onto America's musical stage with a bang.

In late 1939 he met the playwright and librettist Moss Hart, an extremely experienced Broadway man. Born in the Bronx in 1904, Hart had become instantly famous as a result of a comedy he had written jointly with George S. Kaufman, *Once in a Lifetime,* a brilliant satire of Hollywood. Since then, in addition to writing more plays with Kaufman, mostly comedies *(You Can't Take It with You* won the Pulitzer Prize in 1937), he had written librettos for musical comedies by Cole Porter *(Jubilee,* 1935) and Richard Rodgers *(I'd Rather Be Right,* 1937, a play about President Roosevelt, portrayed by George M. Cohan).

Moss Hart had undergone psychoanalysis in 1939; at that time Freud's method was established in the United States not only as a serious science but as an outright fashion. It was "in" to have oneself psychoanalyzed, to have appointments with one's psychoanalyst. Moss Hart wanted to write a play about this; it was to be the story of a female journalist from a fashion magazine. For a long time he saw the actress Katharine Cornell

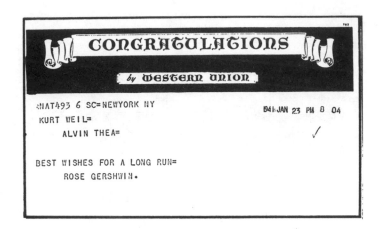

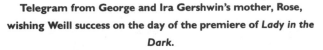

Telegram from George and Ira Gershwin's mother, Rose,
wishing Weill success on the day of the premiere of *Lady in the Dark*.

in the lead role, but then Hart changed his mind. Now he wanted to turn the material into a musical for the celebrated Gertrude Lawrence. This actress and singer had already made her Broadway debut in 1924 and had appeared in numerous roles since then. In 1936–37 she had celebrated another triumph with her part in Noel Coward's *Tonight at 8:30*.

When Moss Hart approached Weill (whom he had already asked to write the music for the play he was originally planning) about composing this musical, the latter immediately agreed. Ira Gershwin, who had not worked for Broadway since George Gershwin's death in 1937, was asked to write the song lyrics. He also agreed.

Out of their joint work between February and November 1940 came the musical *Lady in the Dark*. Moss Hart observed that, from the very beginning, the music was "part and parcel of the basic structure of the play. One cannot separate the play from the music, and vice versa. More than that, the music and lyrics carry the story forward dramatically and psychologically."[7]

Lady in the Dark tells the story of Liza Elliott, editor of a fashion magazine. A woman in her late thirties, she finds herself in a mental crisis. The first scene shows Liza visiting a psychoanalyst. Having been her married publisher's lover for many years, she is now having doubts about the relationship. She is also worried about having thrown a letter-opener at the advertising manager's head. She escapes from all these events at the beginning of the analysis in a "Glamour Dream."

The next scene shows Liza back at her office. When the publisher tells her of his intention to divorce his wife, Liza has another dream—a "Wedding Dream," in which a film star appears and falls in love with her. The advertising manager shows her the layout for the magazine's Easter issue, which is devoted entirely to the circus, and now Liza has a "Circus Dream." The next scene shows her back with her psychoanalyst, who has almost completed the treatment. The resolution of a childhood neurosis leads to a fourth and final dream, a "Childhood Dream." Relaxed, she leaves the analyst's office and decides

**The "Circus Dream" scene from the premiere of *Lady in the
Dark* at New York's Alvin Theatre, 23 January 1941. Gertrude
Lawrence as Liza Elliott is standing on the platform, rear left.**

on the young advertising manager, whom she now prefers to either the publisher or the
film star. The two decide to marry.

Kurt Weill's music makes high points of the four dream scenes. All the musical's
important numbers are to be found there. As Hart remarked, "What more natural than
that the dreams be conveyed by music and lyrics so that the plane of reality and that of the
dreams would be distinct?"[8]

In the first dream, of elegance and beauty, Liza is surrounded by a swarm of admirers
in a luxurious atmosphere as she drives through New York to an elegant nightclub. The
musical hits are "Oh, Fabulous One" and "Girl of the Moment"; the first is sung by
twelve men, as a chorus of admirers, and the second is also a chorus presented by her
admirers. The wedding dream opens with the film star's song, "This Is New," and ends
with "The Princess of Pure Delight," a confusing hodgepodge of Liza's memories that
turns into a nightmare and closes the sequence. The circus dream contains several musical
climaxes. In the song "Tschaikowsky," the lyrics to which Ira Gershwin had written in
1924 under the title "The Music Hour," the names of forty-nine Russian composers are
rattled off in a Gilbert and Sullivan style of patter. Liza's song "The Saga of Jenny," the
story of a woman who can't make up her mind, became a hit. Finally, in the childhood
dream a melody that has appeared in all the previous dream scenes as a musical tag,

**Cover of the premiere's program, featuring Gertrude Lawrence
as Liza Elliott.**

hummed by Liza or played by the orchestra, is presented in full. When Liza's childhood neurosis is resolved, she remembers the song in its entirety: "My Ship." It is a song she had sung with her father: "My ship has sails of white satin." The text seems to vibrate with the romance of another, earlier ship, the "ship with eight sails" from the Berlin days of long ago, but such reminiscences cannot be heard in the music. "My Ship" is the quintessential Broadway number; with the violins caressing the voice in unison, it is also a piece of musical glamour—albeit, one must objectively acknowledge, perfect in every detail. One can only agree with David Drew when he writes: "If *Lady in the Dark* is outwardly the least 'personal' score Weill had yet written, inwardly it is the nearest to being a subconscious form of autobiography. After seven hard years . . . he had now

First American Weill record album, of music from *Lady in the Dark*, issued in spring 1941.

succeeded at last in banishing from his music almost every trace of his musical background and upbringing."[9]

Lady in the Dark became a huge success, thus assuring Weill's complete financial independence. The premiere took place on 23 January 1941 at the Alvin Theatre. The director was Hassard Short, the conductor was Maurice Abravanel, and the cast included Gertrude Lawrence as Liza and the later Hollywood star Danny Kaye, who became a darling of the public with his rendition of "Tschaikowsky." This production had a run of 467 performances and then went on an extended and similarly successful American tour.

The reactions from the press were effusive, even by American standards. Even during the tryouts in Boston, *Lady in the Dark* was being celebrated as the "theatre's new sensation" and as a "wonder work."[10] In New York the press announced: "Six days after opening, 'Gertie the Goddess' has $120,000 advance sale."[11] The reference was to Gertrude Lawrence, whose performance was hailed as outstanding by the critics. Brooks Atkinson dealt extensively with the play:

> Moss Hart's musical play, "Lady in the Dark," which was put on at the Alvin last evening, uses the resources of the theatre magnificently and tells a compassionate story triumphantly. Note the distinction between "musical play" and "musical comedy." What that means to Mr. Hart's mind is a drama in which the music and the splendors of the production rise spontaneously out of the heart of the drama, evoking rather than embellishing the main theme. . . . Mr. Hart and his associates have carried it out as close to perfection as any one except an academician can require. Eschewing for the moment his blistering style of comedy, Mr. Hart has written a dramatic story about the anguish of a human being. Kurt Weill has matched it with the finest score written for the theatre in years. Ira Gershwin's lyrics are brilliant. Harry Horner's whirling scenery gives the narrative a transcendent loveliness. As for Gertrude Lawrence, she is a goddess: that's all.[12]

Cover of sheet music from *Lady in the Dark*.

Eight months later Atkinson attended another performance and then wrote an article entitled "Remarks on the Theatre Wonders of 'Lady in the Dark'—with Special Reference to Kurt Weill and Gertrude Lawrence." About Weill's music he wrote:

In the case of "Lady in the Dark" the catalytic agent is Kurt Weill's music. It not only tightens the transitions from the analyst's office to the dream sequences but also expresses the modern unearthly mood of the play. . . . He is not a song writer, but a composer of organic music that can bind the separate elements of a production and turn the underlying motive into song. He can orchestrate a score as well as compose it, and, as a matter of fact, his fresh, versatile orchestrations are highly enjoyable. . . . Mr. Weill is a composer of theatre music in the original sense of that term. . . . Without Mr. Weill's beautifully integrated music it would be difficult to evoke the

Starring

GINGER   RAY
ROGERS ☆ **MILLAND**
WARNER   JON
BAXTER ☆ **HALL**
In Glorious Technicolor
Screen Play by FRANCES GOODRICH and ALBERT HACKETT
Based Upon the Play by MOSS HART
With Music by KURT WEILL and Lyrics by IRA GERSHWIN

A **MITCHELL LEISEN** Production
Directed by MITCHELL LEISEN
Associate Producer: RICHARD BLUMENTHAL
A Paramount Picture

**Advertisement for the 1944 Paramount film of *Lady in the Dark,*
with Ginger Rogers playing the lead. The film was a huge success
at the box office, but Weill's music took a beating.**

strange imagery that distinguishes this musical play from the ordinary run of musical comedy.[13]

Shortly after the premiere the most successful songs appeared on five records, performed by Gertrude Lawrence and Robert Hannon. By May 1941 Paramount was negotiating for the film rights to *Lady in the Dark*. United Artists had already secured the rights to *Knickerbocker Holiday*. When both films were made in the summer of 1943, Weill once more went to Hollywood. But in addition to receiving only modest financial returns, he had to endure seeing his music mangled.

Lady in the Dark, starring Ginger Rogers and Ray Milland, was released to the movie theaters in February 1944. Mitchell Leisen was the director, and the screen play, based on Weill and Hart's play, was written by Frances Goodrich and Albert Hackett, who rose to

**Weill and Lenya on the porch of Brook House in New City,
Rockland County, to which they moved at the end of May 1941.**

fame after the war with their dramatization of *The Diary of Anne Frank*. The color picture was a big success at the box office, but Weill's music was badly mutilated by revisions and deletions. Of the play's major songs, "My Ship" was missing altogether, and only "The Saga of Jenny" was accurately taken over and sung well by Ginger Rogers.

Weill did not fare any better with the United Artists production of *Knickerbocker Holiday*, which was released in April 1944. Harry J. Brown was the director, and the lead roles were played by Nelson Eddy, Charles Coburn, and Constance Dowling. The producers had hired four arrangers and scriptwriters; and they obviously did not trust Weill's music, because the credits list a total of five Hollywood composers (including the Berlin émigré Werner R. Heymann) for "additional musical numbers." The film had little artistic quality; even "September Song" was poorly sung by Charles Coburn: "The Stuyvesant role . . . was the best part in the original, but it has had all the vitality boiled out of it; and, sad to say, Mr. Coburn just hasn't got the voice for the September song, even aided by sound track's amplifier."[14]

Let us return, though, to the time of the premiere of *Lady in the Dark*. Lotte Lenya had also just taken on a large piece of theater work. After the couple had moved into their house in New City and settled in there, she took a part in Maxwell Anderson's new play *Candle in the Wind* and went on an extensive American tour with the play. Not only was Weill now established as a composer, but his reputation—unusual in the United States—for orchestrating his own music led to additional offers. In the summer of 1942 the producer Russell Lewis, who wanted to bring Offenbach's *La Belle Hélène* to Broadway, asked Weill to reorchestrate and revise the work. Weill had to decline because of time constraints but recommended his old friend Darius Milhaud, who had emigrated from France in the summer of 1940. Weill and Lenya had greeted Darius and Madeleine Milhaud when they arrived in New York on 15 July 1940. Then the Milhauds had gone to California, where Milhaud took a teaching position at Mills College. Glad of the extra income, he accepted the Offenbach commission and wrote to Weill: "My dear Kurt, I am

Weill and Lenya at Brook House.

very excited about the Offenbach business, and I am going to accept to make this orchestration. But as I have no experience of BROADWAY, pleae tell me exactly what they expect of me. 1)Must I change the harmonies, put 'pep' into it? 2) What kind of orchestra can I use? What instruments? Give me all sort of good advices."[15] The production of *La Belle Hélène* was announced in January 1943, but for various reasons it was never actually performed.[16]

By this time Kurt Weill was already at work on his next musical, which was to take up the old Galatea–Pygmalion theme and feature a "bombshell role" for the leading actress. On 24 July 1942 Weill telegraphed Marlene Dietrich in Hollywood: "Dear Marlene, I have wonderul new set-up for Venus show. The Spewacks will write the book and Ogden Nash who is the foremost light verse writer of America will do the lyrics. We start working immediately and hope to be ready for fall production, with you as Venus. Yours, as ever, Kurt Weill."[17]

But Marlene did not accept; nor did the planned collaboration with Sam and Bella Spewack come about. The new writer of the book was S. J. Perelman. Working together with Ogden Nash, they wrote *One Touch of Venus* between June and September 1943.

The plot is tried and true, but also effective. The first scene is set in the private museum of Whitelaw Savory, a millionaire and patron of the arts, who has just acquired a priceless, 3,000-year-old statue of Venus. The poor, short barber Rodney Hatch arrives as he does

Weill with his dog, Wooley, in the kitchen of Brook House in 1942.

every day to shave Savory. Looking at the statue, he remarks that his fiancée, Gloria Kramer, is much more attractive than this Venus. Alone in the room for a moment, he wants to test his assumption and takes the statue's stretched-out hand in his. Lost in thoughts of his Gloria, he slips the wedding ring he has just purchased over the statue's finger. In a flash of thunder and lightning Venus comes to life. To Rodney's distress she immediately shows herself to have fallen deeply in love with her liberator. But the more she entreats him, the stronger Rodney's refusal becomes.

Perplexed, no longer sure of her charms, the goddess of love ventures out among people at a shopping arcade. There, in the ballet "Forty Minutes for Lunch," she arranges a romance between a young man and woman to prove that love is not dead. Meanwhile

Weill and Lenya at work in Brook House, 1942.

Gloria and her mother scold Rodney for having lost the wedding ring. He is in the barbershop bemoaning his situation when Venus suddenly appears and lovingly ensnares him. The two lie in each other's arms. To dispense with her rival, Venus turns Gloria into a breath of air. Rodney, suspected of having murdered Gloria, is arrested.

The second act begins with Venus helping Rodney escape from prison. The two spend an unforgettable night together in a hotel room. In bed Rodney implores Venus to bring Gloria back to life so that he will be cleared of the murder charge. At that moment a furious Gloria comes out of a closet in a puff of smoke. She curses Venus and Rodney and then disappears forever. Afterward Rodney dreams of his married life with Venus— naturally she will live with him in a little house in the suburbs. In the grand ballet "Venus

Weill and the lead actors at a rehearsal of *One Touch of Venus* at New York's Imperial Theatre in September 1943.

in Ozone Heights" the goddess is torn between the alternatives of becoming a suburban housewife at Rodney's side or returning to her former luxurious life. In the end she decides to rejoin the gods. The statue is returned to the museum. Rodney is standing sadly beside it when a girl who is the spitting image of the goddess enters the room. Speechless, they look at each other and leave the museum hand in hand.

Weill's brilliantly orchestrated score again contains some real hits: the romantic song "West Wind"; "Foolish Heart," a Weill waltz with a Broadway touch; "That's Him," the song in which Venus confesses her love to the barber; and above all the rumba "Speak Low," which rapidly became a worldwide hit. In the midst of this music of 1943, music from the old Berlin days resurfaces once more when three men come to the barbershop looking for the statue. Along with Rodney they sing the quartet "The Trouble with Women," to the same melody as "In der Jugend goldnem Schimmer" (In Youth's Golden Glimmer), one of the Salvation Army songs from *Happy End*. Here the music is no longer caricature but good Broadway entertainment, with full orchestral "sound."

Cheryl Crawford, Weill's old acquaintance from his time with the Group Theatre and now working independently, produced *One Touch of Venus,* which opened at the Impe-

The *One Touch of Venus* team at a rehearsal discussion with (*center*)
Kurt Weill and (*second from the left*) Elia Kazan, the director.

rial Theatre on 7 October 1943. The director was Elia Kazan; the conductor, once again, was Maurice Abravanel; and the lead role of Venus was sung and danced by Mary Martin, who launched a great musical career that evening.

If *Lady in the Dark* had experienced a record run with 467 performances, *One Touch of Venus* did even better, totaling 567 performances. By December 1943 "Speak Low" had already climbed to the top of the popular charts, and records and single sheets of the most important songs were being produced in large quantities. Universal Studios acquired the film rights and released the film version of *One Touch of Venus* (directed by William A. Seiter) in 1948. The commercial success of the production was again extraordinary.

A good six months before the premiere of Weill's new musical, *Oklahoma!* by Richard Rodgers and Oscar Hammerstein II, one of the new genre's boldest ventures, had been premiered (and was to be performed a total of 2,212 times!). It is understandable enough that the critics should have measured *One Touch of Venus* against *Oklahoma!* and—by contrast with the large crowds the latter was drawing—have expressed disappointment in the new musical. After describing the Broadway season as meagre, with the exception of

Oklahoma!, Lewis Nichols made the following assessment: "But in truth 'One Touch of Venus' is not another 'Oklahoma!' although it well may be the best new musical show to have opened since that time. Its earlier sections are not so funny as most of the remarks normally chattering off the Perelman–Nash typewriters, some of the show is neither fast nor brilliant and few of the players are much better than the material with which they are forced to work."[18]

Elliott Carter—after comparing the play with Weill's Berlin works and noting that "his social scene has shrunk to the bedroom"—vouched for the composer's "mastery of Broadway technic" and his ability to "turn out one success after another with a sure hand."[19]

It was unusual enough in the United States for a composer to orchestrate his own works. It was even more unusual for a composer to keep close tabs on the quality of the music through long runs, as Weill did. A reporter who accompanied Weill to the theater gave an eyewitness account of this. Even his headline, "Composer of 'One Touch of Venus' Visits Production Twice Weekly to Make Sure No Let-Down Occurs," expressed his astonishment. "[When] Mary Martin . . . with Sono Osato, Ray Harrison and dancers, went into the 'Forty Mintues for Lunch' ballet . . . Weill dashed a note upon his program. 'They've changed the tempo,' he observed. 'There may be a reason. I'll find out later.' He spoke quietly but very matter-of-fact about it. Presently in the 'Speak Low' number he dashed off another note. 'Brasses a little too loud,' he explained, unemotionally."[20]

One of the interviews that Weill gave after *One Touch of Venus* shows how aware he was that a leading position in the tough business of musicals could be won and retained only by perfection: "In the four weeks that are needed you get about two hours of sleep a night. But it's fun. You can't really start doing the orchestration until the rehearsals begin, because until you know who the singers are going to be, you don't know which key to choose for each number. The American musical is a custom-made job."[21]

Jacket of a record album released by Decca in late 1943, with Mary Martin pictured as Venus.

Cover of the single sheet of the song "Speak Low" published
after Universal Studios released the film version of *One Touch
of Venus*, picturing the lead, Ava Gardner.

Weill kept a close watch over the quality of the
repertory performances of *One Touch of Venus*
after the premiere. This note, presumably
addressed to the conductor, reads: "Your
orchestra sounds absolutely awful, like a
3-piece beergarden-band!"

Weill, the popular composer of musicals,
featured in the comic strip "Casey."

**Weill, with the writer Edwin Justus Mayer, during a rehearsal
of *The Firebrand of Florence*, based on episodes in the life of
Benvenuto Cellini, in March 1945.**

His next "job" was not a success, even though it involved a promising team that had
come together in mid-1944. Edwin Justus Mayer, an experienced Broadway writer, was
reworking his play *The Firebrand*, which had been performed in 1924, into a libretto, and
Ira Gershwin was writing song lyrics. The new musical was called *Much Ado about Love;*
only after the tryouts was the title changed to *The Firebrand of Florence* for the New York
premiere. The play consists of episodes from the life of Benvenuto Cellini, the Florentine
sculptor and goldsmith of the late Renaissance. Surely the material alone was a recipe for
failure. At a time when World War II was exploding with its own "firebrands," Benvenuto
Cellini must have seemed too distant a hero to the audiences of 1944–45.

Lenya as the duchess in the premiere of *The Firebrand of Florence* at New York's Alvin Theatre on 22 March 1945.

The Firebrand of Florence opens with an execution scene. Benvenuto Cellini is to be hanged in Florence's marketplace. But the duke appears and not only pardons him but commissions a statue from him. The private intrigues become apparent in the second part. Cellini is pursuing Angela, who in turn is loved by the duke, and the duchess is smitten with Cellini. In the end all the "firebrands" are settled to everyone's satisfaction. Of Weill's music only one song became well known—"Sing Me Not a Ballad," the duchess's entrance song.

The premiere took place on 22 March 1945 at the Alvin Theatre, with John Murray Anderson directing and Maurice Abravanel conducting. Lotte Lenya played the duchess, and Earl Wrightson sang the part of Benvenuto Cellini. The reactions were the exact opposite of what they had been with *One Touch of Venus*. This time the press liked the play ("a new hit has come to town"[22] and "one of the best scores that the gifted composer has written"[23]), but the public stayed away. The production had to be withdrawn after only forty-three performances.

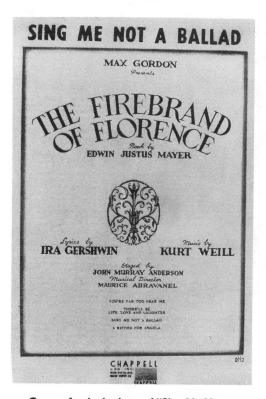

Cover of a single sheet of "Sing Me Not a Ballad," the duchess's entrance song from *The Firebrand of Florence*, 1945. This was the only song from that work which became at all well known.

Cover of the program for the premiere of *Love Life* at New York's Forty-fourth Street Theatre, 7 October 1948.

By this time Kurt Weill was well aware of how routine his work had become, and he was searching eagerly for new forms of expression for American musical theater. We shall speak of this again. He returned once more to the form of pure musical, however. The impetus came in the summer of 1948 from Cheryl Crawford, who had just produced a very successful musical by the then little-known team of Frederick Loewe and Alan Jay Lerner, *Brigadoon* (nine years before their international success, *My Fair Lady*). Now she was looking for a new play. Mindful of the success of *One Touch of Venus,* she suggested to Weill that he write something with Alan Jay Lerner, and so *Love Life* was written in just four weeks in August 1948. The play, which its authors called a "vaudeville," dealt with three centuries of everyday scenes from American marriages.

In the opening scene we see the couple Sam and Susan Cooper as mediums in a magic show. The magician announces that their marriage has been in trouble for a hundred years. The first historical scene is laid in Connecticut in 1791. The Cooper marriage is

Weill with the book writer and lyricist Alan Jay Lerner at a rehearsal for *Love Life* in September 1948.

presented in a pastoral-moral paradise. By the end, however, the shadows of the economic progress that threaten to destroy this paradise can already be sensed. The next scene shifts to the year 1821. Cooper is starting a factory and no longer spends the whole day in the bosom of his family. In the next scene (1857) Sam is a railroad king and no longer has time even to beget the child his wife yearns for. The following scene takes place in 1890. Now Susan is too busy for love, as she has become part of the women's rights movement. The retrospective ends in 1920; now the Coopers are on a steamship, both flirting with other partners. The second act shows the Coopers in a New York apartment in 1948. The marriage is defunct, and they decide to get a divorce. The play ends with a big vaudeville revue in which all the faces and stages are presented again.

Weill's music shows his perfect mastery of the conventions of the musical one last time. New hits were born for the star parade: "Green-Up Time" and "Here I'll Stay." The premiere took place on 7 October 1948 at the Forty-sixth Street Theatre. As with *One*

Cover of sheet music from *Love Life*.

Touch of Venus, the director was Elia Kazan, and the conductor was Joseph Littau. The reaction from the press was largely positive, and with 252 performances the production was also moderately successful financially. But Brooks Atkinson hit the nail on the head when he spoke of its creators' stagnation at a point they had long since reached: "Unless it is illegal to do so, this column would like to express a feeling of general disappointment over 'Love Life.' . . . It is cute, complex and joyless—a general gripe masquerading as entertainment. This may be a thoroughly illegal opinion, since some of the most honored people in show business have worked at it."[24]

Kurt Weill did not see himself in this field any longer either. *Love Life* was nothing more than a way station for him, since he had already turned to a new arena–Broadway opera.

12

Interlude: We Fight Back

World War II broke out in Europe when Hitler and his *Wehrmacht* invaded Poland on 1 September 1939. The Roosevelt administration continued its policy of isolationism and nonintervention well into 1941. Only after the Japanese attack on Pearl Harbor on 7 December did the United States enter the war. In 1942 it joined with Great Britain, the Soviet Union, and other members of the Atlantic Charter in the fight against Nazi Germany.

A large mobilization campaign for the war against Hitler was mounted in all

The painter Arthur Kaufman at work on his triptych *Geistige Emigration* (Intellectual Emigration), New York, 1939. In the center panel we see (*in front*) Albert Einstein, flanked by Heinrich and Thomas Mann, and next to them Erika and Klaus Mann. The front row of the right panel shows (*left to right*) Kurt Weill; Max Reinhardt; his wife, Helene Thimig; and Ernst Toller.

parts of the country. Kurt Weill participated in this campaign with great seriousness and through so many activities that it seems appropriate to devote a separate chapter to them.

His decision to break with Germany and henceforth seek new artistic expression in America had quickly led to a determination not only to apply for citizenship but to become an American in thought, feeling, and speech. From 1936 on, Weill started to write and speak in English—even in his personal life and in his correspondence with Lotte Lenya. In a radio interview he gave in March 1941 he declared, "I am an American."[1] Weill and Lenya became American citizens in 1943. When a 1947 article in *Life* magazine referred to him as a German composer, he protested energetically: "I have a gentle beef about one of your phrases. Although I was born in Germany, I do not consider myself a 'German composer.' The Nazis obviously did not consider me as such either, and I left their country (an arrangement which suited both me and my rulers admirably) in 1933. I am an American citizen, and during my dozen years in this country I have composed exclusively for the American stage. . . . I would appreciate your straightening out your readers on this matter."[2]

Announcement of the pageant play *Fun to Be Free* on 5 October
1941 in New York's Madison Square Garden.

So there was no question in Weill's mind but that he would offer his services when war broke out. Along with Maxwell Anderson he volunteered for civil service as an air warden near New City. A newspaper printed a picture of the two and wrote: "From this tower on a hilltop between New City and Haverstraw, N.Y., Maxwell Anderson, the playwright, listens for enemy planes over the High Tor. . . . With composer Kurt Weill (on steps), his friend and next-door neighbor on South Mountain Road three miles away, he makes the windy, ten-minute climb every other week; watches four hours. On duty, Anderson wears an Alaska fur cap; little bald Weill goes bareheaded. They haven't heard a plane—not even a friendly one."[3] It was surely because of the last, sarcastic sentence that Brecht cut out the photograph in California and pasted it into his work journal.

Weill participated quite early on, at a time when isolationism still had the upper hand, in the actions of the organization Fight for Freedom, which called for American entry into

**Kurt Weill (*right*) and Maxwell Anderson (wearing a hat) on duty
as air wardens in the early summer of 1942.**

**Weill's identification card as an air warden, a
volunteer position in the U.S. Army's Aircraft
Warning Service.**

the war. On 5 October 1941 Fight for Freedom held a large event in New York's Madison
Square Garden that was attended by six thousand people. Along with the playwrights
Ben Hecht and Charles MacArthur (who had become famous in 1928 with their play *The
Front Page)* Weill wrote the pageant play *Fun to Be Free* for this occasion. The perfor-
mance was a big success.

Likewise, long before the United States entered the war, Weill reflected on ways in
which the many artists who had emigrated to this country could be united and mobilized.
On 17 June 1940 Weill wrote identical letters to Erika Mann and Bruno Frank in which
he asked:

Cover of the piano reduction of the radio
cantata *The Ballad of Magna Carta*, published
in New York in 1940.

What can we do to help America in her inevitable fight against Nazism? . . . What can
we do to prove to our American friends that we are loyal citizens of this country? . . .
My idea is to form immediately an organisation called something like "Alliance of
Loyal-Alien Americans" with the purpose of convincing the authorities and the public
opinion in this country that we are strongly anti-Nazi, that they can count on us in
every effort to save American democracy and that they can consider us in every way as
faithful American citizens.[4]

Both Frank and Erika Mann replied affirmatively by return mail. Such an organization
was not founded, however.

A further project that Weill suggested shortly before American entry into the war was
partly realized in the following years. On 12 December 1941 he wrote to the shortwave
service of CBS: "There are in this country now the greatest German writers, poets,
playwrights, composers, musicians, actors, and directors. What I would like to do is to
mobilize all this talent for a cultural attack on the German people. We would write radio
plays, pamphlets, songs, and comedy scenes. . . . In word and music we would tell them
the truth about their leaders."[5] Since 1938 the New York radio station WEDV had been
broadcasting a weekly German-language radio program (called "We Fight Back" from
1942 on) in which many émigrés spoke, but this program was directed toward German-
Americans already living in the United States. Propaganda broadcasts over shortwave

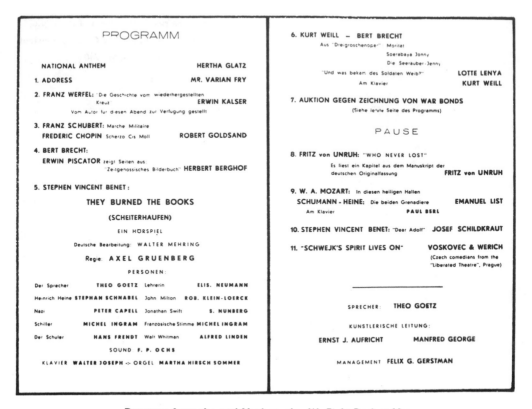

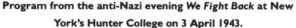

Program from the anti-Nazi evening *We Fight Back* at New
York's Hunter College on 3 April 1943.

radio to Germany were introduced only after the establishment of the Office of War
Information (OWI), a coordinating office for all questions of war propaganda that re-
ported directly to the president. It was thanks in part to Weill that, along with verbal
contributions, samples of anti-Nazi art were broadcast to Germany. Lotte Lenya re-
corded two songs for shortwave transmission by the OWI in 1943 on poems that Bertolt
Brecht had written and sent to Weill from California: "Lied einer deutschen Mutter"
(Song of a German Mother), with music by Paul Dessau that Brecht had sent along, and
"Und was bekam des Soldaten Weib?" (And What Did the Soldier's Wife Get?). Kurt
Weill set the second text to music. Later he worked on the play *Schwejk im zweiten
Weltkrieg* (Schweik in the Second World War) with Hanns Eisler's music. A comparison
of the Eisler and Weill settings shows what a range "epic music" can have, for this is what
both compositions were. This also applies to Weill's setting of "Nannas Lied," which
Brecht had sent him in 1939 but which became part of the play *Die Rundköpfe und die
Spitzköpfe* (The Round Heads and the Peak Heads) in Eisler's setting. In 1944 Lotte
Lenya sang another song for shortwave radio that Weill had composed, on a text by
Walter Mehring: "Wie lange noch?" (How Much Longer?).

The OWI's shellac records were broadcast not only from the United States to Europe but also by the American radio stations operating at the front lines in Europe. A letter that the OWI sent to Weill in 1944 said: "This organisation wishes to express its deep appreciation and to thank you and Mrs. Weill for your fine work on the song 'Wie lange noch.' These recordings, which have a very definite place in the prosecution of the war, have been received, reshipped, and by the time this note reaches you, they will have reached their ultimate destination. At some day in the future we hope it will be possible for us to show you more definitely how your song assisted in the total war effort."[6]

The circumstances of the anti-Fascist war brought Weill and Brecht somewhat closer together again. Weill and Lenya saw Brecht on a visit to Hollywood in October 1942; it was the first time the three had met since 1935. Lotte Lenya must have sung Weill's setting of "Nanna's Song" on that occasion, because soon thereafter Brecht sent a new text to Weill, "In Sturmesnacht" (On a Stormy Night), with a handwritten note saying, "I am naturally thinking of Lenya's unforgettable rendition of 'Where Are the Tears of Yesterday Evening' "[7] In the end it was Eisler, though, rather than Weill, who set this song to music.

On 3 April 1943 Lotte Lenya and Kurt Weill appeared at Hunter College in New York as part of a big anti-Nazi evening with the programmatic title *We Fight Back* that Manfred Georg and Ernst Josef Aufricht had organized to commemorate the tenth anniversary of the book burning. The four-hour-long program included presentations by the writer Fritz von Unruh and the actors Erwin Kalser and Joseph Schildkraut. Lotte Lenya, accompanied by Kurt Weill, sang three songs from *Die Dreigroschenoper,* as well as "Und was bekam des Soldaten Weib?" Two days later Georg wrote to Weill: "On Saturday I was congratulating *us* that you were with us and were thus to a considerable extent creating and assuring the evening's success, but today I would like to congratulate *you* on your new composition of the Brecht song. This simple, unforgettable melody will live on as only a few major folk songs do. And one cannot wish more for it."[8]

Record cover for a collection of six Weill songs that Lenya recorded for Bost in 1943.

Record cover for a performance of the patriotic melodrama
Mine Eyes Have Seen the Glory, by Helen Hayes in 1942.

Jacket of a recording of Weill's settings of three
poems by Walt Whitman, 1943.

Cover of an advertising brochure for *The Lunch Hour Follies*.
The photographs convey an impression of the anti-Nazi
entertainment programs provided for dock workers and
arms factory workers.

Soon thereafter, in May 1943, Brecht came to New City for a week of joint work. Prompted by Aufricht, whose activity had not slackened in the United States, Weill was to write music for Brecht's *Schweik* play. In addition, Brecht himself asked him to write music for *Der gute Mensch von Sezuan* (The Good Person of Szechwan). But neither project came to fruition; their artistic conceptions differed too much by now. Brecht's admiration for Lotte Lenya was unchanged, however. In the summer of 1943, again accompanied by Weill, she recorded a set of songs for the Bost label. This set included six Weill songs: two old Berlin hits, two songs from his time in France, and two songs from

Weill's certificate of naturalization, which he received on 27 August 1943. Lenya also became an American citizen.

the uncompleted *Ulysses Africanus*. Brecht bought the records immediately in California and wrote in a letter to Weill, "Give my regards to Lenya. I have been playing her French record constantly for encouragement. (Lenya has grown incredibly!)"[9]

Weill's activities as part of the American mobilization campaign were even more extensive than his anti-Nazi work directed at Germany. In 1942 he worked with the famous actress Helen Hayes on two records of patriotic melodramas. "I took the words of 'America,' 'The Star Spangled Banner,' and 'Battlehymn of the Republic' and wrote a musical setting for them, based on the original tunes, but dramatising the words for Helen's reading. On the fourth side we took one of my Walt Whitman songs ('Beat! Beat! Drums!') which Helen speaks in rhythm of the music."[10] Around the same time he wrote music for Maxwell Anderson's radio broadcast *Your Navy*, as well as the "Song of the Free" on a poem by Archibald MacLeish.

Since the OWI was enlisting every kind of artistic production in its mobilization of the American people, Broadway was also asked to create special programs for the personnel of the large arms factories in the New York area. Weill worked with Moss Hart and other artists on one of these projects, *The Lunch Hour Follies*, in 1942–43. This project involved creating small shows that could be performed in the factories at lunchtime. Along with pure entertainment, they contained sketches and songs satirizing the Nazis. The troupe started out performing for workers at the Brooklyn shipyards and was soon taking the show all over the state of New York. Weill wrote to Archibald MacLeish about his impressions of the first performance:

Yesterday I went with Moss Hart who is in charge of this project to see the first tryout

**Scene from the premiere of the pageant play *We Will Never Die*,
a protest against the Holocaust, in New York's Madison
Square Garden, 9 March 1943.**

of the "Lunch Hour Follies" at the Wheeler Shipyard in Whitestone, L. I. It was a 45-minutes show—some songs, some dancing, a sketch "Hitler in Russia" by Kaufman and Hart, and a pep-talk by a naval officer. It was completely successful and a very exciting experience for everybody connected with it. At 12 o'clock sharp, about 1,200 men rushed from their place of work to a little square near the water where they had built a little stage. They took their seats on benches, on the floor and high up in the scaffolds and watched the show while they were eating their lunch. They had a wonderful time, and when it all was over we heard them saying: "We'll do twice as much work this afternoon." We all felt that here is the most natural field of activity for all those writers, musicians and artists who are desperately looking for their place in the nation's War effort.[11]

Weill composed at least eight songs for this project to words by Maxwell Anderson, Oscar Hammerstein II, and others. Among them is a biting satire on Hitler entitled "Schickelgruber," with lyrics by Howard Dietz.

In 1942, as part of a fund-raising drive to send military equipment to the Soviet Union in support of its struggle against the German invasion, J. P. McEvoy and Weill wrote the song "Russian War Relief," with the recurring line in the refrain "Russia needs a helping hand."[12]

In 1943 Weill wrote a second pageant play with Ben Hecht. Called *We Will Never Die*, this was an urgent protest against the Nazi Holocaust. It was premiered on 9 March 1943 in Madison Square Garden before twenty thousand people. Moss Hart was the director, and Edward G. Robinson and Paul Muni, two of the most popular American film stars of the day, were also involved in the project. Musically Weill continued here what he had already begun in 1935–36 with *The Eternal Road,* integrating Jewish folk music into the score and alternating large choral and solo scenes with acted, purely narrative passages.

Cover of a single sheet of the "Song of the Rhineland" from the
Hollywood anti-Nazi film *Where Do We Go from Here?*, 1945.

Four large sections depict, first, the centuries-old history of the Jewish people ("The Roll
Call"), then the heroic participation of Jewish soldiers in the war on various fronts ("The
Jew in War"), next the uprising in the Warsaw ghetto ("The Battle of Warsaw"); and
finally the victims of the ghettos and concentration camps ("Remember Us"). The evening was so successful that it had to be repeated, by popular demand, the next day. This
was followed by performances, with partially different casts, in Washington, Philadelphia, Chicago, Boston, and Hollywood. More than twenty thousand people saw this
work in the Hollywood Bowl, the largest open-air stage in America, in May 1943. A
number of radio stations broadcast the performances both nationally and locally. It

would not be an exaggeration to say that *We Will Never Die* brought the tragedy of the Holocaust into the consciousness of many tens of thousands of Americans that year. Sinclair Lewis wrote in the program: "Here is one of the first examples of the great art that should, but scarcely has yet, come out of the War for Democracy."[13]

In 1944 Weill took part in a program for American troops by providing a number of song compositions. Although these works have not been preserved, a letter from the "Entertainment Section" of the U. S. Army, which was responsible for the program, gives us evidence of their impact: "May I take this opportunity to thank you for your efforts in connection with the Soldier Shows Production *Three Day Pass*. After a tryout at a military installation in the vicinity of New York City, the production will be 'blueprinted.' The complete script, full orchestral score, and design for improvised costumes and scenery, will be sent to military installations all over the world. I feel certain that the songs you have written for *Three Day Pass* will prove a tremendous incentive to our fighting men here and overseas in staging their own shows."[14]

Finally, Kurt Weill also took part in Hollywood's anti-Nazi output of the 1940s with two film compositions (beyond the unsuccessful 1937 project *Blockade)*. Here, too, all genres were included; the musical film was no exception.

Weill composed music to lyrics by Ira Gershwin for the film *Where Do We Go from Here?* (directed by Gregory Ratoff) from November 1943 to January 1944. This was the only time that Weill was able to realize his vision of a musical film—unfortunately, with a very weak book. The film's plot is rather confusing: Bill Morgan signs up to serve in the U.S. Army but is declared unfit for the front. He is required to serve in an army canteen when he wants nothing so much as to fight against the Nazis. A ghost appears in an old lamp and grants Bill three wishes. Bill has only one wish, to get into the army. But the old ghost changes the century, and Bill finds himself in the army of George Washington. Having survived this, he still does not make it into the army but travels even farther back in time and finds himself aboard one of Christopher Columbus's ships. He helps Columbus discover America, buys Manhattan from an Indian, and participates in the founding of New Amsterdam. Finally, the ghost takes him on a flying carpet to the U.S. Army of 1944, and Bill takes part in the opening of the Second Front in Europe.

Weill and Gershwin had a free hand musically, and they came up with a number of successful songs, especially in the two historical sequences. These included, from the Columbus scene, "The Nina, the Pinta, the Santa Maria"; from the Washington scene, the "Song of the Rhineland" (macabre in its depiction of Hessian recruits who have been forced to come to America singing a ditty about the German Rhineland in high spirits); and, from the final scene in which Bill—accompanied, of course, by a girl—goes off to World War II, the love song "If Love Remains." This song became quite popular when the film was being shown in 1945, as did the rousing title and closing song, "Morale." All in all, *Where Do We Go from Here?* must be counted as one of the few successful anti-Nazi films.

Renowned Hollywood directors, such as Frank Capra and John Ford, were then working in the area of documentary films, which were being produced both to inform the American people about the progress of the war and—especially after 1944—for use in

**First postwar German production of a Weill work: *Die
Dreigroschenoper* at Berlin's Hebbel-Theater, directed
by Karlheinz Martin and premiered on 15 August 1945, with
Hubert von Meyerinck as Macheath.**

freed Europe. In April and May 1944 Kurt Weill was able to secure a collaboration in this
field that he had been seeking ever since his arrival in Paris in 1933. Jean Renoir was
filming a semi-documentary film, *Salute to France,* on a script by Maxwell Anderson.
Three Allied soldiers—an American, a Briton, and a Frenchman—report on the struggle
to liberate France. Acted scenes alternate with documentary sequences from the war.
Weill's music contains, along with instrumental passages, adaptations of French songs,
including the famous "Chant de libération."

By the time the film was completed, the Red Army had already brought about a decisive turn in the war. Four weeks later, in June 1944, the United States opened the Second Front with the landing of troops in Normandy. The end of Hitler's Germany was only a few months away. A few days before the capitulation, Weill wrote to his parents in Palestine: "I do not believe that in all of human history any nation has experienced as terrible a defeat as Germany—or that any people has deserved humiliation as much as these barbarians who have taken it upon themselves to destroy everything good and decent that people have achieved over millennia."[15]

Kurt Weill as a Vansittartite? That would not be a correct interpretation of this letter. Rather, these are words written by a sensitive Jewish person and artist, still shocked to the core twelve years after his expulsion, who has long since reclassified himself as a "loyal-alien." In this respect Weill also eludes any groupings or trends among those who considered themselves to be in exile in the United States.

13

Broadway Opera

Two years after Kurt Weill's arrival in America, the respected journal *Modern Music* published a lengthy article he wrote entitled "The Future of Opera in America," in which he stated:

The development of opera in Europe, which had a sudden upsurge after the war, has been stagnant for many years. I was therefore greatly interested in discovering the state of the theatre when I came to America about twenty months ago.

What we have known for years in Europe is even more applicable here. The concept of opera cannot be interpreted in the narrow sense that was prevalent in the nineteenth century. If we substitute the term "music theatre," the possibilities for development here, in a country not burdened with an opera tradition, become much clearer. We can see a field for the building of a new (or the rebuilding of a classical) form.[1]

A number of American composers were taking up the problem of an "American opera" at the same time as Weill. For them, too, the stimulus had come from experiences in Europe in the 1920s: for George Antheil from a stay first in Berlin from 1921 to 1923 and then in Paris from 1923 to 1933; for Marc Blitzstein from studies with Schönberg in Berlin in 1927; and for Virgil Thomson from time spent in Paris starting in 1925. In the United States their efforts made them outsiders. Virgil Thomson, looking back on his country's opera scene, described it thus:

Progress towards a true American opera was inhibited by an age-old suspicion of the theatre that lingered in puritanical minds. One of America's earliest opera houses was called the Boston Museum, another the Howard Street Athenaeum. . . . As late as 1900 Thomas Whitney Surette, a most influential music educator, branded opera as a sin. And when American composers attempted to compete in the operatic field, more often than not their works were denied performance by the foreign-dominated companies or sabotaged by singers who had never learned to vocalize English. . . . After such a history few composers could be expected to waste their time on opera.[2]

The few real experiments in opera during the 1930s took place outside of opera houses; they were produced by progressive theater people or under the auspices of the Federal Theatre Project. George Antheil's *Helen Retires* and Virgil Thomson's *Four Saints in Three Acts* were performed in 1934, followed by Marc Blitzstein's *The Cradle Will Rock* in 1937, all without any particular public success. Even George Gershwin's *Porgy and Bess* was given only 124 performances after its premiere on Broadway in 1935.

Kurt Weill observed all this carefully. During the 1940s, while he was still writing hit musicals for Broadway, he was devoting increasing attention to the question of how a new form of musical theater such as he envisaged could be realized independently of opera houses (which were closed to any kind of innovation) and of a rarified experimental scene (which had virtually no public impact). The only solution he saw was to tie the new form of opera to Broadway. It seemed equally important to him to put American material on the stage and to draw on the rich resources of American folk music. The successful revival of *Porgy and Bess* on Broadway starting in 1942, which ran to 400 performances, strengthened Weill in his convictions. In a 1947 essay entitled "Broadway and the Musical Theatre" he wrote:

It has been my opinion for a long time that the Broadway stage can become an important outlet for the American composer and might even become the birthplace of a genuine American "musical theatre" or, if you wish, an American opera. . . . I never could see any reason why the "educated" (not to say "serious") composer should not be able to reach all available markets with his music, and I have always believed that opera should be a part of the living theatre of our time. Broadway is today one of the great theatre centers of the world. It has all the technical and intellectual equipment for a serious musical theatre.[3]

In 1945 he was also turning to radio as a means of helping a new kind of opera gain a broad influence. He was thinking of the old English "ballad opera" in the style of John Gay infused with American folk songs and ballads. Weill's acquaintance with a number of radio people from his work on OWI programs led to a commission for a short opera. Together with the playwright Arnold Sundgaard he wrote the radio opera *Down in the Valley* between August and November 1945, and it was recorded at the end of 1945. Afterward Weill wrote to the producers: "For our radio program we have found a new way of making the folksong the basic element of an American art-form. We decided to dramatize the folksong itself, to exploit the old American habit of story telling and to present the folksong in its most natural surrounding: in scenes from the American life. What could be a more natural medium for the presentation of these modern 'ballad operas' than the radio? . . . The new combination of the three elements music–drama–radio which we have found in our program, is what we in show business call a 'natural.' "[4]

Various factors prevented the opera from being broadcast, however, and Weill's whole project of radio operas was discontinued. This first version of *Down in the Valley* has never been broadcast.

In January 1946, just as the radio project was falling through, Weill began work on a theater project that was to transform his idea of a Broadway opera into reality. As with *Knickerbocker Holiday,* the starting place was the Playwrights' Company, with which Weill had kept up an association through Maxwell Anderson. For a long time Weill had thought of *Street Scene,* the successful play by Elmer Rice, as a good basis for his project. Premiered in New York in 1929, *Street Scene* had won the Pulitzer Prize that same year and had immediately been translated into a number of languages. Weill had seen it in Berlin in 1930 (in Hans Reisiger's translation, *Die Straße,* performed by a prominent ensemble that included the actors Albert and Else Bassermann as well as Grete Mosheim), and had been favorably impressed by it. As early as 1936, when he first met Rice during a rehearsal for *Johnny Johnson,* Weill had asked the playwright for permission to write a musical adaptation of the play. At that time Rice (who had already received quite a few such requests from various composers) had said that it was too early for a musical adaptation.[5] Now, ten years later, Rice thought the time was right, and he agreed to Weill's plan. America's leading black poet, Langston Hughes, was persuaded to write the lyrics. From the very beginning it was clear that this would be a production with the apparatus of opera—trained singers and a thirty-five-member orchestra.

Work on *Street Scene* took up all of 1946. First Weill and Rice began working on the book, but soon Hughes, who stayed with Weill and Lenya in New City for a while, joined the team. Hughes took the composer to black neighborhoods of New York, to simple entertainment spots, to slums where unkempt children were playing in the streets, so that

The creators of the Broadway opera *Street Scene*. *Left to right:*
Kurt Weill, Elmer Rice, and Langston Hughes.

Weill could absorb the milieu. During these visits he got to know a side of America that he had not yet seen in all its reality. The collaboration between Weill, Rice, and Hughes was extraordinarily close and egalitarian and probably accounts in large measure for the opera's strength.

Hughes wrote about their collaboration:

It didn't seem strange or unusual to either Kurt Weill or Elmer Rice that I, a black American, should write the lyrics for *Street Scene*. Both of them wanted a lyricist who understood the problems of small people. Blacks certainly do. . . . Weill wanted a poet. I am happy that he considered me one. . . . By writing a "Broadway opera" like *Street Scene* in a national idiom that could be understood by the American people, Weill reached this American people and stirred it to compassion, concern, and self-awareness.[6]

And Weill wrote about his work: "As soon as I began to think about the music for 'Street Scene' I discovered that the play lent itself to a great variety of music, just as the

Scene from the Berlin production of Elmer Rice's play *Street
Scene*, translated as *Die Straße*. Directed by Heinz Hilpert, this
production was premiered in the Berliner Theater on 24 January
1930, with Albert and Else Bassermann as the Maurrant couple
and Grete Mosheim as Rose. Weill saw this production, and it
made a strong impression on him.

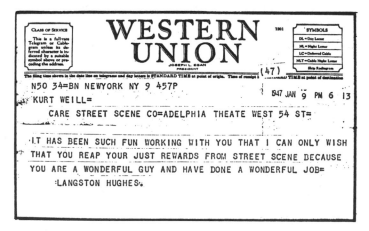

Telegram from Langston Hughes on the day of the premiere
of *Street Scene*.

Scene from the well-received premiere of *Street Scene* at New York's Adelphi Theatre, 9 January 1947.

streets of New York themselves embrace the music of many lands and many people. I had an opportunity to use different forms of musical expression, from popular songs to operatic ensembles, music of mood and dramatic music, music of young love, music of passion and death—and, overall, the music of a hot summer evening in New York."[7]

Weill worked more intensively than he had for a long time. Before he started composing, he studied Verdi scores as well as American folk songs. In September 1946 he wrote to his parents: "The composition is about 80 percent finished, and I have been working on the orchestration for the last four weeks. I sit at my desk from eight o'clock in the morning till late at night and write about eighteen pages a day. But Lenya makes sure that I don't overwork, and that I do something for my health in between times—bicycling, gardening, etc."[8] Two months later he wrote to his brother Hans: "I am working like never before in my life, and so far it looks awfully good. It is without doubt the most important piece I have written since *Bürgschaft* and it might turn out to be the best of all my works."[9]

Street Scene is the story of a New York apartment house and its inhabitants during two hot summer days. It is a tale of simple people. The Maurrant family is at the center of the plot. Frank Maurrant, a heavy drinker, is often away from home on business. His wife, Anna, keeps house and cares for their two children, young Willie and Rose, their grown daughter, who works in a real estate agency. Unhappy with her life, Anna Maurrant has started having an affair with a neighbor, Mr. Sankey. Rose is drawn to the young Sam Kaplan; but her boss, Harry Easter, is chasing her. The first act introduces the plot and the characters, and the second act brings the dramatic climax.

Frank Maurrant leaves on one of his trips. After warning her mother that everyone is already gossiping about her relationship with Sankey, Rose meets Sam Kaplan, and the two make plans for the future. Harry Easter picks up Rose to go to the funeral of the head of their company. Now Mr. Sankey appears, Anna Maurrant waves to him to come up, and at that very moment her husband unexpectedly returns and sees Sankey entering the house. The situation suddenly becomes clear to him. Furious, he storms into the house. Sam Kaplan tries—in vain—to stop him and then tries to warn Mrs. Maurrant, but at that moment screams and several shots are heard from above. With his revolver drawn, Maurrant storms back out of the house and disappears before the police arrive. Rose returns from the funeral and sees her mother's and Mr. Sankey's bodies being carried out of the house. Soon thereafter the police arrest Frank Maurrant and take him away. Rose and Sam Kaplan see each other one last time, and she decides to leave him and start a new life elsewhere.

Weill's score is extremely varied. Pieces that are very closely related to Gershwin's *Porgy and Bess* alternate with grand opera arias in the style of Puccini; jazz-inspired songs are juxtaposed with large choral scenes and smooth musical instrumentation.

Weill described the opera's most important musical numbers in conjunction with the plot:

> We see, in the beginning, the women who live in the house, sitting on the steps, complaining about the heat ("Ain't it awful, the heat"), talking to the janitor who comes up from the cellar singing his blues song ("I got a marble and a star"), gossiping about Mrs. Maurrant's love life ("Gossip") and making fun of young Buchanan whose wife is having a baby ("When a woman has a baby"). Then we hear Mrs. Maurrant's aria ("Somehow I never could believe"), expressing her troubled mind and her secret desires; the song of the young girls coming home from the graduation exercises ("Wrapped in a ribbon and tied in a bow"); Sam Kaplan's song of adolescent melancholy ("Lonely House"); then Rose Maurrant's scene with her "boss," Mr. Easter, who is trying to lure her into a different sort of life ("Wouldn't you like to be on Broadway?"); Rose's decision to live her own kind of life ("What good would the moon be?") and the scene of young love between Rose and Sam, dreaming of lilac bushes and happiness ("Remember that I care").
>
> The second act opens with the morning music, the awakening of the house and the "Children's Game," and goes on to Mrs. Maurrant's touching song to her little son ("A boy like you"), to a passionate duet of the two lovers, Sam and Rose, who have decided to take life in their own hands ("We'll go away together") and the horror-stricken death scene of Mrs. Maurrant ("The woman who lived up there"). In the last scene we see the two nursemaids trying to sing the babies to sleep, while at the same time gossiping about their parents ("Lullaby"); we see Rose meeting for the last time her father who has killed his wife and is being taken away by the police ("I loved her too"); and finally Rose saying goodbye to the one she loves ("Farewell Duet").[10]

Rehearsals began in December 1946, and the premiere of *Street Scene* took place on 9 January 1947 at the Adelphi Theatre, with Charles Friedman directing and Maurice Abravanel conducting.

Kurt Weill had posted a letter to the ensemble on the theater's bulletin board: "Dear Friends, the show we are giving to-night is to me the fulfillment of an old dream—the

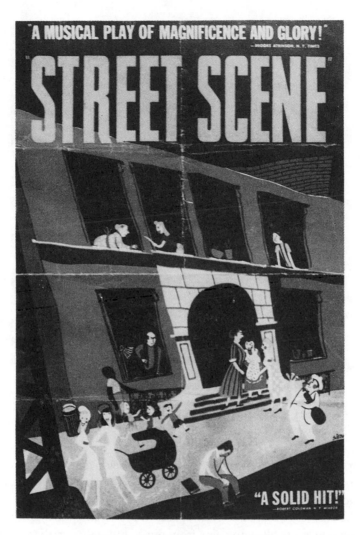

Poster for *Street Scene*, January 1947.

dream of a serious, dramatic musical for the Broadway stage which might open up a new field of activity for singers, musicians, writers and composers. This dream comes to life to-night. . . . Now it is all yours, and I want you to go out to-night in the spirit of fighting an important battle. . . . Good luck to you all! Kurt Weill."[11]

Weill received a telegram from Elmer Rice on the evening of the premiere that read: "Dear Kurt: Working with you has been one of my happiest experiences in the theatre and one that I hope will be repeated. You have written a beautiful score and I hope it gets the recognition it deserves."[12]

The authors could not complain about the attention it received. The audience at the premiere was enthusiastic, and the press also praised the play, agreeing fully with Weill's

Record cover of *Street Scene*, showing the cast of the premiere, Columbia, spring 1947.

intentions for it. One headline read " 'Street Scene' Real American Opera,"[13] and the *New York Times,* which had sent both its theater critic, Brooks Atkinson, and its music critic, Olin Downes, spoke of "Opera on Broadway." Downes declared: "We had long entertained the suspicion that American opera, in the vital, contemporaneous sense of that word, would be more likely to come from our popular theatre than from our august temples of the operatic art. After seeing and hearing 'Street Scene' at the Adelphi Theatre we feel that this supposition was wholly justified." Then he described how Weill's concept of a connection between Broadway and opera worked:

> It was interesting to observe the wording of the advance notices of the show. In them the word "opera," which still is strongly suspect to the American man on the street, was carefully avoided. "Street Scene" was billed as a "dramatic musical," a term understood and not abhorred on Broadway. So the audiences came to the show, as they probably would not have done if the operatic element in it had been stressed as such, and found themselves excited, astonished and entertained. Opera had crept up and caught them unaware. The word "opera" got inextricably into the dramatic critics' reviews. For it was as a play musically expressed that the work was taken—as opera always should be taken—and the sum of the two elements make opera.[14]

IT DOESN'T TAKE BURNING FAGOTS TO STAGE A WITCH HUNT. BLAZING FLASH BULBS AND KLIEG LIGHTS WILL SERVE.

* * *

We, the undersigned, members and non-members of the ADA which is paying for and sponsoring this advertisement, ask you to send in a contribution so that it may appear in every city in the land.

Franklin P. Adams	Dorothy Fields	Chester Kerr
Agnes Rogers Allen	Herbert Fields	Rollin Kirby
Frederick Lewis Allen	Wolcott Gibbs	Howard Lindsay
Theodore Amussen	Alan Green	George Macy
Maxwell Anderson	Harold K. Guinzburg	Leopold Mannes
Lemuel Ayres	John Gunther	Dolores Martin
Peggy Bacon	Robert Haas	Dorothy Norman
Maximilian Becker	Philip P. Hamburger	Donald Oenslager
Ulric Bell	Oscar Hammerstein, II	Paul Osborn
Aline Bernstein	Moss Hart	Sol Pernick
Harry Brandt	Helen Hayes	Bill Robinson
Louis Calhern	John Hersey	Richard Rodgers
Bennett Cerf	Laura Z. Hobson	Bella and Sam Spewack
Thomas Chalmers	Quincy Howe	Isaac Stern
Hector Chevigny	Charles Jackson	Dorothy Stickney
Dorothy Claire	Bessie Rowland James	Rex Stout
Vincent Connolly	Marquis James	Barnard Straus
Allan Correli	Eliot Janeway	Edith Sulkin
Norman Cousins	Elizabeth Janeway	James Ramsey Ullman
Thomas Coward	E. J. Kahn, Jr.	David Wayne
Russell Crouse	MacKinlay Kantor	Jerome Weidman
Homer Croy	Fred C. Kelly	Kurt Weill

Americans *for* **D**emocratic **A**ction

Americans for
Democratic Action,
9 East 46th Street,
New York 17, N. Y.

Enclosed find $_____ to help pay for advertisements like the above.
Name_____
Address_____
Please send membership blank and further details of the ADA program.

Americans for Democratic Action advertisement in the *New York Herald Tribune*, 27 October 1947. Kurt Weill and Maxwell Anderson were among the many prominent Broadway artists and others who signed a petition protesting the hearings of the House Un-American Activities Committee.

Unfortunately, *Street Scene* did not achieve financial success, because two big Broadway musicals opened at almost the same time. The day after Weill's Broadway opera opened, *Finian's Rainbow,* by Burton, Harburg, and Saidy, was premiered; and Lerner and Loewe's *Brigadoon* followed in March. So *Street Scene* had to close after only 148 performances—"a mediocre run for a 'dramatic musical,' but an unprecedented string of consecutive performances for an opera!"[15]

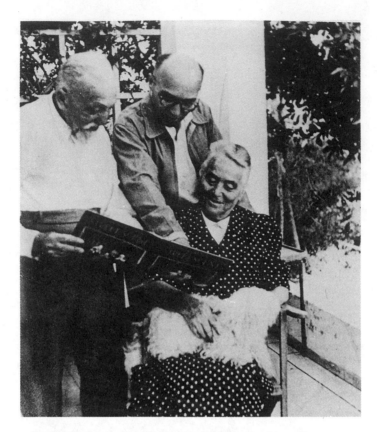

**Reunited after fourteen years: Kurt Weill on a visit to his parents
in Naharia, Palestine, in May 1947, proudly showing them the
program from *Street Scene*.**

Street Scene made headlines again a good two years after its premiere. On 30 July
1949, during the New York Philharmonic Orchestra's annual summer concerts in
Lewisohn Stadium (New York's largest open-air arena), Maurice Abravanel conducted
first a suite from *Lady in the Dark* orchestrated by Robert Russell Bennett and then
excerpts from *Street Scene* with a first-class ensemble of singers for an audience of six
thousand. A few days later, more than ten thousand people heard the same concert in the
legendary Hollywood Bowl.

On 1 March 1947 Kurt Weill's brother Hans, who had also lived as an émigré in New
York since 1938, died. Afterward, Weill decided finally to visit his parents in Palestine and
to take a big trip through a number of European countries. True to the fundamental
decision he had made, he excluded Germany from his itinerary. On 6 May 1947 Kurt
Weill left New York on the SS *Mauretania,* accompanied by Meyer Weisgal. Stopping in
London, Paris, and Zurich, he arrived in Palestine on 20 May and spent two weeks there.

**Reunited after thirteen years: Lotte Lenya with her mother,
who visited New City from Vienna in 1947.**

After a separation of fourteen years, he saw his parents again; they were now living in the small village of Naharia. Weill of course also visited his sister, Ruth, and his brother Nathan and their families. The return trip took him via Rome, Geneva, and Paris to London, where he boarded an airplane back to New York, arriving in mid-1947.

Since the end of the war Kurt Weill had frequently agreed to write music for Jewish organizations and friends. He wrote a *Kiddush* for cantor, chorus, and organ for the Park Avenue Synagogue in March 1946. That same summer he worked with Ben Hecht again, on a new pageant commissioned by an organization that was collecting money for suffering Jewish survivors in Europe. With well-known actors in the main roles (Paul

Program for the pageant play *A Flag Is Born,*
commissioned by an organization collecting
money for Jewish survivors in Europe, at New
York's Alvin Theatre, 5 September 1946.

Muni, Celia Adler, and the young Marlon Brando), *A Flag Is Born* was premiered on 5 September 1946 at the Alvin Theatre and ran for a number of weeks. In November 1948 Weill wrote an orchestral version of the *Hatikvah,* the Israeli national anthem, to commemorate the founding of the state of Israel in May of that year.

In the spring of 1948 a request reached the composer from Indiana University in Bloomington, which supported an accomplished opera workshop made up of both students and faculty. Hans Busch, son of the one-time director of the Dresden Opera Fritz Busch, who had premiered Weill's first opera, asked Weill for a work suitable for this ensemble. This led the composer to write a new version of *Down in the Valley* with Arnold Sundgaard in April 1948. "We changed the original radio piece into a musico-dramatic form, about twice as long as the original, with new scenes, new lyrics and new music, and a brand-new orchestration for the special requirements of school orchestras."[16]

The play tells a balladlike love story. Brack Weaver, accused of murder, escapes from prison to see his beloved Jennie Parsons again. In a flashback the two relive their recent experiences. Brack had met Jennie at a church service and then accompanied her to her parents' house. Shy about declaring his love to her, he invites her to a dance on Saturday in Shadow Creek. Jennie's father forbids her to go because he has already promised his

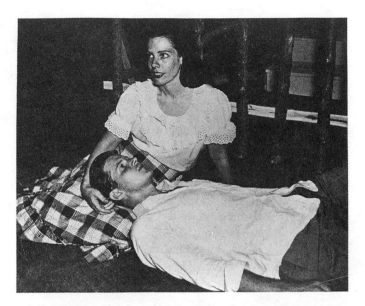

James Welch as Brack and Marion Bell as Jennie in the premiere
of the second version of *Down in the Valley* in the auditorium of
Indiana University at Bloomington, 15 July 1948.

daughter to his creditor, Thomas Bouché. Jennie resists this match and instead goes to the
dance with Brack. There a drunken Bouché goes after Brack with a knife. During their
struggle, unfortunately, he is killed by Brack. The plot returns to the present. Before Brack
is apprehended and sent back to jail, he spends his last hour with his beloved, "down in
the valley, the valley so low."

Weill's music emphasizes the character of folk opera with its simple texture and
original American idiom. A narrator, a chorus, and the soloists alternate with one another in the stream of musical narrative, which centers around four old American folk
songs besides "Down in the Valley." The style of the work is deliberately simple, suited for
amateur performance. The parallels to the school opera *Der Jasager* are obvious, and the
performance run that this new opera was soon to have in America also suggests such a
comparison.

Kurt Weill and Lotte Lenya drove to Bloomington for the premiere on 15 July 1948.
Along with Hindemith's *Hin und zurück* (There and Back—had Hans Busch wanted to
create an echo of Baden-Baden in 1927 with this pairing?), *Down in the Valley* was given
an enthusiastic reception. Only a few weeks later the University of Michigan in Ann
Arbor put on a performance that was broadcast nationwide by NBC. After this, Weill's
new work was known all over the United States. Between August 1948 and June 1949
Down in the Valley was performed by no fewer than eighty-five amateur ensembles
(mostly at colleges and universities),[17] a number that can only be compared with the
success of *Der Jasager* in 1930–31.

At a Bloomington, Indiana, radio station: Weill and the leads of
***Down in the Valley* on the day after the premiere, 16 July 1948.**

On 4 July 1949 *Down in the Valley* was given its New York premiere by the energetic off-Broadway ensemble Lemonade Opera. Weill proudly reported to his parents:

My folk opera *Down in the Valley*, which has already been performed in one hundred American cities, has now come out in New York, in a small theater where a group of young singers has been performing operas with great success for a few years. They call themselves "Lemonade Opera" because they sell lemonade during intermission to emphasize their difference from grand opera (just as we did back in the days of *Die Dreigroschenoper*). . . . The critic from the *Times* is comparing my opera with the original *Beggar's Opera*, which was the source of English opera, and says that *Down in the Valley* will go down in history as the "fountain head" of American opera. You can imagine what that means to me, since this kind of recognition allows me to work in opera again, which was always my real field.[18]

Cover of the piano reduction of *Down in the Valley*, 1948.

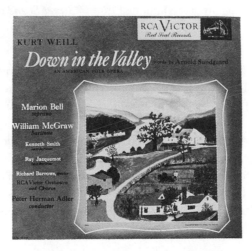

Record cover of *Down in the Valley*, RCA
Victor, 1949. This recording was made under
Weill's supervision.

The South African writer Alan Paton (*left*) with Weill and
Maxwell Anderson, discussing *Lost in the Stars*, based on Paton's
Cry, the Beloved Country, in the summer of 1949.

What Weill was hinting at in the last sentence was the difficulty he and Maxwell Anderson had been having after the financial flop of *Street Scene* to get the Playwrights' Company to produce a new musical project. Anderson tells the story of the new project's genesis:

> When I read "Cry, the Beloved Country," early in 1948, I immediately called Kurt Weill and told him I thought I had found the story we'd been searching for during the last ten years. He read the novel and agreed with me at once. We cabled Alan Paton in South Africa . . . and the matter was quickly settled. . . . Kurt and I were both at work on other plays at the time, but we paused long enough to decide on a form and a story line that could be used in a play, based on Mr. Paton's novel, which would probably be called "Lost in the Stars." . . . I picked up the plan for "Lost in the Stars" at the end of December 1948. By the middle of February 1949 the play was written, and so was Kurt's music, for he had kept pace with me as I brought him successive lyrics and scenes.[19]

A letter to the author of the novel discusses the form of the dramatization: "To keep the plot and the dialogue in the form you gave them would only be possible if a chorus—a

Rehearsal of *Lost in the Stars* with Todd Duncan as
Stephen Kumalo.

sort of Greek chorus—were used to tie together the great number of scenes, and to comment on the action as you comment in the philosophic and descriptive passages. Of course, I should have to put some of that comment into verse, but some of the lyric prose could be lifted out intact and set to music. Kurt Weill, who would make the musical setting, is as enthusiastic about the book and about this dramatic method for it as I am. We have worked together before, and you no doubt know of him."[20]

Alan Paton agreed with Anderson's and Weill's suggestions; he also had no objections to their using material from the uncompleted *Ulysses Africanus* of 1939, including the title song. The novel, the odyssey of a black clergyman in Johannesburg, presents both a sharp protest against apartheid and, at the end, a programmatic hope for reconciliation.

The play opens in the village of Ndotsheni, where the black clergyman Stephen Kumalo lives with his wife. Kumalo wants to go to Johannesburg to visit his sister, a prostitute, and to look for his son, Absalom, whom he has not heard from for a year. While Kumalo waits at the station for a train to Johannesburg, the chorus sings that a black person never returns from Johannesburg. The rich white planter Jarvis is also waiting for the train with his son, Arthur, a well-known lawyer and advocate for blacks from Johannesburg, and Arthur's young son. To his father's disapproval, Arthur Jarvis greets the black clergyman Kumalo.

**Scene from the premiere of *Lost in the Stars* at New York's
Music Box Theatre, 30 October 1949, with Todd Duncan as
Kumalo and Leslie Banks as Jarvis.**

Next we see Kumalo in Johannesburg, in his cynical brother John's tobacco shop. John gives him an address in a slum neighborhood where he might be able to meet his son, Absalom. Kumalo is unsuccessful, though, and he returns to his miserable lodgings ready to travel back to his village with his sister's little boy.

The next scene shows Absalom in a bar, where he is planning with an accomplice to break into Arthur Jarvis's house. When they carry out their plan, Absalom shoots Arthur Jarvis. The father Kumalo finally sees his son, who has been rightfully accused of murder, in prison.

The second act takes Kumalo back to his brother's shop, where the two are talking about Absalom's upcoming trial. Kumalo goes to see the victim's father, but the white

THE PLAYWRIGHTS' COMPANY
Maxwell Anderson, Elmer Rice, Robert E. Sherwood, Kurt Weill, John F. Wharton
presents

LOST IN THE STARS

THE MUSICAL HIT
(based on ALAN PATON'S novel
"CRY, THE BELOVED COUNTRY")

Words by   *Music by*
MAXWELL ANDERSON   **KURT WEILL**

Production Directed and Supervised by
ROUBEN MAMOULIAN
with
TODD DUNCAN   **LESLIE BANKS**

Warren Coleman   Inez Matthews   Julian Mayfield
William Greaves   Frank Roane   Sheila Guyse

Settings by GEORGE JENKINS   *Conducted by* MAURICE LEVINE
Costumes by Anna Hill Johnstone
Musical arrangements and orchestrations by Mr. Weill

Program from the premiere of *Lost in the Stars*.

planter insists that Absalom must die. Stephen Kumalo visits his son a last time on death row and then returns to his village. He tells his congregation that he will resign from the pulpit because of what has happened. When Jarvis learns of this, he gives up his rigid position. On the night that Absalom is to be executed, he visits Kumalo to be reconciled with him. The men spend the whole night together.

Weill's music for *Lost in the Stars* avoids any artificial Africanisms, drawing instead on powerful elements of spirituals. The music is of two main sorts: solo songs (among which "Stay Well" and "Cry, the Beloved Country" and the accessible title song, "Lost in the Stars," are especially moving) and extensive choral passages, making *Lost in the Stars* the largest choral work that Weill wrote in the United States. The music is serious and measured. In places a bitterness breaks through—for example, in the large finale of the first act, which builds into a mighty chorale. The juxtaposition of large choral passages with occasional songs results in a remarkable dramatic effect. Weill wrote in a letter to the *New York Times:*

> It must be somewhat surprising indeed to find a serious subject treated in a form which (in this country at least) has been used so far only for a lighter form of entertainment. But that was exactly the nature of my experiment—to do a "musical tragedy" for the American theatre so that the typical American audience (not a specialized audience) can accept it; and the real success of the piece to me is the fact that the audience did accept it without hesitation, that they accepted a lot of very serious, tragic, quite un-Broadwayish music of operatic dimensions, together with some songs written in a more familiar style.[21]

Weill had again remained true to his intention of realizing a new form of musical theater—this time a "musical tragedy"—with the help of Broadway. It took a long time both to find a suitable director for this unusual work and to cast the lead role of Stephen Kumalo, which of course needed to be played by a black singer. In Rouben Mamoulian a director was finally found who was as experienced as he was famous. Mamoulian's Broadway credits included the premiere of Gershwin's *Porgy and Bess* (1935) and the Rodgers and Hammerstein hits *Oklahoma!* (1943) and *Carousel* (1945). Since 1931 he had also been sought after as a Hollywood director and had made films with Greta Garbo, Marlene Dietrich, and others. After a long, unsuccessful search among many would-be Kumalos, it was Mamoulian who suggested engaging Todd Duncan, who had played Porgy in the Gershwin premiere. Duncan was in Australia when Mamoulian's

Record cover for *Lost in the Stars*, Decca, late 1949.

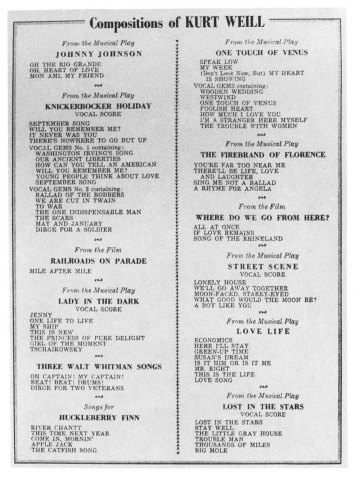

Advertisement of 1949 in which Chappell listed all of Weill's
American sheet-music publications since *Johnny Johnson* (1936).

offer reached him, but he immediately accepted. This time it was the director who asked for an additional musical number during rehearsals. Mamoulian thought that Kumalo should sing a musical soliloquy when he discovers that his son has become a criminal. So in a short time Weill and Anderson wrote "O Tixo, Tixo, Help Me," one of the score's strongest numbers.[22]

The premiere of *Lost in the Stars* on 30 October 1949 (with Maurice Levine conducting) was an extraordinary success. "A rich musical," one could read, "developing a difficult theater form to a high degree. Although the connotation of the word has been completely altered, it should properly be called melodrama. It is one of the most difficult idioms of the theater, but when it is employed with clarity and eloquence it brings a stage to vibrant life. 'Lost in the Stars' . . . is melodrama in its original sense: a stage play in which songs are interspersed and in which music accompanies the action."[23]

A double-page spread from Weill's diary, 7–9 January 1950.
The note on 7 January begins: "Worked with Max [Anderson]
all day on story for Huck Finn." And on 9 January: "Worked
with Max from noon to 6."

With 273 performances the production was also a financial success for the Play-wrights' Company. Weill, Anderson, and Mamoulian immediately agreed to embark on another collaboration. They decided to turn Mark Twain's *Huckleberry Finn* into a musical called *Raft on the River*.

Weill's ideas for Broadway opera were not carried forward, however. As Brooks Atkinson wrote about the years from 1950 on: "Broadway had not become a musical academy in which gifted composers and visionary writers transmuted the regulation song-and-dance show into artistry. Mediocrity struggled along, as usual."[24]

On 2 March 1950 Weill celebrated his fiftieth birthday in New City. "It is not partic-ularly remarkable to turn fifty," he wrote to his parents, "and I don't even feel as if I were fifty."[25] Shortly beforehand he had described his situation as follows: "In the meantime all sorts of things have happened with my works and it almost looks as if I will have a time of harvest after 25 years of hard, untiring work, not in a material sense but in a purely idealistic sense."[26]

But Kurt Weill was granted neither the time to enjoy this harvest nor a chance to realize the new projects that he was already working on. On 17 March 1950 he suffered a

"The Catfish Song" was one of five completed songs from Weill
and Anderson's unfinished musical based on Mark Twain's
Huckleberry Finn, published after the composer's death by
Chappell.

heart attack in New City, and two days later Lotte Lenya took him on their physician's advice to New York's Flower Hospital, where he died on 3 April 1950 of heart failure. On 5 April he was buried in the Mount Repose Cemetery in Haverstraw, near New City. Kurt Weill's tombstone is engraved with the melody and lyrics of four lines from his last work, *Lost in the Stars,* which was still running on Broadway as successfully as ever when he died:

> This is the life of man on earth
> Out of darkness we come at birth
> Into a lamplit room, and then—
> Go forward into dark again.

On 10 July the New York Philharmonic Orchestra presented a "Kurt Weill Memorial Concert" in Lewisohn Stadium. The program included excerpts from *Down in the Valley*

Weill's study in Brook House, photographed shortly after his death, in April 1950.

and *Lost in the Stars,* as well as a selection of the best-known songs from Weill's American works. Maxwell Anderson gave a eulogy for his friend.

Six months later, on 3 February 1951, Ernst Josef Aufricht organized a "Kurt Weill Concert" in the New York Town Hall. In the first part Grete Mosheim, Nina Valery, Victor Clarke, and Inez Matthews sang German, French, and American songs from Weill's stage works. The second part consisted of a concertized cross-section of *Die Dreigroschenoper* sung in German by Lotte Lenya and other soloists.

That evening provided the impetus for a long-overdue project to which Weill had, without success, devoted considerable energy and fifteen years of his life in the United States. Twenty-three years after the premiere of *Die Dreigroschenoper* in Berlin, Brecht's text was finally adequately translated into English. Marc Blitzstein did the new translation, and in 1952 it was given a tryout at Brandeis University under the direction of Leonard Bernstein, with Lotte Lenya playing the role of Jenny.

All who were present immediately sensed that the "Americanization" of this work had succeeded, and with Lotte Lenya's active participation it was immediately prepared for a theater performance in New York. Carmen Capalbo directed and Samuel Matlowsky conducted the premiere of *The Threepenny Opera* on 10 March 1954 in the Theatre de Lys, an off-Broadway stage in Greenwich Village. Scott Merrill played Macheath, and, as

STADIUM PROGRAMS • SEASON OF 1950

THE PHILHARMONIC-SYMPHONY ORCHESTRA

Monday Evening, July 10, at 8:30

(In case of rain this program is postponed until the next clear night)

KURT WEILL MEMORIAL PROGRAM

MAURICE LEVINE, *Conductor*

TODD DUNCAN, *Baritone*

in excerpts from

"LOST IN THE STARS"

with

Virginia Paris   Herbert Coleman

Narrator: ALAN JAY LERNER

1.	Hills of Ixopo	Duncan and Chorus
2.	Train to Johannesburg	Chorus
3.	Thousands of Miles	Duncan
4.	Little Gray House	Duncan and Chorus
5.	Trouble Man	Virginia Paris
6.	Lost in the Stars	Duncan and Chorus
7.	Big Black Mole	Herbert Coleman
8.	Fear	Chorus
9.	Tixo	Duncan
10.	Stay Well	Virginia Paris
11.	Cry the Beloved Country	Duncan and Chorus
12.	Finale	Duncan and Chorus

INTERMISSION

Spoken Tribute to Kurt Weill by MAXWELL ANDERSON

"DOWN IN THE VALLEY"

One Act Folk Opera

Libretto by Arnold Sundgaard

with

Elaine Malbin   Victor Clarke, *Tenor*   Norman Atkins, *Baritone*   Randolph Symonette, *Baritone*

Staged by: DINO JAMOPOULOS   Dances by: ANNA SOKOLOFF

POPULAR CLASSICS BY KURT WEILL

TODD DUNCAN

Virginia Paris

1.	Green-Up Time	Chorus
2.	Here I'll Stay *(from "Love Life" — Lyrics by Alan Jay Lerner)*	Todd Duncan
3.	Speak Low *(from "Love Life" — Lyrics by Alan Jay Lerner)*	Duncan and Virginia Paris
4.	September Song *(from "One Touch of Venus" — Lyrics by Ogden Nash)*	Todd Duncan

(from "Knickerbocker Holiday" — Lyrics by Maxwell Anderson)

Musical supervision by: MAURICE LEVINE

(Program continued on page 23)

Program from the memorial concert for Kurt Weill at New York's Lewisohn Stadium, 10 July 1950. After the intermission Maxwell Anderson gave a eulogy for his deceased friend.

Kurt Weill's and Lotte Lenya's final resting place in the Mount Repose Cemetery in Haverstraw, near New City. A few measures from *Lost in the Stars,* Weill's last completed work, are engraved on his tombstone. Lenya died on 27 November 1981. The last name on her tombstone, from her third marriage, to the painter Russell Detweiler, is misspelled.

Advertisement in the German-language *Aufbau* for the Weill concert organized by Ernst Josef Aufricht at the New York Town Hall on 3 February 1951 and repeated two weeks later.

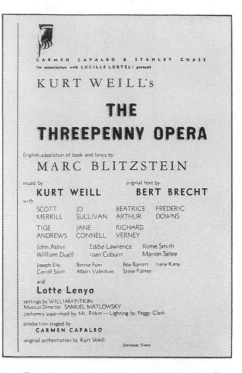

Program from the first staging of the Weill–Blitzstein *Threepenny Opera* at New York's Theatre de Lys on 10 March 1954. This production launched *Die Dreigroschenoper*, twenty-six years after its creation, on its triumphant progress through the English-speaking world.

in Berlin in 1928, Lotte Lenya sang the part of Jenny. This production had an almost uninterrupted run of more than seven years, until December 1961. It broke all New York records, with a total of 2,611 performances seen by some 750,000 people. Kurt Weill was not able to enjoy this late triumph of what is still today his most successful work.

For a long time after his death it seemed that he would live on only in this version of the *Threepenny Opera* and in a few popular songs. The splitting of his biography and of his work, necessitated by the events of the century into which he was born, led to an ignorance of his works and a lopsided, ill-informed reception of them, both in Europe and in America. Only gradually and rather hesitantly did the journey of rediscovery begin into the multi-faceted cosmos of the music that Weill left behind. The 1980s finally brought a worldwide Weill revival that was no longer confined to the works of one hemisphere or

The first concert performance of Marc Blitzstein's English
adaptation of *The Threepenny Opera* during Brandeis
University's Festival of the Creative Arts in the new Adolph
Ullmann Amphitheatre in Waltham, Massachusetts, on 14 June
1952, with Leonard Bernstein (*left*) conducting and narrating and
Lotte Lenya playing the role of Jenny.

the other. What Maxwell Anderson said in 1950 is reality four decades after the composer's death: "He left his music for us, and his music will keep his name and his spirit
alive."[27]

Rouben Mamoulian's epitaph for Kurt Weill, these lines from Shakespeare, make a
fitting close for this book as well:

> His life was gentle, and the elements
> So mixed in him that Nature might stand up
> And say to all the world, "This was a man!"[28]

Chronology of Kurt Weill's Life and Work

1900 2 March: Kurt Weill born as the third of four children to Albert Weill (1867–1955), cantor of the Dessau synagogue, and Emma Weill, née Ackermann (1872–1957), in Dessau's Jewish quarter, the "Sand Suburb."

1906 Enters school.

1907 Passover: The Weill family moves into an apartment in the new Dessau synagogue's parish house.

1909–18 Attends the Herzogliche Friedrichs-Oberrealschule in Dessau.

1913 First surviving composition, "Mi Addir: Jüdischer Trauungsgesang."

1914 Fall: Caught up in the wave of German nationalism after the outbreak of World War I, Weill becomes a member of the youth organization Dessauer Feldkorps. This national pro-war sentiment also infuses the composition "Ich weiß wofür" (for male chorus a cappella, text: Guido von Güllhausen) and "Reiterlied" (text: Hermann Löns).

1915 Following three years of piano instruction and his first compositional efforts, Weill begins his systematic musical education as a private pupil of Albert Bing, principal conductor of Dessau's Herzogliches Hoftheater. Bing instructs him in piano, composition, theory, and conducting through the end of 1917. January: First public appearance as an accompanist at a concert of the Dessauer Feldkorps.

December: First public appearance as a pianist at a concert at the ducal palace. Weill plays a Chopin nocturne and Liszt's "Liebestraum" no. 3.

1916 Song compositions: "Sehnsucht" (text: Eichendorff), "Im Volkston" (text: Arno Holz), "Volkslied" (text: Anna Ritter), and his most important early work, *Ofrahs Lieder* (a cycle of five songs on Hebrew verses by Jehuda Halevi in modern German translation).

Weill becomes the piano teacher of Duke Frederick's two nephews and niece. First operatic effort: *Zriny* (based on a tragedy by Theodor Körner; now lost).

1917 Thanks to Albert Bing, Weill becomes an adjunct *répétiteur* at the Herzogliches Hoftheater. Further song compositions: "Das schöne Kind" (author unknown), "Maikaterlied," and "Abendlied" (two soprano duets on poems by Otto Julius Bierbaum).

December: Piano Intermezzo.

1918 March: Completes the Oberrealschule.

April: Matriculates at the Staatliche Hochschule für Musik in Berlin. Attends philosophy lectures by Max Dessoir and Ernst Cassirer at the university. Weill's teachers at the Hochschule are Rudolf Krasselt (conducting), Friedrich E. Koch (counterpoint), and Engelbert Humperdinck (composition).

1919 July: Breaks off his studies in Berlin and returns to Dessau.

End of August: *Répétiteur* at the Friedrich-Theater in Dessau under its new musical director, Hans Knappertsbusch.

Orchestral Suite in E Major.

Die Weise von Liebe und Tod des Cornets Christoph Rilke (symphonic poem on a text by Rilke).

Schilflieder (cycle of five songs on poems by Nikolaus Lenau).

Die stille Stadt (song on a text by Richard Dehmel).

December: On Humperdinck's recommendation, becomes conductor at the newly founded Stadttheater in Lüdenscheid (Westphalia).

1920 January–May: Conducts opera, operetta, and singspiel in Lüdenscheid.

Sonata for Violoncello and Piano.

Ninon von Lenclos (one-act opera on a play by Ernst Hardt; now lost).

End of May: At the end of the season Weill leaves Lüdenscheid and goes to visit his parents in Leipzig, where his father has been overseeing a Jewish orphanage since 15 May.

Sulamith (choral fantasy for soprano, women's chorus, and orchestra).

September: Returns to Berlin.

December: Interview with Ferruccio Busoni, who, after looking at some of Weill's compositions, accepts him as one of five pupils in his master class in composition at the Preußische Akademie der Künste in Berlin.

1921 January: Begins three years of study with Busoni (through the end of 1923). Since Busoni does not teach counterpoint, Weill takes counterpoint lessons from Philipp Jarnach.

Plays the piano in a beer hall to earn some money.

Symphony (no.1) in One Movement.

Song compositions: "Die Bekehrte" (Goethe) and two songs on texts by Rilke for voice and piano.

1922 Spring: Weill joins the music division of the Novembergruppe.

Weill's arrangement for flute and piano of Busoni's Divertimento for Flute and Orchestra, op. 52, is published by Breitkopf & Härtel in Leipzig.

Psalm VIII for six-part chorus a cappella.

Divertimento for Small Orchestra with Male Chorus, op. 5.

Sinfonia sacra: Fantasia, Passacaglia, and Hymn for Orchestra, op. 6.

18 November: Premiere of Weill's first work for musical theater, *Die Zaubernacht* (children's pantomime in one act, sets by Wladimir Boritsch), at Berlin's Theater am Kurfürstendamm.

1923 To help his finances, Weill begins to give private lessons in theory and composition. His pupils through 1924 include Claudio Arrau, Maurice Abravanel, and Nikos Skalkottas.

String Quartet, op. 8.

Quodlibet (orchestral suite from the pantomime *Die Zaubernacht*), op. 9.

Frauentanz (seven poems from the Middle Ages for soprano, flute, viola, clarinet, horn, and bassoon), op. 10.

Recordare for four-part chorus and children's chorus a cappella (text: Jer. 5), op. 11.

Well-received premieres: op. 6 (12 March; conductor: Alexander Selo) and op. 5 (10 April; conductor: Heinz Unger) in concerts by the Berlin Philharmonic Orchestra; op. 8 by the Hindemith–Amar Quartet during the Frankfurt Chamber Music Festival on 24 June.

December: completes his studies with Busoni at the Preußische Akademie der Künste.

1924 7 February: Premiere of op. 10 at an ISCM concert in Berlin (with Nora Pisling-Boas, soprano; conductor: Fritz Stiedry).

Beginning of January: is introduced by the Dresden opera manager, Fritz Busch, to the playwright Georg Kaiser; they agree to a joint project.

Mid-February–March: Trip to Switzerland and Italy. Stops in Vienna on the return trip to negotiate with Universal Edition, to whom Busoni has recommended him.

22 April: Signs a publishing contract with Universal.

Summer: First meets the actress Lotte Lenya in the home of Georg Kaiser in Grünheide bei Erkner.

27 July: Death of Ferruccio Busoni.

Concerto for Violin and Wind Orchestra, op. 12.

Das Stundenbuch (six songs for baritone and orchestra on texts by Rilke), op. 13.

September: Kaiser and Weill stop work on a ballet pantomime they have begun and start on a one-act opera instead.

1925 January: Weill begins a four-year assignment as critic with the weekly journal *Der deutsche Rundfunk*.

End of March: Completion of *Der Protagonist* (opera in one act; libretto: Georg Kaiser), op. 14.

May: Weill and Lotte Lenya move into the Pension Hassforth on the Luisenplatz.

Summer: Meets the poet Yvan Goll in Berlin.

Der neue Orpheus (cantata for soprano, solo violin, and orchestra; text: Yvan Goll), op. 15.

"Klops-Lied" (for high voice, two piccolo flutes, and bassoon; on a Berlin folk text).

1926 January: Completion of *Royal Palace* (ballet opera in one act; libretto: Yvan Goll), op. 17.

28 January: Weill marries Lotte Lenya, née Karoline Wilhelmine Blamauer.

27 March: Premiere of *Der Protagonist* at Dresden's Staatsoper (director: Josef Gielen; conductor: Fritz Busch).

End of March: Meeting with the Berlin poet and librettist Felix Joachimson and the beginning of collaboration on the comic opera *Na und?* (rejected by Universal at the beginning of 1927; the material is now lost, apart from a few sketches).

June–July: Trip with Lotte Lenya to Switzerland, Italy, and the French Riviera.

1 September: Funkstunde Berlin broadcasts the radio version of Grabbe's tragedy *Herzog Theodor von Gothland* with music by Weill (for soloists, chorus, and orchestra).

1927 2 March: Premiere of *Der neue Orpheus* and *Royal Palace* at Berlin's Staatsoper (director: Franz Ludwig Hörth; conductor: Erich Kleiber).

March: Starts working with Georg Kaiser on a second one-act opera.

End of March: Receives a commission from the German Chamber Music Festival in Baden-Baden for a short opera.

End of April: In the course of looking for a suitable libretto, meets Bertolt Brecht for the first time in the Restaurant Schlichter.

May: Collaboration on the songspiel *Mahagonny* (on the "Mahagonnygesänge" from Brecht's *Hauspostille*). Both authors see this as a preliminary step toward a larger opera that they expect to work on in the coming years, growing out of the same material.

17 July: Premiere of *Mahagonny* at the festival in Baden-Baden (directors: Brecht and Hans Curjel; conductor: Ernst Mehlich). Lotte Lenya is one of the singers and, with her rendition of the "Alabama-Song," launches her career as a congenial interpreter of the Weill song style.

August: Completion with Georg Kaiser of *Der Zar läßt sich photographieren* (opera buffa in one act; libretto: Georg Kaiser), op. 21.

"Vom Tod im Wald" (ballad for bass and ten winds; text: Bertolt Brecht), op. 23.

October: Extensive purely instrumental stage music for August Strindberg's play *Gustav III* (premiere: 29 October in Berlin's Theater an der Königgrätzer Straße; director: Victor Barnowsky; conductor: Walter Goehr).

1928   18 February: Premiere of *Der Zar läßt sich photographieren* at Leipzig's Neues Theater (director: Walther Brügmann; conductor: Gustav Brecher).

March: Stage music for a production of Leo Lania's play *Konjunktur* by the Piscatorbühne (premiere: 8 April at Berlin's Lessingtheater; director: Erwin Piscator; conductor: Edmund Meisel). The music includes the song "Die Muschel von Margate" (text: Felix Gasbarra).

April: Instrumental stage music for Arnolt Bronnen's play *Die Katalaunische Schlacht* (premiere: 25 April at Berlin's Staatliches Schauspielhaus; director: Heinz Hilpert).

May: Trip to the French Riviera with Lotte Lenya, Brecht, and Helene Weigel. Large parts of *Die Dreigroschenoper* are written in Le Lavandou.

June–July: Further work on *Die Dreigroschenoper* in Berlin.

August: The final version of *Die Dreigroschenoper* (play with music based on *The Beggar's Opera* by John Gay, translated by Elisabeth Hauptmann, German version by Bertolt Brecht, music by Kurt Weill) is completed after the dress rehearsal in conjunction with Brecht; the director, Erich Engel; and the musical director, Theo Mackeben.

31 August: Premiere of *Die Dreigroschenoper* at Berlin's Theater am Schiffbauerdamm.

October: Weill and Lenya move into their own apartment in Berlin-Westend, Bayernallee 14.

The song "Berlin im Licht" is written on commission from the Berlin magistrates for the festival of the same name.

November: Stage music for Lion Feuchtwanger's play *Die Petroleuminseln* (premiere: 28 November at Berlin's Staatliches Schauspielhaus; director: Jürgen Fehling). The music includes the petroleum song, "Das Lied von den braunen Inseln" (text by Feuchtwanger).

December: Reacting to the increasing integration of the *Dreigroschen* songs into the spheres of dance and entertainment music, Weill writes a suite version, *Kleine Dreigroschenmusik für Blasorchester*. *Das Berliner Requiem* (cantata for tenor, baritone, male chorus, and wind orchestra on poems by Bertolt Brecht) is written on commission from the Reichs-Rundfunkgesellschaft.

1929   7 February: Premiere of *Kleine Dreigroschenmusik* by the Preußische Staatskapelle in Berlin; conductor: Otto Klemperer.

March: Weill travels to Vienna for the first performance there of *Die Dreigroschenoper*.

April: After two years of work, completion of the first version of *Aufstieg und Fall der Stadt Mahagonny* (opera in three acts; text by Bertolt Brecht).

May: The first version of the didactic play for radio *Der Lindberghflug* (text: Bertolt Brecht; music by Kurt Weill and Paul Hindemith) is written on commission from the German Chamber Music Festival in Baden-Baden.

22 May: First broadcast of *Das Berliner Requiem* by the Frankfurter Sender (conductor: Ludwig Rottenberg).

27 July: Premiere of *Der Linderghflug* in Baden-Baden. Afterward Weill withdraws his part and decides to recompose the entire work.

July–August: Work with Brecht on the songs and choruses for *Happy End* (play with music by Dorothy Lane—i.e., Elisabeth Hauptmann—with songs by Brecht and Weill). The premiere, on 2 September in the Theater am Schiffbauerdamm, is a failure, on account of the play's weak text.

End of August: Stage music for Büchner's play *Dantons Tod* (premiere: 1 September in the Volksbühne am Bülowplatz).

November: The Berlin Schubert-Chor under the direction of Karl Rankl premieres two a cappella choruses on texts by Brecht: "Zu Potsdam unter den Eichen" and "Die Legende vom toten Soldaten." 5 December: Premiere of the second version of *Der Lindberghflug* (cantata for tenor, baritone, bass, mixed chorus, and orchestra) at Berlin's Krolloper; conductor: Otto Klemperer.

1930   January–May: Work on *Der Jasager* (school opera in two acts; text by Bertolt Brecht on the Japanese play *Taniko)*, commissioned by the Festival for New Music, Berlin 1930.

9 March: The premiere of *Aufstieg und Fall der Stadt Mahagonny* at Leipzig's Neues Theater (director: Walther Brügmann; conductor: Gustav Brecher) becomes one of the biggest theater scandals of the Weimar Republic. First organized disturbances by rightist political powers against the "cultural Bolshevists" Weill and Brecht.

23 June: Premiere of *Der Jasager* at Berlin's Zentralinstitut für Unterricht und Erziehung (directors: Brecht and Neher; conductor: Kurt Drabek). After the Festival for New Music rejects Brecht and Eisler's *Die Maßnahme*, Weill withdraws *Der Jasager*. It is premiered independently of the festival as a "counter-event."

Summer: Temporary end of Weill's collaboration with Brecht because of growing aesthetic and political differences.

August: Begins working with Casper Neher on a new project for a large opera.

19 October–4 November: Brecht and Weill sue Nero-Film AG for neglecting their author's rights and intentions in the planned filming of *Die Dreigroschenoper*. The "Dreigroschen trial" ends in a settlement.

1931   19 February: Premiere of the film *Die Dreigroschenoper* (director: G. W. Pabst). The French version, *L'Opéra de quat'sous,* filmed at the same time, makes Weill's songs extraordinarily popular in France.

May–June: Extended trip to France and Spain, where Weill continues his work with Neher on the new opera.

October: Completion of *Die Bürgschaft* (opera in three acts; text by Caspar Neher on Johann Gottfried Herder's *Der afrikanische Rechtsspruch)* in Berlin.

21 December: First performance in Berlin of *Aufstieg und Fall der Stadt Mahagonny* at the Theater am Kurfürstendamm (director: Neher; conductor: Alexander von Zemlinsky). For the performance, produced by Ernst Josef Aufricht (with Harald Paulsen, Lotte Lenya, and Trude Hesterberg in the lead roles as singing actors), Weill makes some revisions and cuts. In the course of the rehearsals he breaks with Brecht.

1932   March: Weill buys a house and moves to the Berlin artists' suburb, Kleinmachnow, Wißmannstraße 7. Lenya is in Vienna for a production of *Aufstieg und Fall der Stadt Mahagonny*.

10 March: Premiere of *Die Bürgschaft* at Berlin's Städtische Oper (director: Carl Ebert; conductor: Fritz Stiedry). Renewed political disturbances and open threats by the German Nationals and National Socialists.

26 April: First Viennese performance of *Aufstieg und Fall der Stadt Mahagonny* with Lotte Lenya as Jenny. During the rehearsals she meets the singer Otto Pasetti and decides to live with him. Weill agrees to the separation, and they start proceedings for a divorce.

August: The association with Georg Kaiser never having been ruptured, the two decide once again to work together. Collaboration through the end of October on *Der Silbersee* (a winter fairy tale in three acts).

11 December: Celebrated performance of the *Mahagonny* songspiel and the school opera *Der Jasager* in Paris. After the success of the *Dreigroschenoper* film, Weill's name becomes known in leading Parisian music circles.

1933   18 February: Premiere of *Der Silbersee* simultaneously in Leipzig, Magdeburg, and Erfurt more than two weeks after Hitler's accession to power. Angry protests from the Nazi press lead to its being withdrawn from all three theaters at the end of February and beginning of March.

21 March: Weill leaves Germany. Caspar and Erika Neher drive him to France in their car.

23 March: Arrival in Paris. Weill first stays at the Hotel Splendide, then, starting in mid-April, in the city apartment of the Vicomte de Noailles.

April: Commission for the troupe "Les Ballets 1933." Weill negotiates with Jean Cocteau about a libretto for his project of a *ballet chanté*. When Cocteau declines, the financier Edward James suggests Brecht as an author, and Weill agrees.

Mid-April: Brecht accepts the invitation and comes from Carona, Switzerland, to Paris. Together they write *Die sieben Todsünden* (ballet with song in nine tableaux; text: Bertolt Brecht).

7 June: Premiere of *Die sieben Todsünden* in the Théâtre des Champs-Elysées in Paris (conductor: Maurice Abravanel; Lotte Lenya and Tilly Losch in the lead roles).

1 July: The troupe performs Weill's ballet in London under the title *Anna Anna*.

July–August: Vacation to Italy and Switzerland.

18 September: The divorce is finalized. Weill and Lenya maintain a friendly relationship through correspondence and see each other from time to time at various performances.

31 October: Universal having terminated its contract with Weill on 3 October, Weill signs a new contract with the Parisian publisher Heugel.

Two *chansons*: "Es regnet" (text: Jean Cocteau) and "Der Abschiedsbrief" (text: Erich Kästner).

3 November: First broadcast of *La grande complainte de Fantomas* (fifteen-minute radio ballad; text: Robert Desnos) by Radio Paris (director: Antonin Artaud; conductor: Alejo Carpentier).

Beginning of November: Weill moves to the Parisian suburb of Louveciennes.

December: Trip to Rome for the Italian premiere of *Mahagonny* and *Der Jasager* (29 December at the Accademia di Santa Cecilia).

1934 February: Completion of the Second Symphony, which he had begun composing in Berlin, on commission from the Princesse de Polignac.

Spring: Begins working with Robert Vambery (former *dramaturg* at the Theater am Schiffbauerdamm) on the operetta *Der Kuhhandel*.

Beginning of May: Two *chansons* on texts by Maurice Magre for the popular *diseuse* Lys Gauty: "Complainte de la Seine" and "Je ne t'aime pas."

Mid-May–July: Vacation in Switzerland and Italy.

18 June: Meeting in Venice with Max Reinhardt and the American producer Meyer Weisgal. First discussions about a large musical biblical drama, *Der Weg der Verheißung* (text: Franz Werfel).

Fall: Work on *Der Kuhhandel, Der Weg der Verheißung,* and *Marie Galante* (play with music; text: Jacques Deval).

11 October: Premiere of the Second Symphony by the Concertgebouw Orchestra in Amsterdam (conductor: Bruno Walter).

22 December: Premiere of *Marie Galante* at the Théâtre de Paris is a failure.

1935 January–July: Weill in London intermittently. Further work on *Der Weg der Verheißung.* Stops working on the original German material by Vambery for *Der Kuhhandel* when a performance possibility opens up in London and instead writes an English version entitled *A Kingdom for a Cow* (book: Reginald Arkell; lyrics: Desmond Carter).

May: Lotte Lenya comes to London. The two decide to live together again.

28 June: The premiere of *A Kingdom for a Cow* at the Savoy Theatre in London is a failure.

Summer: Weill's parents emigrate to Palestine.

July: Returns to Louveciennes with Lotte Lenya.

August: Weill in Salzburg. Finishes first version of *Der Weg der Verheißung.*

Mid-August: Further discussions with Reinhardt, Werfel, and Weisgal. The premiere is planned for January 1936 in New York. Weill is to be part of the production team in the American version and is to write some additional numbers for it. Lenya is offered a role in the play. Weisgal invites both of them to travel with him to New York.

10 September: Weill and Lenya arrive in New York. They stay in the St. Moritz Hotel on Central Park for the first four months.

Fall: Work on *The Eternal Road,* as the biblical drama is now called.

October: Meets George and Ira Gershwin during a rehearsal for *Porgy and Bess.*

November: Sees Brecht, who has come to New York for the performance there of *Die Mutter,* and meets the composer Marc Blitzstein.

10 December: The League of American Composers hosts a Weill concert in New York, at which Lotte Lenya sings. The reception is cool.

1936   January: The planned premiere of *The Eternal Road* is postponed indefinitely because of financial problems. Weill and Lenya move into the cheaper Park Crescent Hotel.

March: Establishes contact with the Group Theatre through the director Harold Clurman. First plans for a musical play.

May: Trip to Chapel Hill, North Carolina, with the director Cheryl Crawford of the Group Theatre to meet the playwright Paul Green. First collaborative work on *Johnny Johnson.*

June–August: Weill and Lenya participate with Paul Green in the Group Theatre's "summer camp" at Pine Brook in Trumbull, Connecticut. Weill lectures on theater music and continues working with Green on *Johnny Johnson.*

September: Return to New York. Cheryl Crawford lets Weill and Lenya stay in her Fifty-first Street apartment for a year.

November: Contract with the music publisher Chappell for publication of new works, beginning with *Johnny Johnson.*

19 November: Premiere of *Johnny Johnson* at New York's Forty-fourth Street Theatre (director: Lee Strasberg; conductor: Lehman Engel). With sixty-eight performances the production is a moderate success, and Weill gains recognition.

1937   4 January: After many postponements *The Eternal Road* is premiered at the Manhattan Opera House (director: Max Reinhardt; conductor: Isaac van Grove; Lotte Lenya as Miriam). This monumental production had 153 performances.

19 January: Remarriage of Weill and Lenya in North Castle, Westchester County, near New York City.

End of January–beginning of July: Visit to Hollywood, with many meetings and contacts. First discussions with Fritz Lang of a film project. Weill writes the (later not used) music for *Blockade* (a film on Spain directed by W. Dieterle).

August: Discussions in Chapel Hill with Paul Green of a play project for the Federal Theatre.

27 August: Weill and Lenya take a short trip to Canada; on their reentry to the United States they receive immigrant visas and apply for American citizenship.

September: Weill and Lenya move into their own two-bedroom apartment on Sixty-second Street.

1938   January–March: Work with the playwright Hoffman R. Hays on the play *Davy Crockett* for the Federal Theatre.

Spring: Stops working on *Davy Crockett.* Meets the playwright Maxwell Anderson and agrees on a joint project based on material by Washington Irving.

March–May: In Hollywood to work on the film music for *You and Me* (director: Fritz Lang).

Summer: Weill and Lenya rent a house in Suffern, near New York City. Work on *Knickerbocker Holiday* with Maxwell Anderson, who lives in nearby New City.

19 October: Premiere of *Knickerbocker Holiday* at New York's Barrymore Theatre (director: Joshua Logan; conductor: Maurice Abravanel). With 168 performances the production is a success. The actor Walter Huston creates Weill's first American "hit" with "September Song."

1939   30 April: Premiere of the pageant play *Railroads on Parade,* written for the railroad industry's exhibit at the New York World's Fair.

June: Weill joins ASCAP, the organization of American composers.

Summer: With Maxwell Anderson in Malibu, California, working on the never finished *Ulysses Africanus.*

November: Stage music for the play *Madam, Will You Walk?* by Sidney Howard.

December: Stage music for the play *Two on an Island* by Elmer Rice.

Song compositions: "Stopping by Woods on a Snowy Evening" (text: Robert Frost) and "Nannas Lied" (text: Bertolt Brecht).

1940 4 February: First broadcast of the radio cantata *The Ballad of Magna Carta,* written with Maxwell Anderson, by CBS in New York (conductor: Mark Warnow).

February–November: Work with Moss Hart and Ira Gershwin on the musical play *Lady in the Dark.*

1941 23 January: Premiere of *Lady in the Dark* at New York's Alvin Theatre (director: Hassard Short; conductor: Maurice Abravanel). This production, with Gertrude Lawrence in the lead role, has a run of 467 performances and becomes an outstanding success.

Beginning of May: Paramount acquires film rights to *Lady in the Dark.*

21 May: Weill and Lenya buy a house right next door to Maxwell Anderson's house in New City, Rockland County.

5 October: Premiere of the pageant play *Fun to Be Free* in New York's Madison Square Garden (conductor: Simon Rady).

1942 Spring: After the United States enters World War II, Weill begins various projects for the American war effort.

January: Three *Walt Whitman Songs.*

February: Music for the radio program *Your Navy* by Maxwell Anderson.

March: Four patriotic melodramas for the actress Helen Hayes.

April: Weill chairs a production committee for *The Lunch Hour Follies,* an entertainment series for workers at ammunitions factories and navy docks on the East Coast.

Spring and summer: Various songs for *Lunch Hour Follies* on texts by Maxwell Anderson, Oscar Hammerstein II, and others.

Song compositions: "Song of the Free" (text: Archibald MacLeish), "Und was bekam des Soldaten Weib?" (text: Bertolt Brecht).

August: "Russian War Relief" (text: J. P. McEvoy).

Late summer: First discussions with Cheryl Crawford of a new Broadway musical production.

Beginning of October: Weill in Hollywood. First meeting with Brecht since 1935 in Santa Monica.

1943 9 March: Premiere of the pageant play *We Will Never Die* in New York's Madison Square Garden (conductor: Isaac van Grove).

May: Brecht and Ruth Berlau visit Weill in New City for a few days: make plans (which are not carried out) for a *Schweik* opera.

June: Weill in Hollywood for the filming of *Lady in the Dark* and *Knickerbocker Holiday.* Second visit with Brecht in Santa Monica.

June–September: Work on the musical play *One Touch of Venus* with Ogden Nash and S. J. Perelman.

August: Weill and Lenya become American citizens.

7 October: Premiere of *One Touch of Venus* at New York's Imperial Theatre (director: Elia Kazan; conductor: Maurice Abravanel). With 567 performances, the production is another big success.

November: Weill goes to Hollywood for six months, where he writes the musical film *Where Do We Go from Here?* (director: Gregory Ratoff) with Ira Gershwin for 20th Century Fox's "anti-Nazi production."

1944 Spring: Discussion with Brecht of *Der gute Mensch von Sezuan.* Song composition for the Office of War Information: "Wie lange noch?" (text: Walter Mehring).

April–May: Music for the anti-Nazi documentary film *Salute to France* (director: Jean Renoir).

May: Begins working with Ira Gershwin and Edwin Justus Mayer on the operetta *The Firebrand of Florence.*

1945 22 March: Premiere of *The Firebrand of Florence* at New York's Alvin Theatre (director: John Murray Anderson; conductor: Maurice Abravanel). The production has to be withdrawn after only 43 performances, making it Weill's only failure on Broadway.

April–June: Weill in Hollywood again for the filming of *One Touch of Venus.*

August–November: Works with Arnold Sundgaard on a preliminary version of the radio opera *Down in the Valley,* which was not broadcast.

1946   January–November: Nearly a full year's work on the Broadway opera *Street Scene* with Elmer Rice and Langston Hughes.

March: *Kiddush* for cantor, chorus, and organ.

1 August: Weill becomes a member of the Playwrights' Company.

5 September: Premiere of the pageant play *A Flag Is Born* at New York's Alvin Theatre (conductor: Isaac van Grove).

1947   9 January: Premiere of *Street Scene* at New York's Adelphi Theatre (director: Charles Friedman; conductor: Maurice Abravanel). With 148 performances, Weill sees the success of his efforts to create a new genre of musical theater on Broadway.

March: First discussions with Alan Jay Lerner of a new musical project.

6 May–12 June: Trip to Europe. Weill visits Great Britain, France, and Switzerland, and travels to Palestine, where he sees his parents again for the first time since 1933.

November: *Hatikvah,* arrangement of Israel's national anthem for orchestra.

1948   Spring: Writes a new version of *Down in the Valley* for a performance at the University of Indiana.

15 July: Premiere of *Down in the Valley* by the Opera Workshop at the University of Indiana in Bloomington, with Weill present.

7 October: Premiere of *Love Life* at New York's Forty-sixth Street Theatre (director: Elia Kazan; conductor: Joseph Littau). With 252 performances, the production is reasonably successful.

1949   February–September: Works with Maxwell Anderson on the musical tragedy *Lost in the Stars.*

30 October: Premiere of *Lost in the Stars* at New York's Music Box Theatre (director: Rouben Mamoulian; conductor: Maurice Levine). With 273 performances, this demanding work is a big success.

1950   January–March: Works with Maxwell Anderson on an unfinished musical version of Mark Twain's *Huckleberry Finn.*

3 March: Weill celebrates his fiftieth birthday in New City.

17 March: Heart attack; is taken to New York's Flower Hospital on 19 March.

3 April: Kurt Weill dies in the hospital.

5 April: Burial in the Mount Repose Cemetery in Haverstraw, near New City.

10 July: Memorial concert for Weill in New York's Lewisohn Stadium with a eulogy by Maxwell Anderson.

Notes

Most letters, postcards, and telegrams cited here can be found as originals or copies at the Weill–Lenya Research Center in New York. Unless otherwise noted, all correspondence by Kurt Weill is in German.

PREFACE

1. Maxwell Anderson, eulogy given at the Weill memorial concert on 10 July 1950 in New York.
2. Kurt Weill, liner notes for *Street Scene,* Columbia OL 4139.
3. Kurt Weill, letter to G. W. Stegmann, 14 Feb. 1949.
4. David Drew, "Kurt Weill," in *The New Grove Dictionary of Music and Musicians,* vol. 20 (London, 1980), 302.

I
CHILDHOOD AND YOUTH IN DESSAU

1. Registry of the city of Dessau.
2. For a more detailed account, see Franz Brückner, "Geschichte der Juden und der jüdischen Gemeinde in Dessau," in *Häuserbuch der Stadt Dessau,* vol. 11 (Dessau, 1983), 935–58.

3. *Jahresbericht der Baronin von Cohn-Oppenheimer-Stiftung zu Dessau für das Jahr 1908* (Dessau, 1908), 34, quoted and translated in Ronald Sanders, *The Days Grow Short*, 11.

4. Dr. Willy Krüger, interview with the author, Dessau, 5 Apr. 1984.

5. Ibid.

6. Louis B. Simon, "Up the Rungs from Opera," *New York Times*, 13 Apr. 1941.

7. Ibid.

8. Dr. Werner Spielmeyer, interview with the author, Dessau, 5 Apr. 1984.

9. Kurt Weill, "Topical Dialogue about *Schuloper* between Kurt Weill and Dr. Hans Fischer," in Kowalke, *Kurt Weill in Europe,* 522. Translation of "Aktuelles Zwiegespräch über die Schuloper," *Die Musikpflege,* 1 Jan. 1930.

10. Kurt Weill, letter to Hans Weill, 15 May 1917. Although Dessau records list his name as "Hans Jakob," Kurt addresses him throughout their correspondence as Hanns; this spelling was presumably a familial peculiarity.

11. Weill, "Topical Dialogue about *Schuloper,*" 522.

12. Kurt Weill, letter to Hans Weill, 15 Oct. 1917.

13. *Anhalter Anzeiger,* Dessau, 7 Feb. 1918.

14. Krüger, interview.

15. Kurt Weill, letter to Hans Weill, late 1917.

16. Quoted in Sanders, *Days Grow Short,* 26.

17. Kurt Weill, letter to Hans Weill, 20 Aug. 1917.

2
FIRST PERIOD OF STUDY IN BERLIN

1. Kurt Weill, letter to Hans Weill, 8 Aug. 1917.

2. Ibid.

3. Kurt Weill, letter to Hans Weill, late May 1918.

4. Kurt Weill, letter to Hans Weill, early July 1918.

5. Kurt Weill, letter to Hans Weill, 9 Aug. 1918.

6. Kurt Weill, postcard to Hans Weill, 12 Nov. 1918.

7. Kurt Weill, letter to Hans Weill, 15 Nov. 1918.

8. Kurt Weill, postcard to Hans Weill, 3 Dec. 1918.

9. Kurt Weill, letter to Hans Weill, 27 Mar. 1919.

10. Kurt Weill, letter to Hans Weill, spring 1919.

11. Kurt Weill, letter to Hans Weill, 30 Jan. 1919.

12. Kurt Weill, letter to Hans Weill, spring 1919.

13. Heinrich Strobel, "Kurt Weill," *Melos,* Oct. 1927: 429.

14. Kurt Weill, letter to Hans Weill, spring 1919.

15. Kurt Weill, postcard to Hans Weill, 28 Aug. 1918.

16. Kurt Weill, postcard to Hans Weill, 13 Sept. 1918.

17. Kurt Weill, letter to Hans Weill, 4 Sept. 1918.

18. Kurt Weill, postcard to Hans Weill, 20 June 1919.

19. Kurt Weill, letter to Hans Weill, 27 June 1919.

20. Kurt Weill, postcard to Hans Weill, 14 July 1919.

3
THEATER EXPERIENCE IN DESSAU AND LÜDENSCHEID

1. *Anhalter Anzeiger,* Dessau, 5 Sept. 1919.

2. Kurt Weill, letter to Hans Weill, 5 Sept. 1919.

3. Quoted in Sanders, *Days Grow Short,* 31.
4. Simon, "Up the Rungs from Opera."
5. Kurt Weill, letter to Ruth Weill, 2 Apr. 1920.
6. Kurt Weill, letter to Ruth Weill, 16 Jan. 1920.
7. Kurt Weill, liner notes for *Street Scene.*
8. Kurt Weill, letter to Ruth Weill, 28 Jan. 1920.
9. Strobel, "Kurt Weill."
10. Kurt Weill, letter to Hans Weill, 14 Mar. 1920.
11. Kurt Weill, letter to Hans Weill, 26 Apr. 1920.
12. Ibid.
13. Kurt Weill, postcard to Hans Weill, 28 July 1920.
14. John C. G. Waterhouse, "Weill's Debt to Busoni," *Musical Times* 105 (Dec. 1964): 894.

4
MASTER PUPIL WITH BUSONI

1. Carl Zuckmayer, *A Part of Myself,* trans. Richard and Clara Winston (New York, 1970), 219.
2. Edward J. Dent, "The Return of Busoni," *Athenaeum,* 19 Dec. 1920: 844.
3. Kurt Weill, letter to Albert Weill, 29 Nov. 1920.
4. Ferruccio Busoni, *Sketch of a New Esthetic of Music,* trans. T. Baker in *Three Classics in the Aesthetics of Music* (New York, 1962), 93.
5. See also Hans Heinz Stuckenschmidt, *Ferruccio Busoni: Chronicle of a European,* trans. Sandra Morris (New York, 1970).
6. Busoni, *Sketch of a New Esthetic,* 93.
7. Letter of 7 July 1907, in Ferruccio Busoni, *Letters to His Wife,* trans. Rosamond Ley (New York, 1975), 111.
8. Ferruccio Busoni, *Essence of Music, and Other Papers,* trans. Rosamond Ley (London, 1957).
9. David Drew, "Kurt Weill and His Critics," *Times Literary Supplement,* 3 Oct. 1975.
10. Jutta Theurich, "Der Briefwechsel zwischen A. Schönberg und F. Busoni, 1903–1919 (1927): Edition, Kommentierung und Untersuchung unter besonderer Berücksichtigung der im Busoni-Nachlaß der Deutschen Staatsbibliothek enthaltenen Quellen" (Ph.D. diss., East Berlin, 1979), 41.
11. Letter of 30 July 1921, in Busoni, *Letters to His Wife,* 303.
12. Philipp Jarnach, "Ferruccio Busoni," *Berliner Börsen-Courier,* 1 Apr. 1926.
13. Kurt Weill, "Busoni: On the First Anniversary of His Death," unpublished translation by Stephen Hinton of "Busoni: Zu seinem einjährigen Todestage," *Berliner Börsen-Courier,* 26 July 1925.
14. Wladimir Vogel, letter to Ronald Sanders, 21 Mar. 1978; quoted in *Days Grow Short,* 60.
15. Rudolf Kastner, "Kurt Weill: Eine Skizze," *Musikblätter des Anbruch,* July 1925: 454.
16. Kurt Weill, letter to Busoni, 20 Jan. 1921; in "Briefe von Kurt Weill an Ferruccio Busoni," ed. Jutta Theurich, *Musik und Gesellschaft,* Mar. 1990: 113.
17. Kurt Weill, postcard to Hans Weill, 12 Aug. 1921.
18. Kurt Weill, postcard to Hans Weill, 17 Nov. 1920.
19. Strobel, "Kurt Weill," 430.
20. Kurt Weill, letter to Albert Weill, 29 Nov. 1920.
21. Hans W. Heinsheimer, "Kurt Weill: From Berlin to Broadway," *International Musician,* Mar. 1948: 17.
22. Mario R. Mercado, "A Podium with a View: Recollections by Maurice Abravanel," *Kurt Weill Newsletter* 5/1 (spring 1987): 8.
23. *Der Gegner,* Aug.–Sept. 1921: 297ff.
24. Max Butting, *Musikgeschichte, die ich miterlebte* (East Berlin, 1955), 119ff.
25. Quoted in Helga Kliemann, *Die Novembergruppe* (West Berlin, 1969), 76.

26. Strobel, "Kurt Weill."
27. *Der deutsche Rundfunk,* 11 Apr. 1926.
28. *Berliner Börsen-Courier,* 19 Nov. 1922.
29. *Germania,* 19 Nov. 1922.
30. Strobel, "Kurt Weill."
31. At that time in Berlin she was still spelling her name "Lenja." This book follows the American spelling she later adopted, "Lenya."
32. "Lotte Lenya in Conversation with Steven Paul," liner notes for *Kurt Weill,* Deutsche Grammophon 2740 153.
33. Kurt Weill, letter to Busoni, 21 June 1923, in "Briefe," 116.
34. Ibid.
35. Igor Stravinsky, *An Autobiography* (New York, 1936), 170.
36. Kurt Weill, "New Opera," in Kowalke, *Kurt Weill in Europe,* 465. Translation of "Die neue Oper," *Der neue Weg* 55 (16 Jan. 1926).
37. Ferruccio Busoni, *Selected Letters,* ed. Antony Beaumont (New York, 1987), 373.
38. Kurt Weill, letter to Busoni, Oct. 1923, in "Briefe," 116.
39. Kastner, "Kurt Weill."
40. Quoted in *Musikautographen: Antiquariatskatalog 204: Musikantiquariat Schneider* (Tutzing, 1977), no. 37a.
41. Kurt Weill, letter to Busoni, Oct. 1923, in "Briefe," 118.
42. Kurt Weill, letter to Busoni, 25 Feb. 1924, in "Briefe," 118.
43. Kurt Weill, "Busoni and Modern Music," in Kowalke, *Kurt Weill in Europe,* 461. Translation of "Busoni und die neue Musik," *Der neue Weg* 54 (16 Oct. 1925).

5
ONE-ACT OPERAS

1. Fritz Busch, *Aus dem Leben eines Musikers* (East Berlin, 1974), 137.
2. Bertolt Brecht, "Dem fünfzigjährigen Kaiser," *Berliner Börsen-Courier,* 24 Nov. 1928.
3. *Der deutsche Rundfunk,* 11 Apr. 1926.
4. Kurt Weill, letter to Busoni, 6 Mar. 1924, in "Briefe," 119.
5. Kurt Weill, letter to Busoni, 15 Mar. 1924, in "Briefe," 122.
6. See also Kowalke, *Kurt Weill in Europe,* 263. Here, as elsewhere, I have followed Kowalke's excellent analyses.
7. *Die Musik* 18 (1926): 836.
8. Kurt Weill, postcard to Ruth Weill, 1924.
9. Liner notes for *The Lotte Lenya Album,* Columbia MG 30087.
10. "Lotte Lenya in Conversation with Steven Paul."
11. Hans W. Heinsheimer, *Best Regards to Aida* (New York, 1969), 109.
12. Kurt Weill, letter to his parents, 1925.
13. Kurt Weill, letter to Hans Weill, 29 May 1925.
14. Kurt Weill, letter to his parents, 17 Sept. 1925.
15. Kurt Weill, postcard to his father, 23 Sept. 1925.
16. Kurt Weill, letter to his parents, 1 Jan. 1926.
17. Kurt Weill, letter to his mother, 14 Dec. 1925.
18. Jay S. Harrison, "Weill and Lenya—Berlin to Broadway," *New York Herald Tribune,* 27 July 1958.
19. Strobel, "Kurt Weill."
20. *Berliner Börsen-Courier,* 29 Mar. 1926.
21. Kurt Weill, postcard to his father, 1 Apr. 1926.

22. *Berliner Morgenpost,* 29 Mar. 1926.
23. Heinsheimer, *Menagerie in F Sharp* (Garden City, N.Y., 1947), 147–48.
24. Kurt Weill, letter to his parents, 1925.
25. Kurt Weill, letter to Universal Edition (UE), 6 May 1926. Unless indicated by "[trans.]," all quotations are taken from Christopher Hailey's unpublished translation of Weill's correspondence with UE.
26. Kurt Weill, letter to his parents, 7 June 1926.
27. *Deutsche Tonkünstler-Zeitung,* 20 May 1929.
28. Alban Berg, in the questionnaire "Gibt es eine zeitgenössische Weiterentwicklung der Oper?" (Is there any contemporary development of opera?), *Blätter der Staatsoper Berlin,* Oct. 1927: 12.
29. Kurt Weill, "Zeitoper," in Kowalke, *Kurt Weill in Europe,* 482. Translation of "Zeitoper," *Melos* 7 (Mar. 1928).
30. Interview with Lotte Lenya, *Philadelphia Inquirer,* 28 Apr. 1976 [retranslated from German].
31. Kurt Weill, response to the questionnaire "Meine Frau" (My Wife), *Münchner Illustrierte Presse,* 14 Apr. 1929.
32. Felix Stiemer, *Der deutsche Rundfunk,* 12 Sept. 1926.
33. Felix Jackson [Joachimson], "Portrait of a Quiet Man: Kurt Weill, His Life and Times" (unpublished manuscript, Weill–Lenya Research Center, New York), 27–28.
34. Kurt Weill, letter to UE, 4 Apr. 1927.
35. Weill–Lenya Archive, Yale University, box 24, folder 359.
36. UE, letter to Kurt Weill, 7 Apr. 1927.
37. Heinsheimer, *Best Regards to Aida,* 114.
38. Hans Curjel, "Erinnerungen um Kurt Weill," *Melos,* Mar. 1970: 84.
39. Kurt Weill, letter to UE, 23 Mar. 1927.
40. Kurt Weill, letter to UE, 4 Aug. 1927.
41. Kurt Weill, program from the premiere, Neues Theater Leipzig, 18 Feb. 1928.
42. *Neue Leipziger Zeitung,* 19 Feb. 1928.
43. *Sächsische Arbeiter-Zeitung,* 20 Feb. 1928.
44. *Berliner Börsen-Courier,* 15 Oct. 1928.
45. *Die Musik* 20 (1928): 924.

6
COLLABORATION WITH BRECHT

1. *Der deutsche Rundfunk,* 27 Mar. 1927.
2. "Lotte Lenya in Conversation with Steven Paul."
3. Werner Mittenzwei, *Das Leben des Bertolt Brecht oder Der Umgang mit den Welträtseln,* vol. 1 (East Berlin, 1987), 253.
4. Bertolt Brecht, "Über die Kreierung eines zeitgemäßen Theaters," in *Gesammelte Werke,* vol. 15 (Frankfurt am Main, 1967), 130.
5. Drew, "Kurt Weill and His Critics."
6. Fritz Hennenberg, *Das große Brecht-Liederbuch,* vol. 3 (East Berlin, 1984), 371.
7. See also Gunter G. Sehm, "Moses, Christus und Paul Ackermann," in *Brecht-Jahrbuch 1976* (Frankfurt am Main, 1976).
8. Arnolt Bronnen, *Tage mit Bertolt Brecht* (Vienna, 1960), 144.
9. Bertolt Brecht, *Tagebücher, 1920–1922. Autobiographische Aufzeichnungen, 1920–1954* (Frankfurt am Main, 1975), 202.
10. Kurt Weill, *Mahagonny: Songspiel nach Texten von Bertolt Brecht: Textbuch* (Vienna, 1927), 12.
11. Quoted in Jackson [Joachimson], "Portrait of a Quiet Man," 49.
12. Kurt Weill, letter to UE, 4 Apr. 1927 [trans.].

13. Albrecht Dümling, *Laßt euch nicht verführen: Brecht und die Musik* (Munich, 1985), 228.
14. Quoted in Eckhardt Köhn, "Das Ruhrepos: Dokumentation eines gescheiterten Projekts," in *Brecht-Jahrbuch 1977* (Frankfurt am Main, 1978), 60.
15. Quoted in ibid., 61.
16. Dümling, *Laßt euch nicht verführen*, 228.
17. Program from Deutsche Kammermusik Baden-Baden 1927, 4.
18. *Berliner Börsen-Courier*, 19 July 1927.
19. Kurt Weill, "Notes to My Opera *Mahagonny*," in Kowalke, *Kurt Weill in Europe*, 517. Translation of "Anmerkungen zu meiner Oper *Mahagonny*," *Die Musik* 22 (Mar. 1930).
20. Hans Curjel, "Erinnerungen um Kurt Weill," 81.
21. UE, letter to Kurt Weill, 15 Aug. 1927.
22. Kurt Weill, letter to UE, 25 Aug. 1927.
23. Kurt Weill, letter to UE, 18 Nov. 1927.
24. Kurt Weill, letter to UE, 24 Nov. 1927.
25. Kurt Weill, letter to UE, 8 Dec. 1927.
26. UE, letter to Kurt Weill, 16 Dec. 1927.
27. Kurt Weill, letter to UE, 27 Dec. 1927.
28. Kurt Weill, letter to UE, 20 Mar. 1928.
29. "Lotte Lenya in Conversation with Steven Paul."
30. Ernst Josef Aufricht, *Erzähle, damit du dein Recht erweist* (Munich, 1969), 55ff., quoted and translated in *Kurt Weill: The Threepenny Opera*, ed. Stephen Hinton, (Cambridge, 1990), 16–17.
31. Werner Hecht, "Die 'Dreigroschenoper' und ihr Urbild," in *Brecht: Vielseitige Betrachtungen* (East Berlin, 1978), 23, 26.
32. Lotte Lenya, "That Was a Time!" *Theatre Arts* 5 (1956).
33. Aufricht, *Erzähle*, 50.
34. Ibid., 63, translated in *Kurt Weill: Threepenny Opera*, ed. Hinton, 23. [A *Moritat* is a traditional form of German ballad which relates gruesome criminal deeds—trans.]
35. "Correspondence Concerning 'Threepenny Opera' between Hans Heinsheimer, editor of *Anbruch*, and Kurt Weill," translated in *Kurt Weill: Threepenny Opera*, ed. Hinton, 124–25.
36. Theodor W. Adorno, "'The Threepenny Opera,'" translated in *Kurt Weill: Threepenny Opera*, ed. Hinton, 131–32.
37. *Anbruch* 11 (1929) : 327.
38. *Deutsche Zeitung Bohemia*, 21 Oct. 1928.
39. *Völkischer Beobachter*, 23 July 1929.
40. Kurt Weill, letter to UE, 12 Sept. 1928 [trans.].
41. Kurt Weill, postcard to UE, 11 Oct. 1928.
42. UE, letter to Kurt Weill, 13 Sept. 1928.
43. Adorno, "'Threepenny Opera,'" 129–33.
44. *Anbruch* 11 (1929) : 317.
45. *Berliner Morgenpost*, 29 Nov. 1928.
46. *Die Musik* 11 (1928) : 155.
47. Kurt Weill, "A Note Concerning *Das Berliner Requiem*," in Kowalke, *Kurt Weill in Europe*, 504. Translation of "Notiz zum Berliner Requiem," *Der deutsche Rundfunk* 7 (17 May 1929).
48. Kurt Weill, letter to UE, 29 Dec. 1928.
49. Jan Knopf, *Brecht-Handbuch Theater* (Stuttgart, 1980), 73.
50. Kurt Weill, letter to UE, 4 June 1929.
51. Bertolt Brecht, *Briefe* (Frankfurt am Main, 1981), 149.
52. Karl Holl, in *Frankfurter Zeitung*, 2 Aug. 1929.
53. *Der deutsche Rundfunk*, 5 Aug. 1929.

54. Kurt Weill in an advertisement for *Der Lindberghflug,* by Universal, *Anbruch* 1 (1930) : 28.
55. *Berliner Tageblatt,* 6 Dec. 1929.
56. *B. Z. am Mittag,* 6 Dec. 1929.
57. This copy resides in the Missouri Historical Society in St. Louis.
58. Kurt Weill, letter to UE, 25 May 1929.
59. *Die literarische Welt,* 13 Sept. 1929.
60. *Berliner Tageblatt,* 3 Sept. 1929.
61. Kurt Weill, letter to UE, 14 Oct. 1929.
62. *Sinn und Form: Zweites Sonderheft Bertolt Brecht* (East Berlin, 1956), 243.
63. For a more detailed account of the development of this theory, which is merely sketched in broad strokes here, see Werner Hecht, *Brechts Weg zum epischen Theater* (East Berlin, 1962).
64. Kurt Weill, "Correspondence," in *Kurt Weill:* Threepenny Opera, ed. Hinton, 124.
65. Bertolt Brecht, "The Modern Theatre Is the Epic Theatre," in *Brecht on Theatre: The Development of an Aesthetic,* ed. and trans. John Willett (New York, 1978), 37. Translation of "Anmerkungen zur Oper 'Aufstieg und Fall der Stadt Mahagonny,' " in *Gesammelte Werke,* vol. 17 (Frankfurt am Main, 1967), 1010.
66. Weill, "Notes to My Opera *Mahagonny,*" 517.
67. Kurt Weill, "Foreword to the Production Book of the Opera *Aufstieg und Fall der Stadt Mahagonny,*" in Kowalke, *Kurt Weill in Europe,* 512–15. Translation of "Vorwort zum Regiebuch der Oper *Aufstieg und Fall der Stadt Mahagonny,*" *Anbruch* 12 (Jan. 1930).
68. Ibid., 514.
69. Kurt Weill, letter to UE, 13 July 1929.
70. UE, letter to Kurt Weill, 27 Aug. 1929.
71. UE, letter to Kurt Weill, 9 Sept. 1929.
72. Kurt Weill, *Aufstieg und Fall der Stadt Mahagonny, Oper in drei Akten von Brecht: Textbuch* (Vienna, 1929), 2.
73. *Sächsische Arbeiter-Zeitung,* 11 Mar. 1930.
74. Liner notes for *Aufstieg und Fall der Stadt Mahagonny,* Columbia K3L 243.
75. *Leipziger Abendpost,* 10 Mar. 1930.
76. *Zeitschrift für Musik* 4 (1930) : 117.
77. *Berliner Tageblatt,* 10 Mar. 1930.
78. *Die Scene* 3 (1930): 94.
79. Kurt Weill, letter to UE, 4 May 1930.
80. Kurt Weill, letter to UE, 3 Jan. 1931.
81. Kurt Weill, letter to UE, 14 Dec. 1931.
82. Kurt Weill, letter to UE, 13 Jan. 1932.
83. Kurt Weill, "About My Didactic Opera *Der Jasager,*" in Kowalke, *Kurt Weill in Europe,* 530. Translation of "Über meine Schuloper *Der Jasager,*" *Die Scene* 20 (Aug. 1930).
84. Weill, "Topical Dialogue about *Schuloper,*" 524–25.
85. Ibid., 525.
86. *New York World Telegram,* 21 Dec. 1935.
87. *Die Weltbühne,* 8 July 1930.
88. *Hochland,* Feb. 1930 : 411.
89. *Anbruch,* Dec. 1930 : 243.
90. *Die Musik,* Feb. 1932 : 120.
91. *Film-Kurier,* 5 Feb. 1931.
92. *Licht-Bild-Bühne,* 13 Feb. 1931.
93. Kurt Weill, letter to UE, 9 Dec. 1931.
94. *Die Weltbühne,* 21 Apr. 1931.

7
THE DEFENSE OF OPERA

1. Quoted in a letter from UE to Kurt Weill, 31 May 1932.
2. Kurt Weill, letter to UE, 14 Mar. 1930.
3. Kurt Weill, "Zur großen Form!," *Der Montag Morgen*, 24 Aug. 1931.
4. Kurt Weill, "Actually an Operatic Crisis?," in Kowalke, *Kurt Weill in Europe*, 544. Translation of "Wirklich eine Opernkrise?," *Deutsche Allgemeine Zeitung*, 8 July 1932.
5. Kurt Weill, letter to UE, 6 Aug. 1930.
6. Kurt Weill, letter to UE, 27 Aug. 1930.
7. Quoted in Kurt Weill, *Die Bürgschaft: Klavierauszug*, Vienna, n.d. [1932], 11.
8. *Anbruch* 14 (1932) : 207.
9. Carl Ebert, in *Caspar Neher*, ed. Gottfried von Einem and Siegfried Melchinger (Velber, 1966), 125.
10. *Berliner Tageblatt*, 11 Mar. 1932.
11. *B. Z. am Mittag*, 11 Mar. 1932.
12. UE, letter to Weill, 14 May 1932.
13. Paul Bekker, *Briefe an zeitgenössische Musiker* (Berlin, 1932), 113ff.
14. Kurt Weill, letter to UE, 29 May 1932.
15. All these projects are quoted from Kurt Weill, letter to UE, 15 June 1932.
16. Kurt Weill, letter to UE, 7 July 1932.
17. Kurt Weill, letter to UE, 14 Nov. 1932.
18. Kurt Weill, letter to UE, 23 Nov. 1932.
19. Kurt Weill, letter to UE, 24 Nov. 1932.

8
THE NAZIS AND WEILL

1. *Deutsche Allgemeine Zeitung*, 6 Dec. 1932.
2. Kurt Weill, letter to UE, 19 Jan. 1933.
3. Kurt Weill, letter to UE, 6 Feb. 1933 [trans.].
4. UE, letter to Kurt Weill, 8 Feb. 1933.
5. Quoted in liner notes for *Silver Lake*, Nonesuch Records DB 79003, edited by Kim H. Kowalke.
6. Ibid.
7. Unidentified (Berlin?) newspaper clipping in the Weill–Lenya Research Center, New York.
8. *Leipziger Tageszeitung*, 20 Feb. 1933.
9. *Völkischer Beobachter*, 24 Feb. 1933, Berlin edition.
10. *Magdeburgische Zeitung*, 21 Feb. 1933.
11. The details of Weill's last days in Berlin are recounted in David (in the book incorrectly given as Daniel) Drew, "Neher und Weill," in *Caspar Neher*, ed. von Einem and Melchinger, 99.
12. Walter Trienes, "Neudeutsche Opern'kultur,' "*Nationalsozialistische Monatshefte*, Dec. 1931 : 378.
13. Helmut Kötzsch, "Der neue Opernspielplan," *Zeitschrift für Musik*, Oct. 1933 : 321.
14. Friedrich Walter, "Um die deutsche Musik—Ein Bekenntnis," *Die Musik* 10 (1932–33) : 727.
15. Karl Grunsky, *Kampf um die deutsche Musik* (Stuttgart, 1933), 26ff.
16. *Die Juden in Deutschland* (Munich, 1935), 358ff.
17. Hans Severus Ziegler, *Entartete Musik* (Düsseldorf, 1938), 16ff.
18. "Deutsche Juden im neuen Musiklexikon," *Dresdener Anzeiger*, 15 Mar. 1939, quoted in Fred K. Prieberg, *Musik im NS-Staat* (Frankfurt am Main, 1982).
19. Walter Trienes, *Musik in Gefahr* (Regensburg, 1940), 128.
20. *Lexikon der Juden in der Musik*, ed. T. Stengel and H. Gerigk (Berlin, 1941), 210.

21. Paul Bekker, *Wandlungen der Oper* (Zurich, 1934), 216.
22. John Willett, *The New Sobriety* (London, 1978), 7–8.

9
INTERLUDE: EXILE IN FRANCE

1. Kurt Weill, letter to UE, 26 Aug. 1932.
2. *Les Nouvelles Littéraires*, 13 Dec. 1932.
3. *Candide*, 15 Dec. 1932.
4. The details of the genesis of *Die sieben Todsünden* are taken from Kim H. Kowalke, "A Tale of Seven Cities: A Chronicle of the Sins," *On the Next Wave: The Audience Magazine of "BAM's Next Wave Festival*: 3/1–2 (Oct. 1985) : 20–25.
5. Ibid., 22.
6. *New Yorker*, 8 July 1933.
7. *Das neue Tagebuch*, Jan. 1933: 24.
8. *Evening Standard*, 14 July 1933.
9. Kurt Weill, postcard to Ruth Weill, 23 July 1933.
10. Undated letter from Eva Sybille (Billa) Kaiser to Kurt Weill (probably summer 1933).
11. Bankgeschäft Frankenberg, Berlin, letter to Kurt Weill, 3 Mar. 1934.
12. "Maurice Abravanel Remembers Kurt Weill," *High Fidelity/Musical America* 7 (1978) : 66.
13. Quoted in liner notes for *Kurt Weill. Die Sinfonien*, Argo ZRG 755.
14. *New York World Telegram*, 21 Feb. 1935.
15. Quoted in Kim H. Kowalke, liner notes for *The Unknown Kurt Weill*, Nonesuch Records 79019.
16. Marlene Dietrich, *Nehmt nur mein Leben* (Munich, 1979), 186.
17. Telegram of 3 Mar. 1934.
18. The description here of *Der Kuhhandel* is based on David Drew, "Reflections on the Last Years; *Der Kuhhandel* as a Key Work," in *A New Orpheus: Essays on Kurt Weill*, ed. Kowalke (New Haven, 1986).
19. Ibid., 220.
20. Meyer Weisgal, *So Far* (New York, 1971), 116.
21. Ole Winding, "Kurt Weill i Paris," *Aften-Avisen*, 22 June 1934.
22. Weisgal, *So Far*, 121.
23. *New York Post*, 9 Feb. 1937.
24. *American Hebrew*, 2 Jan. 1941.
25. Kurt Weill, letter to Max Reinhardt, 6 Oct. 1934.

10
GROUP THEATRE AND THE PLAYWRIGHTS' COMPANY

1. Kurt Weill, letter to UE, 6 Feb. 1933 [trans.].
2. *New Yorker*, 22 Apr. 1950.
3. Hanns Eisler, "Gespräche mit Hans Bunge: Fragen Sie mehr über Brecht," in *Gesammelte Werke*, ... (Leipzig, 1976) 99.
4. For a more detailed account, see John O'Connor and Lorraine Brown, *The Federal Theatre* ... (London, 1980).
5. Brooks Atkinson, *Broadway* (New York, 1970), 207.
6. Holly Matz, *Die Broadway Story: Eine Kulturgeschichte des amerikanischen Theaters* (...), 1980) 68.
7. Atkinson, *Broadway*, 123.
8. Ibid., 215.
9. Cheryl Crawford, *One Naked Individual* (New York, 1977), 94.